SIX MINUTES OF TORTURE

December 7, 1998.

DA Inspector Tim Kiely: "So you got on top of her, is that right?"

Annibel: "Uh-huh."

Detective Kurt Smallcomb: "Show me how you did that."

Annibel: "I just grabbed her like this."

Kiely: "Okay, you lay her on her back. Is she under the covers or over the covers?"

Annibel: "Over the covers."

Kiely: "And you're naked and she's naked."

Annibel: "Yeah."

Kiely: "Okay, if this is her neck . . . show me how you position your hands."

Annibel: "Like that."

Kiely: "And your two thumbs, are they right here on the windpipe?"

Annibel: "Yes."

Kiely: "How long did you have your hands on her neck until something happened?"

Annibel: "I only had it on there a minute, and then . . . I didn't want to kill her. I let go. She just started making clucking noises. Kind of like, *cluck, gasp.*"

Kiely: "Did you notice a change in her after this clucking noise?"

Annibel: "Yes."

Kiely: "What happened?"

Annibel: "She died."

DEADFALL

ROBERT SCOTT

PINNACLE BOOKS
Kensington Publishing Corp.
http://www.kensingtonbooks.com

This book is dedicated to Sherry, Andrea, Georgina, and Debbie.

Deadfall: *n* 1. A trap so constructed that a weight (or heavy log) falls on an animal and kills it or disables it. 2. A tangled mass of fallen trees and branches.
—*Webster's Collegiate Dictionary.*

PROLOGUE

Branscomb Road, Mendocino County, California,
November 29, 1998, 4 AM

The killer opened his vehicle door as rain pounded down through the redwood trees. It drummed steadily on the hood of his car like a dirge, cascading across cold metal onto the pavement. There were no other sounds in the forest besides the pouring rain that streamed down through the branches. The pitch-black forest seemed to devour light as well as sound. No stars, no moon, no lights of any kind. Even the roadway was dark and forboding under the sheets of falling rain.

The killer knew this road well. He traveled on it every day to go to work. From experience he knew there was little chance of any traffic at this late hour. The odds of him being discovered were almost nil since the nearest spot that could even be called a town was far away down the twisting, narrow two-lane road. In fact, no one lived within miles of the place he had purposefully parked alongside a dark ravine.

Nonetheless, out of caution, the killer quickly looked up and down the roadway before hauling a sleeping bag out of the backseat of his car. The contents of the sleeping bag made it heavy and unwieldy, causing him to stagger a little under its shifting weight. But he had strong arms from working in a lumber mill, and he was able to carry the heavy sleeping bag to the margin of the road. In fact, the sleeping bag contained the nude body of a forty-two-year old female. Only hours before he'd had sex with her in a motel room, then beat her head and strangled her to death.

The strangulation had not been swift or merciful. He'd taken his time, savoring every moment of it. His hands were powerful from grading lumber at the mill, and he'd choked her for a while, only to let her gasp for breath before applying pressure again. At two minutes her face began to turn red. By three minutes of alternating force and release, her face was blue. Five minutes into the strangulation she lost consciousness, and a few minutes later she was dead—an inert body lying on a bed in a small, sparsely furnished motel room. She had come into the room for sex and a good time—she wound up dead instead.

When the killer was finished strangling her, and she lay still, he rolled her dead body into a blanket and then into a sleeping bag he owned and placed it into his car. Then he'd driven from the small town of Laytonville west onto Branscomb Road en route to his nocturnal dump site.

As streaming rivulets of water poured down into the ravine, the killer carried the sleeping bag and body to the muddy edge and emptied its grisly contents. The woman's nude body slid out of the bag and down about ten feet into the brush. It wasn't perfect, but unless someone stopped at this exact same spot and looked intently down into the brush, the body would never be discovered. It would be just like in 1980 when his girl-friend Andrea had disappeared. The police had been looking for her for the past eighteen years and had always come up empty. They'd even arrested him at one point and tried to make a case against him for her disappearance, saying that he'd murdered her, but eventually they let him go. Without enough physical evidence at the time and no body, there wasn't enough against him to make it stand up in court. Or at least that was the thinking at the time.

Even more than that, this spot on Branscomb Road very much resembled the 1976 dump site not far from his then-home on Eel Rock Road in Humboldt County. A fifteen-year-old female victim named Sherry had been sexually molested, strangled to death, and left in the forest. If it hadn't been for the fluke person stopping at the dump site, she might have ended up like Andrea—just another missing person. And just like this spot on Branscomb Road, it had been on a dark night beneath the towering branches of redwood trees where her body had lain.

The authorities had questioned him on that murder as well, but as with Andrea, they could never quite connect all the dots. They'd even asked him to take a lie-detector test. When the results were questioned, he was asked to take another, but by then he'd "lawyered up" and refused to take a second polygraph. All of the cops' theories and suspicions went round and round in spirals, never quite coming full circle to ensnare him as the killer.

Now as he looked up and down Branscomb Road before jumping back into his car, it seemed that his luck was still holding. There were no headlights of vehicles, nor vehicle noise, nor sounds of human life. Only the steady drumming of the raindrops that echoed in the black heart of the emerald forest.

CHAPTER 1

The Fatal Dance

Southern Humboldt County, April, 1976

Fifteen-year-old Sherry Lynn Smith was going home—the Avenue of the Giants in the small town of Miranda, the heart of the Redwood Empire. The Avenue of the Giants was so named because of the groves of massive Coastal Redwoods (*Sequoia sempervirens*) along this stretch of the roadway. Some of the tallest living trees on Earth were located here, especially in the Founders Grove, close to where Sherry lived. Recently, Sherry had been staying with her father and step mother in the Bay Area at the city of Los Gatos. Los Gatos was definitely a different environment than Miranda. Miranda was small, countrified, and "hippie-fied," with many alternative-lifestyle people living out in the wooded hills. Los Gatos was upscale, fast-paced, and filled with freeways, fast-food outlets, and the bustle of the business world.

Paul Smith, Sherry's dad, remembered her from that time. "Sherry was full of energy. After a week she missed her friends in Humboldt County and wanted to go back. We had breakfast in Mountain View, where I had my business, and I put her on the bus for Eureka. She did not go home that week and wanted some freedom with her friends."

The bus Sherry was on took her across the Golden Gate Bridge, and as soon as it did, it was no longer on the El Camino Real, the old Spanish mission trail, but on the Redwood Highway—US 101. 101 wound up through the suburbs of Marin County and the large city of Santa Rosa in Sonoma County. To the north of Santa Rosa, it rolled through the famous wine country, with acres of vineyards that carpeted the hills and valleys. This scenery remained the same until Ukiah, where the terrain became more forested with oaks and occasional groves of redwood trees, but it was in southern Humboldt County that the landscape grew wild and dense with woods. It was the land of the giant redwoods and fogs creeping in off the Pacific Ocean. It was the land of the sun-dappled, winding Eel River. It was Sherry's home.

Sherry Lynn Smith was the middle child born to Paul and Marilyn Smith in 1961. Sherry's sister, Pam, was three years older than her, and they grew up in the small community of McKinleyville, north of Eureka. Like most of the towns in this region, McKinleyville depended on two industries—timber from the inland hills, and fishing in the ocean to the west. It still had a Wild West flavor to it, with lumberjacks and Native Americans who came into town from the neighboring Hoopa Indian Reservation.

Pam recalled of Sherry, "As a toddler, she was always on the move. One time my mom went outside and found that Sherry had climbed up on the roof of the house. Another day she made it out the front door. She walked around the block and knocked on someone's door. They took her in. When they went looking for her home, my mom and dad had been out for over an hour looking for Sherry. She was adventurous even as a child. That day, luckily, had a happy ending."

In fact, Sherry was lucky to make it past her third birthday. Her mom was in the hospital, giving birth to another daughter, Paulette, on April 4, 1964. On that day, Sherry darted out in front of car in Eureka, was hit, and sent flying. The local paper even called her a "flying rocket." Incredibly, Sherry wasn't hurt badly. Luck truly seemed to be on her side.

Pam recalled about that same year, "When I was about six years old, a little boy knocked me off my tricycle outside. I went in the house crying to my mom. Sherry being three years younger than me, was going to go out and beat him up for being mean to her sister. She was always looking out for her family."

The Smith family, however, could not hold together. Paul and Marilyn split up, and the girls stayed with their mom. All of them moved in with Marilyn's sister and her husband for awhile down at the Burgh Ranch on Salmon Creek in Humboldt County. While living there the girls had a ball. They were able to raise young lambs, goats, puppies, and other animals. Pam recalled, "We would bottle feed the lambs and goats. One day, when Mom wasn't home, we let the lambs into the house. Paulette and Sherry dressed them up like little dolls. We woke up the next morning all flea-bitten. My mom and uncle had to fumigate the whole house. We didn't bring the lambs in to play after that.

"Sherry and Paulette, with our cousins Kenny and Steve, would still go out and play in the bushes. They'd come back with ticks stuck on them. But they sure had fun."

By 1975, Pam, Sherry, Paulette, and their mom had moved to a residence of their own in Miranda. Pam said, "Sherry was so good to her little sister, Paulette. To Paulette, Sherry was everything. Sherry was her best friend, her caretaker, her mother, her whole world!"

In 1975 and 1976, Sherry attended South Fork High School in Miranda. The yearbook, the *Redwood Log*, was called "The Spirit of '76" that year, since 1976 was the bicentennial year. A quote in the book stated, "America in the 1760s and 1770s was a nation of young people. Three eights of the signers of the Constitution of 1787 were in their twenties and thirties. We often pay tribute to the brilliance of this generation, but we overlook its youthfulness."

Sherry's class held a Halloween ball during her sophomore year and according to the yearbook it was a great success. In that year, teacher Gary Rocha was a counselor and one of Sherry's teachers. He said of her later, "She was a fine young lady. Really sweet."

Another one of Sherry's teachers was Mike Foster. He recalled, "She was in my science class. Sherry was a nice, pleasant girl. She was involved in activities and an above average student. She was always full of spirit and a trusting person."

Sherry took a photography class, but the area where she really shined was as a cheerleader. Pam recalled, "Sherry was a cheerleader for the Pop Warner Football team. She was supposed to be a South Fork High School cheerleader, as well, but they miscounted the votes. Sherry actually won out over another girl, but she took it well. My mom did not take it well. She was angry for Sherry and called the school and tried to raise hell over it."

To compensate for their error, the school asked if Sherry wanted to be the mascot for the basketball team. She accepted, and became "Yogi." Yogi was named after the cartoon character Yogi Bear.

South Fork High School that year was a product of its time and place. The Redwood region still resonated with the back-to-the-earth movement and its laid-back nature. At South Fork High, students on Tuesdays and Thursdays were able to attend classes of their choice, go to the library and study, work on projects for more than one period, or listen to special speakers on certain subjects. There was a school magazine called *Middle Earth* which portrayed students' stories, poetry, and essays. There was even something called Society for the Prevention of Brain Atrophy. Interestingly enough, one if its members had the last name of Kafka.

As Sherry Smith rode back home on the bus that late April day in 1976, she passed through the small redwood community of Piercy. Nearby was the tourist attraction known as Confusion Hill. It was a locale that claimed that the laws of nature and gravity did not apply there. Balls rolled uphill, and a taller person could seem shorter than a diminutive one. It was an area of fun and fantasy and seemed to encompass the other-worldliness of the "Redwood Empire," as it was sometimes called.

Piercy claimed a more forboding and sinister past, however. It was here that one of southern Humboldt County's first killings took place. In 1863, Samuel Piercy took in an Indian wife, even though she was already pregnant by another white man. When a baby girl was born, he took her on as his own. A few years later, Elizabeth was born to Piercy and his Native American wife. When the girls grew up, one of the neighbors, a rough character named Marson, vowed he was going to kill Piercy and have the girls for his own. But it was Piercy who won out in a gun battle up in the redwoods, killing Marson in the process.

Ninety-five years later, almost to the day, Sherry's bus rolled through Piercy on Highway 101. If she had known, she could have looked up the hillside and seen an old rotting redwood grave marker that marked the spot where Marson had been buried. He may have been the first white man to die a violent death in this area, but he certainly wasn't the last. Just across the mountains, near Round Valley, the area became a hotbed of cattle rustling and murder. By Sherry's day, the back country was filled with illegal marijuana patches, guarded by gun-wielding guards. Every year some people wandered into the backcountry of southern Humboldt, near Alderpoint, Blocksburg, Zenia, Fort Seward, and Eel Rock and were never heard from again.

In fact, Sherry was headed for Alderpoint. When she got to the town of Garberville, she didn't contact her mom or sisters. She wanted to visit her friend, Glenda Massey, up in the hills of Alderpoint and stay with her before going home. Apparently Sherry did just this for a few days. Glenda would recall later, "Sherry liked an Indian guy named Terry Robinson, even though he was a lot older than her. So maybe that's why she came to Alderpoint when she rode the bus back to Humboldt. On the morning of April thirtieth, Sherry and I helped my mom clean the yard. In the early afternoon we walked down the road to the bridge. We saw a van with New York plates on it driving by. Sherry was the one who noticed the New York plates. She waved at the guys inside the van. They waved back. Sherry and I were acting silly."

Glenda recalled that the color of the van was either yellow or cream. It had a canoe on top and it looked as if the guys had been canoeing and camping in the area.

Glenda remembered, "Me and Sherry, my mom, Uncle Charlie Stillwell, Aunt Nada Stillwell, and Charlie Smith all went to a dance in Garberville [on April 30]. It was at the Fireman's Hall. We arrived at about 9:30 PM and a little later on, we saw one of the guys from the van at the dance. The guy was older than Sherry, but he was kind of handsome. Sherry talked to him for quite a while, but did not dance with him."

The band at the hall that evening was the Jezebell Cain Band out of Marysville, California. It consisted of several young men and women, mostly in their twenties, except for seventeen-year-old Angela Burrows. Angela had actually gone to South Fork High School in Miranda.

Various people would remember events differently as the dance progressed, and one of the most reliable sources was Sherry's friend Glenda Massey. She said later, "Sherry told me that after the dance, she was going to visit her sister, Pam, [who was staying at a different place], because her mom would be sleeping by 2 AM, and she didn't want to wake her up. We [Sherry and Glenda] went in and out of the dance two times and maybe three times that evening."

As far as rides went for Sherry, Glenda would recall certain things. She said that even before the dance, Sherry had asked Fred Lane, who lived up on Fruitland Ridge, for a ride home, but then changed her mind. Glenda recalled, "She told him not to worry. She had another ride." Glenda was sure the ride was with a guy named John Annibel.

Before the dance was over, Glenda told Annibel, "Don't forget Sherry."

John responded, "I won't. I won't forget Sherry."

Glenda also recalled one more thing. "Sherry got her luggage out of Uncle Charlie Stillwell's car at about 2 AM. It was either right before the lights came on, or right after that time.

I didn't want Sherry to go back home. I liked having her at Alderpoint. I started crying and didn't say goodbye to her at the door."

One person, James Emmons, said later that he saw Sherry walk out the door with eighteen-year-old John Annibel. They seemed to be heading toward Annibel's car.

A young man who was a railroad worker for the NWP at Fort Seward up on Eel Rock Road, had been out for the weekend with friends. On Sunday, May 2, 1976, he got on his motorcycle in Weott and headed up Eel Rock Road back to where he lived in Fort Seward. He recalled later, "I went off on a little side road to urinate, and I wanted to take a picture of that rock. [There was a large unusual rock in the area.] I had my camera and I went down the little road to take a leak. That's when I saw the body.

"I didn't know if she was dead, but she wasn't moving and it scared the hell out of me. I was pretty sure she was dead. I could see her vagina exposed and her pants pulled down. I just went to find the nearest person to call.

"I was at the scene [body dump site] at about 6 PM—maybe 6:30. I arrived at the Kinnebrews' place up there around 6:30 PM. We knew each other. I told Kinnebrew what I saw, and he radioed down to the sheriff's office. Then me and the Kinnebrews met Mr. Roberts [a Sheriff's deputy] at the scene. That was probably around 7:15 PM. I even told Roberts, 'Look at the gravel road [the main road near the little dirt road]. 'It looks like somebody skidded through the gravel there.'"

At 7:30 PM, Assistant Coroner Russell Allen received a dispatch that there was a 187 (homicide) at a location off of Eel Rock Road in southern Humboldt County. Allen and Deputy Coroner E. Moore departed from Eureka at 7:45 PM. It was roughly sixty miles to the spot on Eel Rock Road. Allen would later report on everything that happened at the crime scene.

It was 9:45 PM by the time Allen and Moore arrived at the body. They were met there by Coroner Edward Nielson and

Deputy Sheriff D. Roberts. The crime scene was already roped off by Lieutenant Roy Simmons, Detective Leo Bessette, Detective James Ivey, and ID Tech Bud Thompson. A few minutes later, District Attorney John Buffington and Investigator Bob Hickok arrived. The crime scene was then investigated by all of these individuals.

Assistant Coroner Allen noted that the victim was an unidentified white female, age unknown, later determined to be between the ages of fifteen and twenty. She was lying on her back with her head facing downhill. The victim was partially disrobed and Allen noticed signs of trauma on her body. The victim was removed by Allen, Coroner Nielson, Deputy Moore, and Lieutenant Simmons, and taken to the Pierce Mortuary in Eureka. The rest of the crime scene crew secured the area. It was 10 PM, May 2, 1976. Officer Roberts stayed at the scene until after 2 AM and then it was handed over to Deputy John Hutchins.

At the Pierce Mortuary, the victim was taken to a prep room at 11:30 PM. The victim was visually examined by Coroner Nielson, Assistant Coroner Allen, Lieutenant Simmons, and other investigating officers of the Humboldt County Sheriff's Office. The victim's statistics were noted as being 5' 7" tall and weighing 125 pounds. She had light brown hair and brown eyes. She was wearing braces on her teeth.

The victim was wearing orange-colored bell bottom pants, green panties with white trim, red boot socks, brown boots, white-colored peasant blouse, and a white bra, size 34B. She also wore a gold-colored band ring on the small finger of her right hand and a turquoise-and-silver ring on the index finger of her left hand. On her ears she wore one-and-a-half-inch earrings, pyramid in shape and covered with multicolored dots.

The victim was noted to be in full rigor, with a great deal of cyanosis of the face, which probably meant she had been struck there in various locations. She was cold to the touch and a lot of trauma to the face and head was noted. The knees and buttocks showed numerous cuts, contusions, and abrasions. This may have been from moving around in the dirt and rocks while being attacked. Assistant Coroner Allen and Lieutenant Simmons went through her pockets for identification, but came up empty.

It was decided that nothing more could be done at that time. Coroner Nielson was to make arrangements for a complete postmortem examination, BA, drug screen, and vaginal smear for the following day.

Coroner James Sundeen was the one who actually did the autopsy. He began at 10 AM on May 3, and his report was very specific in many areas. He noted that the victim's orange-colored pants had a torn buttonhole and broken zipper. They had been pulled down around her ankles. There was a great deal of caked dirt on the seat area of the pants. The hiking boots were 7D, and she wore three pairs of socks. There was a large tear on her blouse, and a few spots of blood on the right sleeve and left shoulder area.

Leaves, pine needles, and twigs were matted in her hair and there was a small amount of blood in the hair near the hairline and scratches in the scalp. The skin in this area was violet in color and suggested ecchymoses. The skin on the forehead had superficial irregularities and indentations and was bordered by purple livor spots, suggesting that there were ecchymotic areas on the forehead and temporal regions. There was bruising on the upper left eyelid and over the bridge of the nose. There was also a small abrasion below the right eyebrow, and the medial eyelashes on the upper and lower lid were quite short and appeared to be beaded at the ends, suggesting they had been singed.

Blood was noted to have run from the left eye into the left auditory canal. A small amount of blood was also on the right cheek. Her tongue protruded slightly from her mouth and there was a moderate amount of foam mixed with blood in her mouth. There was also a small amount of dirt and twigs present around the mouth.

Her neck revealed a small amount of blood spattered on the upper portion and there were small abrasions on the neck suggestive of fingernail marks. The skin on the neck revealed considerable postmortem livor as did the upper chest and shoulders. There were a small amount of superficial abrasions widely scattered over the surface of her back and a longer abrasion was present on the midline of one buttock.

No lacerations were found on her abdomen, and only one single superficial abrasion on the left thigh. Superficial abrasions were found on the left arm and flattened irregular abrasions on the right arm. Examination of the right hand revealed an ink stamp that read "Do Not Bend."

Examination of the genitalia revealed no obvious signs of semen or blood in the pubic area. The labia minora showed a small ecchymosis. Two swabs were taken from the vagina and another swab from the rectum. Swabs of the mouth were taken as well.

On her head there was a considerable hemorrhage on the masseter muscle. There was no fracturing of the skull, however. On the ventral surface of the left temporal lobe there were two small contusions, and on the right temporal lobe as well.

The victim's neck was carefully opened using a U-shaped incision, and the soft tissue external to the muscle fascia revealed two areas of hemorrhage. The most prominent one was on the right side, level with the thyroid cartilage. The trachea and larynx contained a moderate amount of clear frothy fluid, as well as some bloody mucus, and the lungs contained a moderate amount of blood-tinged frothy fluid. The bronchioles also contained frothy fluid.

Swabs for acid phosphates and analysis for presence of sperm were taken from her mouth, vagina, and anus. Blood was also taken from her body to determine if alcohol or drugs were present.

Results of the chemistry analysis were that her blood type was A-positive and she had no drugs in her system. The swab for acid phosphatase in the vagina was strongly positive. (Phosphatase tests were the standard method in that era to determine if semen had been present.) Acid phosphatase tests were negative for the mouth and anus.

Dr. Sundeen's autopsy summary was:

1. Abrasions to skin of neck, and hemorrhage into superficial soft tissues of neck.

2. Petechial hemorrhage.

3. Moderate pulmonary edema and vascular congestion.

4. Evidence of blunt force trauma to head.

   A. Left forehead.

   B. Left temporal area.

   C. Eyelids showing edema.

5. Multiple cerebral contusions on right and left temporal lobes.

Dr. Sundeen's conclusion was that, "The patient's demise was a result of strangulation. Besides the abrasions on the neck and hemorrhage into the soft tissues, the findings of petechial hemorrhages in the scelerae pulmonary edema and vascular congestion are confirmatory findings in a death of asphyxia. In addition, however, there is multiple evidence of blunt trauma to the head."

Ed Moore was also part of the process of the autopsy. After extended examination he removed the victim's clothing, and placed the items in paper bags that were tagged and given to officers of the Humboldt County Sheriff's Office. Coroner Edward Nielson and Assistant Coroner Allen removed the victim's rings and put them in paper bags for collection as well. Coroner Nielson also took samples of pubic hair, hair from the victim's head, and blood samples.

All of the photos snapped during the autopsy were taken by Deputy Bert Craven, ID tech for HCSO (Humboldt County Sheriff's Office). While the autopsy was being conducted, Richard Wolven, DDS charted and examined the victim's teeth and dental work. Dr. Wolven requested Dr. Everett Hart, an orthodontist, to come to the Pierce Mortuary and examine the braces on the victim's teeth. Dr. Hart arrived about 2:30 PM, examined the braces and thought they might be the work of Dr. Johnston, DDS of Fortuna.

Dr. Hart called Dr. Johnston and described the dental work

and gave him the victim's physical description. Dr. Johnston said that it sounded like the orthodontic work he'd done for a girl named Sherry Lynn Smith of Miranda. Dr. Johnston gave him the phone number of Sherry's mother, Marilyn Jensen.

At approximately 6 PM, Coroner Nielson and Assistant Coroner Allen took the victim's body to Dr. Wolven's office on G Street in Eureka. X-rays were taken of her teeth by Dr. Wolven and comparisons were made with dental charts that Allen had obtained from a dentist in Rio Dell. Positive identification was made by Dr. Wolven that the victim was Sherry Lynn Smith, age fifteen.

Detectives Leo Bessette and James Ivey had the sad task of informing Sherry's mom about her murder. The news was absolutely devastating. Pam Smith would recall, "My mom said when she first got the call about Sherry's body being found she just started screaming and hung up the phone. She then called my Aunt Linda. My aunt must have driven really quickly because she got to the house so fast. My aunt just got there when the detectives came to the door."

One of the first persons detectives talked to was Sherry's friend, Glenda Massey. She told them about Sherry staying at her house after coming back from the Bay Area, and the guys in the van from New York State. She also spoke of going to the dance in Garberville. Glenda said, "Sherry danced with John Annibel five times; Jeff Fox two times; Kenny Robinson one time; and Mike Stillwell one time. Terry Robinson didn't dance with her. Even though she liked him, he was much older than Sherry. He avoided her at the dance."

One of the detectives asked, "Who was Sherry going home with?"

Glenda answered without hesitation, "John Annibel."

Glenda added, "When the lights came on and the band quit at 2 AM, John Annibel was still at the dance. I hung around with my mom until 2:15 AM or 2:20, so my mom could finish a drink. She didn't want to finish it outside."

Glenda also related that when John Annibel said, "I won't forget Sherry," he was heading toward his car.

Glenda told them one more thing of interest, she said that John Annibel's buddy, Ron Stone was also at the dance. Stone lived up on Fruitland Ridge near John. Glenda said that she didn't know Ron Stone until Sherry pointed him out at the dance, but Glenda did know the woman with Stone, Paula Wise, and so did Sherry. Glenda declared, "We saw Paula take off. I'm not sure of the time. It might have been around 1 AM. Sherry even waved goodbye to Paula, but Paula did not wave back. Sherry turned to me and said, 'That bitch didn't even wave.' Later on, Paula Wise and that guy [Ron Stone] returned to the dance and stayed until it was over."

The detectives also spoke with Glenda's mom, Glynnis Leggett. Glynnis said that they'd arrived at the dance at about 9:30 PM. She saw Sherry around 2 AM when the band stopped and the lights came on.

Glynnis said, "Sherry was friendly with everybody. She was pretty easy to get along with and a real nice girl. She was a good friend to my daughter.

"Sherry [at the end of the dance] was waiting on two guys who were waiting for her. They were John Annibel and Frank something." (Glynnis may have gotten the name Frank mixed up with Fred, as in Fred Lane.)

Glynnis told a detective that right at the end of the dance she had a conversation with Sherry.

Glynnis: "Are you all right? Are you going home with those two guys?"

Sherry: "Yeah."

This statement would be different from everyone else's on this matter. Every one else would speak of only one guy. Glynnis spoke of two. She told the detective, "You should call Mrs. Annibel and have her give you the name of the two guys. I'll write them down. One of the guys was Sherry's sister's boyfriend's brother." (Sherry's sister Pam, had a boyfriend, James Annibel, who was John Annibel's twin brother. They did not look alike, however, since they were fraternal, not identical twins. The other guy Glynnis referred to was John Annibel's stepcousin, Fred Lane.)

The detective asked Glynnis if Sherry would fight back if attacked. Glynnis answered, "Absolutely!"

When the detectives talked with Glenda Massey again, she said that Sherry had been wearing a headscarf that was blue and red, or blue and white, in color. She had a pink bag that normally was for a hair dryer, but Sherry had put a pair of white roller skates in it instead. Sherry also had a medium-sized suitcase that contained a white short-sleeved sweater, a green V-neck sweater, and a long-sleeved maroon/multicolored sweater. Glenda said that Sherry always wore a wooden and glass-bead necklace and never took it off.

The detectives had already found a necklace matching that description in the main road not particularly distant from Sherry's body. It was broken and looked like it might have been ripped off her neck in a struggle.

Junior Stillwell was questioned and said that he was at his Uncle Charlie Stillwell's car at around 2 AM. He added that Sherry came to the car and got her luggage at the end of the dance. It was Junior Stillwell's understanding that Sherry was getting a ride home with John Annibel.

Michael Stillwell's sister-in-law was Glynnis Leggett. Michael told a detective about a person Sherry was to get a ride with from the dance. He said, "It was her [Sherry's] sister's boyfriend's cousin." (This would have made it Fred Lane.) Then Michael added one more important bit of information. "But Fred Lane didn't take her home. That other guy did."

He didn't say who the other guy was, but other people had mentioned the "other guy" as being John Annibel.

A detective spoke with a woman named Christine Beer. (Though he may have gotten the spelling wrong. It may have been Christine Bear.) Christine was a Native American woman who was a friend of Glynnis Leggett. Christine said, "I saw Glenda and Sherry come out of the dance and go to the Blue

Room in Garberville. I was there with Nada [Stillwell]. I said to the girls, 'Well, you might as well go back and dance.' That was sometime between 10 and 11 PM. Sherry was talking to [word deleted], and she was crying." Why the name was deleted from the report has not been explained.

Later Christine added, "Sherry didn't want to go back home. She wanted to go back to Alderpoint."

Christine almost gave in and agreed to take Sherry back to Alderpoint, but then she realized all the school Sherry had been missing, and refused to take her there. Christine added, "Sherry was going to get a ride with Pam's boyfriend's brother [in other words, John Annnibel]."

James Emmons, who was at the dance, was questioned, and told Lieutenant Simmons that he saw Sherry leave the dance hall with John Annibel. Emmons was the only eyewitness to see Sherry Lynn Smith and John Annibel actually walk out the door together. Emmons did admit, however, that he didn't see Sherry get into John's car.

Friends and relatives of Glenda Massey, friends of Sherry Lynn Smith and those who knew Smith only slightly were questioned. One of these was Fred Lane, John Annibel's cousin— the other young man who was supposed to give Sherry a ride after the dance. Lane told the detective that Sherry had asked him for a ride early in the dance. Then she came up to him later and said she had a different ride after the dance. She indicated that the driver would be John Annibel.

Since John's mother, Lyla, was Lane's aunt, Lane said, "[Whit Lewis—Lyla's brother] was staying at my Aunt Annibel's at the time. Whit told Lyla that Sherry had been staying in Alderpoint. And I guess Lyla told Pam. Then Pam phoned her mother and said that Sherry was back in the area."

Lane noticed that Sherry danced with John Annibel a lot that night. He said that after 2 AM the lights came up and Sherry was standing near the restroom. She was not with John at that point and there were a lot of people milling around. Lane said that a little after 2 AM he gave a guy named Mike Kelly a ride to Redway.

Many people who were at or near the dance were questioned,

including Michael Moore. Moore's parents lived on Cooper Ranch near Alderpoint. James Emmons had been with Moore since Wednesday of that week. Moore didn't actually go into the dance hall, but stayed outside and talked with friends. At one point he said he saw Glenda Massey outside of the dance, but not with Sherry. He thought this was about 10 PM. Then at around 11:30 PM he said he saw Sherry and Glenda down near "Des's in Garberville." A girl with Moore, Christine Anderson, waved at Sherry. He wasn't sure if Sherry waved back at her.

At some point, Christine Anderson got into Moore's vehicle, and according to Moore they went up the hill to drink some beers. Moore said that James Emmons was with them, but Moore was very reluctant to speak about this matter. He was twenty years old at the time and Christine was fourteen. Moore told detectives he didn't have intercourse with her; they just sat up there and drank beers and then returned to the dance in Garberville.

James Emmons's statements differed from Moore's, however. Emmons said that he and Moore went to the dance and picked up Christine Anderson on the way there. According to Emmons, Mike Moore and Christine Anderson did have "sexual relations." Emmons said he was there to witness it. Emmons said it happened around 11 PM and then they all went back to the dance. He went inside and Moore and Anderson stayed outside.

James Emmons said he stayed at the dance until 2 AM, and he saw John Annibel and Sherry and another male all leave the dance together. Emmons didn't indicate who the other male was. Perhaps he didn't know him. In some ways it corroborated Glynnis Leggett's statement that Sherry had left with two males.

Emmons said that he left the dance with Christine Anderson in Fred Lane's car, which Lane drove, and they all went over to Mike Kelly's residence in Redway.

Thelma Diffin spoke with a detective and said that she had given Sherry the glass-bead-and-wooden necklace. Diffin said Sherry never took it off, even to shower. Diffin's description matched the necklace found in the road not far from Sherry's body.

Since the name John Annibel kept coming up so often, he became a "person of interest" to the authorities. In John's first interview with detectives, he said that he had gone home at midnight and didn't really know what happened to Sherry Lynn Smith. Then as other people started placing John at the dance hall at 2 AM, he began to change some of his story.

John had a second and more lengthy interview at 5:15 PM on May 4 the place he worked: the Pacific Lumber Company. Now the detectives were looking at him more as a suspect than a witness. One of them advised him of his Miranda rights, and John waived his rights and decided to talk to them. John told the detectives that Sherry had asked for a ride home about midnight. He said he had driven his mother's car, a 1969 lime-green Mustang to the dance. A detective asked John, "Where was Sherry going after the dance?"

John answered, "She was going to her mom's house. And she'd already phoned her mom and told her to leave the porch light on and the door unlocked." (Sherry's mother would later deny she ever received a phone call like this from Sherry. And even Sherry had told Glenda Massey that she didn't want to go home because it would be after 2 AM and it would wake her mom up.)

John said that Sherry never indicated to him later whether she was going to get a ride with him or Fred Lane. John said that he was at the dance at 2 AM, when the lights came up and that at that time, "I was drinking a beer. And Glenda [Massey] came up and asked me if I was going to give Sherry a ride home. And I said yeah. I would if she [Sherry] needed one. But she had to go get her luggage. I went out to my car, which was parked near the red building [fire station]. I was parked near the cement ramp. I waited there. She didn't come out, so I went—"

Detective [interrupting John]: "Did you tell her where your car was?"

John: "Yeah. So I went back into the hall and looked around. I couldn't see her outside, so I went inside. I didn't see her, so I just went back to my car and drove home."

Detective: "You went directly home?"

John: "Yeah."

The detectives later determined that it normally took John anywhere from twenty to forty minutes to get from Garberville to his home. It took him an hour and fifteen minutes that night, or maybe even an hour and thirty minutes. Where had he been in that time? The detectives decided this was enough time to kill Sherry Lynn Smith and drag her body to the dump site.

Asked about his twin brother, James, John told the detective that James did not look like him and could not be confused with him.

Detective: "Could he [James] have been with Sherry?"

John: "No. He was in Fortuna with Sherry's sister, Pam." (This was later confirmed by police.)

When asked about the Mustang, John related that another Mustang of similar vintage had been parked near the dance and was blue in color. He tried saying that someone might have confused it with his. He also said that he saw Fred Lane near the end of the dance, but he never asked Fred if he was giving Sherry a ride. Then John added, "When I went home, I assumed Sherry was with Fred."

The detective asked John if he knew Ron Stone. John's answer was evasive at best and did not address the fact that he knew Ron very well. John said, "We know each other. I've visited with him, but we are not really good friends. Um, he bought his Ford Falcon from my dad." (Pam Smith would later say that John and Ron were "thick as thieves.")

The questions about Ron Stone was a whole new angle on the case. It was determined that Ron Stone and John Annibel were indeed good friends and didn't live that far from each other up on the "Ridge." In fact, both of them lived not that far from where Sherry's body had been found. One of the people who knew both of them was Helen Barber of Garberville. She told a detective that she and her friends Wanda Young, Lynn Lyons, and Donna Evans had gone to the dance. Barber and Lyons were standing near the ticket booth when they saw Glenda Massey at about 10:30 PM. Barber knew Massey's uncle and aunt, Charlie and Nada Stillwell, as well.

Barber said she didn't know Sherry Lynn Smith, but she did know Ron Stone. Barber had been at a dance the previous week and according to Barber, Ron had been "hitting on me."

Barber saw a tall young girl at the dance with dark hair who might have had a bandana in her hair, go to Ron Stone's car sometime that night. Barber thought that it might have been 11:30 PM. Ron's car was parked near the Fireman's Hall.

After the dance, people were talking about where parties might be taking place. They heard that one party was going to be at Ron Stone's residence. Lyons spoke up and said, "Oh, he lives up on Eel Rock Road," and Barber added, "Who wants to go way up there!"

Barber said that Fred Lane was sitting next to Ron Stone for a while at the dance. She also heard that Ron Stone and Paula Wise had been arguing because Ron had been flirting with her (Helen Barber). Barber described Stone as 5' 5" or 5' 6" tall. He had dark hair. There was another guy hanging around with him who she didn't know. This guy was taller than Stone and had been arguing with a girl at one point at the dance.

The detective asked if this guy could have been John Annibel.

Barber said, "No, I know all of the Annibels."

Lynn Lyons told a detective that she'd seen Sherry Lynn Smith put her luggage into a brown Ford at some point that evening. Ron Stone owned a brown Ford Falcon.

Jessie Lyons was questioned as well. She lived in Redway and had known Sherry Smith for about three years. Jessie said that there had been a lot of activity around Ron Stone's car that evening.

Jessie said, "I knew Ron Stone and Paula Wise. I saw Ron and Paula together at the dance at about 2 AM. Russell [no last name] was also standing near Ron Stone at the end of the dance. This Russell, according to Jessie Lyons, was about 5'6" or 5'7" tall and had curly blond hair.

Angela Burrows, one of the members of the band was questioned. She had gone to South Fork High School and knew a guy named "Rusty" who worked at French's Camp. She thought that he had recently "gotten out of prison." She also said that this Rusty was a friend of Ron Stone. He had curly blond hair.

Mary Ann James also saw Ron Stone and Sherry Lynn Smith. Mary Ann got to the dance at around 10:30 PM and saw a girl bending over the trunk of Ron's car. The girl was either putting something into or taking something out of the trunk. Mary Ann said it could have been Sherry Lynn Smith.

Not only had civilians seen Ron Stone and his car around the dance, a couple of Sheriff's Deputies had as well. In a report by Deputy D.R. Roberts, the same man who would be first officer on the scene at Sherry's body, Roberts said that he was with Reserve Officer John Hutchins near the dance at 12:40 AM on May 1. They did a drive-by check of the Fireman's Hall dance and turned onto Locust Street in Garberville and saw a male putting a package or something into the trunk of his car. It was a brown Falcon. There were a male and female in the front seat. There were passengers in the backseat. Robert knew Ron Stone's car and said later that the vehicle was Stone's car. The female in the backseat had long brown hair and was young. She wore a white-colored blouse.

Roberts spoke with a male (not Stone or John Annibel) who was in the backseat with the female who had long brown hair. Roberts didn't know this guy. The male had curly, light brown hair. He was about 5' 9", in Roberts's estimation. He was neatly dressed. Later in the report, for some reason Roberts noted that this person worked at French's Camp Resort as a night manger. (Russell Rude worked there in that capacity.)

Since the female looked underage, and was drinking in the car, Roberts told the male to tell her to dump her beer out before they left. She was drinking from a cup that said Coors on the side. Robert's exact words were, "Will you make the female get rid of the booze? It is illegal to have booze in a vehicle."

The male was polite and assured Roberts that he would do just that.

The next day, May 2, at 7:30 PM, shortly after Sherry's body was found, a reporting officer saw a Falcon on Eel Rock Road with a male with curly hair in the passenger seat. The driver was urinating by the side of the road. A short time later that same evening, California Highway Patrol Sergeant Ed Sabbera saw the same vehicle going at a high rate of speed away from the area. (This may have been on Highway 101, once the vehicle had descended the ridge area.)

Lieutenant Simmons would later talk with Ron Stone's sister, Doris Perna, who said the curly-haired man was Russ Rude.

Then there was an Angela (no last name) who told a detective that "Rusty" or Russ Rude had recently gotten out of prison. He worked at French's Camp. He was a friend of Ron Stone's.

An even more intriguing comment was made by K.C. Bowman to a detective. Bowman phoned the sheriff's office about information overheard at the Roadrunner Café in Phillipsville. Bowman learned that Sherry Lynn Smith had been sitting next to Stone at the dance. While at the Roadrunner Café, Stone had supposedly said in a loud voice so others could hear, "The sheriff's office can't question me on the Smith case, because I left the dance at 10 PM. I didn't like the music." Bowman said that Ron Stone took great lengths to have other people hear this comment.

Most witnesses, however, at the dance said that Ron Stone and Paula Wise did leave the dance at 10 PM, but came back later and stayed until 2 AM, when the lights came on.

One more thing Bowman said was that Ron Stone had declared just a week before Sherry's murder, "You can't enter the old piece of road by the Eel Rock Junction from the bottom anymore. You have to drive in from the top because of a fallen tree across the road."

It was on that "old piece of road" that Sherry's body was discovered.

In another bit of information on the Ron Stone angle, Lieutenant Del Frame noted that Ron Stone's burl shop was closed for three days after the news that Sherry Lynn Smith's body had been found. A waitress told Frame she'd seen scratch marks on Ron Stone's hands and arms after the murder. He told her that he'd fallen off his horse while riding it.

Jessie Lyons saw Ron Stone on about May 8, and she recalled him saying, "If I die tonight, I know what I did last week." He didn't offer any explanation about what he meant by the remark.

Another ongoing mystery since the discovery of Sherry Lynn Smith's body was the fact that fourteen-year-old Christine Anderson had disappeared. Then in mid-May a short article appeared in the *Eureka Times-Standard*, with the headline: MISSING GIRL FOUND, HELD. Among other things it reported that fourteen-year-old Anderson had last been seen in the company of Sherry Lynn Smith, when they both left the dance together. How the newspaper came to the conclusion is unknown. None of the witnesses mentioned Christine Anderson leaving with Sherry.

The article went on to say that Anderson had been reported missing by South Fork Principal Don Swanson. This was another mystery, since Christine did not go to South Fork High, but her sister did.

Christine was reported to have been intercepted in a truck that also held two young men. Just who these men were, the article did not say. The truck had been stopped by officers on Alderpoint Road, two miles east of Garberville. The article stated, "Investigators reported that when the vehicle was stopped, the Anderson girl jumped from the truck but was immediately apprehended."

Christine Anderson was taken to Eureka and booked into juvenile hall for "disobeying authority." At the end of the article was a statement about Sherry Lynn Smith. It stated, "Apparently the victim of rape, [Smith] had been choked to death, much in the same manner as two other young women brutally killed in Humboldt County." These murders had occurred within the last six months.

When Christine Anderson finally spoke with a detective, she said that she and Mike Moore arrived at the dance at around 10:30 PM. She and Moore didn't want to pay the entrance price, so they stayed outside and talked with friends. Anderson said she mostly stayed in the pickup. (She didn't mention anything about going up the hill to drink beers or a sexual encounter.) She did say that she had seen Glenda Massey and Sherry Lynn Smith outside the dance hall and had waved at them.

Christine's statement also differed from that of James Emmons. She said that instead of staying at Mike Kelly's residence in Redway, she had spent the night in a tent on Sprowel Creek. Anderson would not say what she had been doing since May 1, though in a later statement Glenda Massey said that Christine Anderson had come by Alderpoint on May 2, the day following the dance. Even before Sherry's body was found, according to Massey, Christine had asked, "Did Sherry get home okay?" She seemed to be worried about Sherry's welfare. Why she was worried was not explained. Massey also said that Mike Moore asked where Sherry was, and he seemed concerned.

The investigative waters were muddied even more when a detective spoke with Debra Mullins, nineteen. She said that Sherry had danced with Terry Robinson, whereas everyone else said he had avoided her. According to Mullins, she spoke with Fred Lane on May 5 and said that Lane had told her he thought John Annibel and Terry Robinson had killed Sherry.

Mullins also talked about a time in 1972 when she had nearly been raped by four boys near Alderpoint. They had disrobed her, but were scared off by a passing car. Some of the names she gave were individuals who had been questioned in Sherry's case, though these names did not include John Annibel, Ron Stone, or Russ Rude.

Another person the detectives talked to was Joan Moody of Alderpoint. She knew Whit Lewis, who was John Annibel's uncle. According to Moody, Sherry borrowed some money from her on Friday, April 30, 1976 to go to the dance. Moody stated that Sherry told her she would go to the dance and then home.

This seemed to indicate Miranda, where her mom lived. Sherry told Moody this about 7:30 PM, however, Sherry may have changed her mind later in the evening without telling Moody.

Moody also told the detective that someone with the last name of Robinson had at one time had sexual relations with Sherry. This had supposedly occurred in the previous six weeks. Moody said that Sherry had a crush on this guy, and she indicated the person was Terry Robinson. According to Moody, Terry Robinson was a lot older than Sherry, and he worried about having sex with a minor. Robinson avoided Sherry during the dance and Robinson was later polygraphed and passed the test.

Alton Whitley Lewis, John Annibel's uncle, was interviewed by detectives. His girlfriend, he said, was Gayle Anzini of Alderpoint, and in the late-night hours of April 30, he took her to Payton Ranch between Blocksburg and Bridgeville. While he was there, there was a drunk man named Dennis who didn't have a ride home, and Lewis took Dennis to his residence near Fort Seward and dropped him off.

Lewis told a detective, "On the way to the Annibels' place, where I was staying, I came down on top of the ridge where you start to go down to the Eel Rock hill toward Fruitland Ridge. I came upon a car 250 to 300 yards ahead of me, and the car's taillights came on when I drove up. They just really took off, and I figured it was probably somebody poaching a deer or something. I thought I would scare him. So I sped up, but I couldn't catch him.

"I was going really fast, and I thought it had to be somebody I might know. All I ever got to see was two round taillights—one on each side. One big taillight on each side. The person driving the car was really flying down the road and had to have known it. He had to have lived in the area.

"John [Annibel] got home around 3 AM or 3:30 AM. It was darker than a son-of-a-gun and I had some stuff I had bought at the commissary there at Fort Miley. Shorts and socks and stuff. I was packing some stuff in the house and I went to get a blanket and John came in. He had been partying quite a bit.

Drunk or stoned or something. John said, 'I'm going to bed.'
I said okay.

"Then I made a pot of coffee because my sister [John's
mother] gets up at 4 AM. She's a morning cook at the Benbow
Inn. I went in and woke her up. She took my car and went to
work. I stayed up and fixed the water pump on her car. Then
I went to bed around one o'clock in the afternoon."

Pam Smith, who was at the Annibel residence when John
arrived, said later she looked at her clock and it was 3:15 AM.
She said, "John was only home for a while and then he went
out again at around 6 AM or so. It didn't make much sense. He
had just gotten home not long before that. He was gone for
quite a while. He never talked about where he went or what
he did. I didn't think about it at the time, but it seemed awfully
suspicious later."

Investigator Bob Hickok was sent by Deputy DA Bernard
DePaoli to interrogate Clyde Pomeroy of McKinleyville,
which was about seventy miles in the opposite direction.
Pomeroy had been in trouble in the past, and when Hickok arrived at Pomeroy's residence, the first words out of Pomeroy's
mouth were, "You must have found another body."

Hickok answered, "Yes."

Pomeroy inexplicably said, "That was quick. I didn't think
they could find that lady where she was."

Then Pomeroy mumbled on that he picked up girl hitchhik-
ers, and that they deserved to die for being so careless. He also
said that he wanted to get into a gunfight with Hickok. Pomeroy
was very clearly drunk.

Unfortunately for the investigation, it was proved later that
Pomeroy had been nowhere near Garberville on the dates in
question—he had been out on the ocean fishing. Nonetheless,
DePaoli had Pomeroy's vehicle's tires checked. Apparently, they
didn't match tire treads found up on Eel Rock Road.

Another angle was checked out as well, and it concerned
the young men who had been seen by Glenda Massey and
Sherry Lynn Smith up at Alderpoint in a van on April 30. Detectives discovered that the van had been parked at a camp in
the redwoods on April 29, and the owner of the van was

Doug Eitelman. He lived in Vernon, Connecticut, even though his van had New York plates. Detective Leo Bessette flew all the way back to Connecticut to question Eitelman.

Eitelman agreed to take a polygraph test to prove his innocence. He was asked the following questions:

Tester: "Do you know who killed Sherry Smith?"

Eitelman: "No."

Tester: "Did you kill Sherry Smith?"

Eitelman: "No."

Tester: "Were you present when Sherry Smith was killed?"

Eitelman: "No."

Tester: "Did you rape Sherry Smith?"

Eitelman: "No."

Chief certified polygraphist Sergeant Jack Schneider said that Doug Eitelman had passed the test.

Eitelman's van passenger was a guy named Edward Roston of Wyoming. He was also given a polygraph test as well, and passed.

Both of Sherry's parents, and her sisters, were devastated by the news of her murder. It seemed impossible that the girl who had survived so many mishaps at a young age was actually dead. Her dad did admit later, "Sherry trusted everyone, and never was in fear of anything." He surmised that she probably knew her killer and did not suspect a thing before she was attacked.

All of the family members were tearful, angry, and confused, but more than anything else, in a daze. The stark reality of the situation was the most unreal thing of all.

The memorial and funeral service for Sherry took place on May 6, 1976. Among the casket-bearers was John Annibel and his brother, James. Sherry was interred at Eureka's Sunset Memorial Park, which faced the Pacific Ocean. Pam would recall later, "John was acting weird that day. It seemed like he was glaring at me. I didn't know why."

An article in the *Eureka Times-Standard* reported that Sheriff Gene Cox had said that a team of four southern Humboldt County detectives was working around the clock to try and uncover evidence about the slaying. Cox told a reporter that they were checking up on Sherry Lynn Smith's last movements. Cox added, "We are making every effort to find the person responsible for this horrible crime."

Even more intriguing was the fact touched upon by newspapers that Sherry Lynn Smith's murder bore a striking resemblance to two other murders of young women in the previous months in the county. The *Eureka Times-Standard* reported, "The method of the girl's [Sherry's] murder bears resemblance to two other brutal killings of young women which have occurred in the county, according to Humboldt County Sheriff Gene Cox. Officials have said in the past, noting that the bodies have been discovered by chance, that there could be others in isolated parts of the county not yet discovered."

The first rape and murder mentioned had occurred late in September or early October 1975. Nineteen-year-old Humboldt State University student Janet Lee Bowman was last seen at the county welfare office at 8:45 AM on September 30. A few days later, the Humboldt County Sheriff's Office received an anonymous letter stating that a girl's body was lying in the brush near the truck scale on Highway 299, north of Blue Lake. According to Lieutenant Roy Simmons of the sheriff's office, the letter had been postmarked on a Saturday, and received the following Monday at 11 AM. The letter accurately described the location where a young woman's body could be found. For some reason, Simmons also stated, "The anonymous letter appears to have been written by someone who knew the location of the corpse and did not wish to get involved, rather than being from the killer." How Simmons came to that conclusion, he didn't say. Nor did he reveal the contents of the letter.

Janet Bowman had recently returned to Humboldt State University in Arcata from her home in San Diego. She rented a room on Pigeon Point Road for the coming school year. Janet lived by herself and was not known to have a boyfriend. Acquaintances said she was shy but did hitchhike once in a while. Hitchhiking by students in the Arcata area was common in the 1970s.

Janet was 5'2" tall, weighed 95 pounds and had short dark curly hair. When her body was found, it was lying in brush and partially disrobed. Her face was bruised, and she had been strangled to death. Just like Sherry Lynn Smith, Janet had personal items that were missing. Sherry's luggage had not been found, and certain items that Janet was known to carry with her were missing.

Three months passed and the police were no closer to solving the murder of Janet Lee Bowman. Then on January 18, 1976, the body of twenty-one-year-old Karen Frances Fisher, a University of Colorado student visiting the area, was discovered in an isolated area near Trinidad Head on the coast. Karen had apparently been raped and strangled. Her pants were found pulled down around her ankles.

Like Sherry Lynn Smith, Karen's body had been found by chance. A hiker discovered it in the brush and called police. Like Smith and Bowman, the body would not have been easily discovered if not for outside intervention, either a hiker or some other means.

Karen Fisher had been visiting friends near Arcata and inquired about nice beaches in the area. They told her about beaches near Trinidad Head. Karen rode on an AMRTS bus to Humboldt State University and then started hitchhiking. A man later told police he gave Karen a ride from the Seventeenth Street entrance at Highway 101 to Clam Beach. He let her off there and did not see her again. Police eventually ruled him out as a suspect.

Karen was described as being 5' 7" tall, and weighed 120 pounds. She had dark blond hair. A *Eureka Times-Standard* article noted, "Officers said the case bears some resemblance to the murder of Janet Lee Bowman. Miss Bowman, a Humboldt

State University student, had also been throttled to death and apparently raped. Both bodies were discovered by chance."

In a curious addition, the article then stated, "Both Miss Bowman and Miss Fisher were discovered by hikers." No mention was given of a mysterious anonymous letter. Nor were there questions if an anonymous letter ever existed in the Bowman case. Another reporter on the Karen Fisher murder had also for some reason reported hikers as having been the discoverers of both bodies. A similar story of a hiker finding the body of Sherry Lynn Smith would soon make its way into the newspapers, even though in reality, it had been a motorcycle rider who found her body. Just why these errors occurred is unknown.

To make matters even more curious, a decomposed body of a young woman was found in June 1976, only weeks after the discovery of Sherry Lynn Smith's body. Nineteen-year-old Vickie Lynn Schneider went missing on June 13, 1976. She had told friends she was going sunbathing on a beach near Samoa, a town to the west of Eureka. A week after the thirteenth, sherriff's marine units and a mounted posse had searched for the missing woman. In the last week of June, four boys who were riding motorbikes in the dunes discovered Vickie's body behind some bushes. She was about fifty yards away from a road. The boys did not touch her body, but instead hurried off to call the police. No mention was later made if she had been raped or strangled. Her story fell from sight in the newspapers.

On May 26, 1976, a memo was sent out by the sheriff's office to be on the lookout for Sherry Lynn Smith's missing luggage. The items included a blue-gray overnight bag, a dark blue or black suitcase, a pink hair-dryer case that contained white roller skates, a multicolored heavy sweater, and a blue-and-white Western-style handkerchief that she wore in her hair.

On that same day, John Annibel was interviewed again. John Lilly, an investigator for the California Department of Justice, was even on hand. Annibel once again said that he left Sherry at the door of the dance around 2 AM. He said he went back to the bar to have one last beer. He stood there for a little while then went back to his car. John said he waited, then went back into the dance hall, but couldn't find Sherry. Once again he said, "I thought she got a ride from Fred Lane."

Christine Anderson was reinterviewed two days later. She proclaimed that she and Sherry were not friends. They had argued about something and according to Anderson, "Sherry threatened to punch my lights out." Just what they had argued about was not revealed in the report.

John Annibel was given a polygraph test in late May by HCSO Detective Hickok. Hickok originally said that John passed the test, but later Hickok stated that the results were inconclusive. These polygraph-test results were sent to the California Department of Justice (DOJ) in Sacramento. The results were studied by Sam Lister and Robert Riburdy. They said that there were "signs of guilty knowledge" on John Annibel's part, and that Hickok's assessment was not correct. Their recommendation was that a second polygraph test be operated by DOJ experts.

On June 3, 1976, DOJ Bureau Agents interviewed John Annibel once again, this time at the HCSO substation in Garberville. Most of John's answers to questions were the same as before, except this time he said that he had spoken with "Doris" (Ron Stone's sister), near the door of the Fireman's Hall at 2 AM. She later denied having any conversation with John at that time.

Because of all the inconsistencies in John's statements, a search warrant was requested and granted for a search on the 1969 Mustang. Items found inside the car were:

1. Loose matches.

2. Matches from the ashtray.

3. Hair from a sweatshirt.

4. Hair from a brush.

5. Hair from the floor of the car.

6. Some beer bottles.

7. An empty box of Havoline Motor Oil.

The tire-tread marks left when a car had skidded on the gravel road had been measured when Sherry's body had been found, and they matched well to those of John's vehicle, the 1969 Mustang.

John was also asked for, and provided hair from his head and pubic area. The cabin in which he stayed (each Annibel boy had his own cabin near the main house) was searched as well. No evidence linked to Sherry Lynn Smith was found in the cabin or car, but by then it had been more than a month since her body had been discovered.

Despite no evidence of Sherry showing up in John's possession, DOJ Special Agent John Lilly wrote in his report to Sheriff Cox, "John Annibel remains the primary suspect."

John was asked to take a second polygraph test. Instead of doing this, he retained a lawyer. The lawyer was William Ferroggiaro, and on advice of counsel, John did not take another polygraph test.

Pam Smith and James Annibel would later ask themselves questions about some strange things that had occurred. Pam wanted to know why it was so important for John to leave so early on May 1, since he didn't get home until 3:15 AM. She said later, "John left again around 6 AM. He was gone for a few hours. I didn't make any sense. He had just been home for a few hours and then left with no explanation. He hadn't done anything like that before. I was in too much of a daze at the time, but later I thought John might have dumped Sherry's belongings off in the forest somewhere."

James realized that the taillights that Whit Lewis saw on Eel Rock Road could not have belonged to a 1969 Mustang. That year's model had rectangular taillights. A 1964 Ford Falcon, however, did have large round taillights like Whit had seen, and Ron Stone drove a Falcon. James wondered if Ron's vehicle was ever inspected for traces of Sherry's presence. He also wondered if John had gone to Ron's house and John, Ron Stone, and Sherry had gotten into Ron's car at some point.

* * *

Almost a year later, in 1977, Bob Hickok and Lieutenant Roy Simmons were present when Dwight and Nada Stillwell were hypnotized to try and recall events at the Garberville dance on the night of April 30/May 1. Dwight was able to be hypnotized, but Nada wasn't. No useful new information came out of Dwight being hypnotized.

That same year, in the fall, Edward Harrison of Redway said to a detective that Christine Anderson had told him that she knew who the killer was. Anderson supposedly told him, "I'm not going to tell the police. I know he'll get out in four or five years and kill me." Anderson did not reveal who she thought the killer was to Harrison. Whether Christine Anderson was reinterviewed is not recorded.

Frustrated by lack of progress on Sherry Lynn Smith's case, her father, Paul, began talking to people on his own, and taking notes. He said later, "Sherry trusted everyone and never was in fear of anything. She put up a fight at the hands of her killer."

Just how he came to this conclusion, he didn't say. Did he know that there was skin of her attacker under her fingernails? Had the authorities told him this? Or did he just surmise this because he knew Sherry's personality? Paul wasn't the only one who would later decide that there was the skin of her attacker under her fingernails. Several people who lived up on Fruitland Ridge heard this story as well, and would claim that it was true.

Paul recalled, "Sherry was found a short distance from John Annibel's house. Only a local person would have picked the area where her body was found, as it was almost hidden from the main road."

Paul started looking into the relationship of John Annibel and his buddy Ron Stone. He was intrigued about Stone because he'd heard that another male had gotten into the car with John and Sherry at the Garberville dance. Paul wrote on a scratch pad, "Ron Stone—John Annibel—suspects? At the dance?"

Then Paul on his notepad added, "John Annibel knows

information about case. Ron, very mean and on parole. Is capable of committing a violent crime." Paul Smith came to these conclusions by talking to several people around the area. Some claimed to have been robbed by the team of Annibel and Stone. Paul would say much later that it was a not-very-well-kept secret that John and Ron were responsible for several burglaries in the area. According to Paul, "John once said that he'd buried a bunch of stolen guns on the property."

One of Paul's more curious notes read, "John and Ron Stone came home about 3:00 AM." How did he know this? Pam, who was there that night, said she only saw John come home about 3:15 AM. She knew that was the time because she had checked the clock. She made no mention of Ron Stone being there.

Then Paul listed the officers who had been at the crime scene. The list included Lieutenant R. Simmons, Detective Leo Bessette, Detective James Ivey, Deputy Hickok, and District Attorney John Buffington. This last one, about Buffington was another mystery to Paul. Usually DAs will leave this kind of work to their subordinates, and Paul wondered why the district attorney himself would come nearly sixty miles from Eureka to be at this murder site. Was it because there had already been the murders of two other young women in the last few months? Two murders with similar MOs? Or was it something else?

Paul Smith was also very curious about the mention of Christine Anderson in the newspaper article. He referred to her as Christine Anderson of Phillipsville, and he noted that she didn't go to South Fork High School, but was a continuation student elsewhere. So why had the principal of South Fork High contacted police about Anderson being missing if she wasn't one of his students? Christine's sister apparently went to South Fork High. Paul wondered if she had told the principal about Christine being missing. It was just one more mystery surrounding the murder of Sherry Lynn Smith.

Paul scratched on the notepad, "She [Christine] with two young men." He underlined two young men and asked, "Who?" That was indeed a big question. Just who they were did not come out in the newspapers, nor was it listed in published police reports. Later he would surmise that the two men were Moore and Emmons.

Paul Smith tried to profile both Sherry and her killer. Of Sherry he said, "Sherry was trusting, but would fight verbally or physically when forced to do something she did not want to do. She always thought she was in control."

Of the killer he said, "This type of guy, I mean the killer, is engaged in serious violence, exhibiting symptoms of paranoia. The psychopathic personality is antisocial, aggressive, and highly impulsive. He feels no guilt and cannot form lasting bonds of affection with others. These kind of guys are present-oriented and rarely plan crimes in detail, and they feel little anxiety or remorse after hurting people. They are loners with a warped capacity for love." After this he wrote in bold letters: "John Annibel."

Wanting to know how far it was from Highway 101 to where Sherry's body had been discovered, Paul drove up the road and gauged the mileage and the time it took to drive there. He noted that the old logging road where Sherry had been found could barely be seen from the main road. He surmised that only a local would know about it. John Annibel was definitely a local. And so was Ron Stone. Paul wrote these names down and underlined them.

No more hard evidence showed up concerning the murder of Sherry Lynn Smith until March 20, 1978. On that date her luggage was found one quarter-mile south of where her body had been discovered. Pam Smith said later, "When John left that morning again, around 6 AM, did he drive down to that spot and get rid of Sherry's luggage? I think he did."

CHAPTER 2

Young John and James

Fraternal twins John and James Annibel were born in Scotia, California on December 4, 1957 to Ted and Lyla Annibel. They already had an older brother, Ted, who was named after their father. In the family oral history, there was a story that the name Annibel could be traced back to Hannibal of Carthage, the legendary hero and famous general of ancient times.

The region that the twin brothers were born into would shape their destiny. It was a land of towering redwood trees, and the timber industry was the preeminent economic force in the area. More than any other timber company, the Pacific Lumber Company dominated Humboldt County. The Pacific Lumber Company (often referred to as PL or PALCO) facilities at Scotia, on the Eel River, were the largest redwood-lumber mills in the world. Their father, Ted Annibel, worked for PL, and in time John would as well.

The place John and James were born was one of the last true company towns in America. Scotia had come into being in the late nineteenth century. The bungalows in town for the workers were built between 1910 and 1925. They were modest homes, painted in pastel colors, with open front porches and unfenced yards, so that one yard blended into another. As the book *In The Peace Zone* stated, "There is a comforting feel of proportion to the houses, a sense of having been planned to human and not automotive scale. There are no driveways or discarded wrecks out front. You can almost hear the voices of your childhood, the admonitions of friends and family dead; the air thick with unsatisfied desire."

If you were a resident of Scotia, you never had to worry about painting your house, inside or out. The company painters did that for you, and the plumbers fixed your pipes and carpenters did repairs. If you lived there your only job was to work at one of the great mills or out in the forest.

There was almost an egalitarian sense in the town. The most prestigious houses, once built for company executives, had only a few more amenities than the regular houses—a fireplace, screened-in porch, and extra bedroom. For some reason the places where Portuguese and Italian families had once grown vegetables in the yards were deemed to be less desirable. There was a subtle pecking order in Scotia, but it was almost invisible to the outsider.

There was very little in town for young people to do. The Winema Theater had closed down in the mid-1950s, and youngsters were left pretty much to their own devices as far as play and entertainment went. For adults the prime social organization was the Volunteer Fire Department. For a town made primarily of wood, being a volunteer fireman was an ironically essential part of the community and a prestigious job.

Generation after generation of a family might work for Pacific Lumber in Scotia, but it was mainly for men. In those days, no women worked on the "Green Chain," the mill line that turned logs into lumber. Women might have jobs as secretaries in the offices, but that was about it. Others might work at nearby cafés, motels, and other small businesses. John and James's mom would eventually work as a cook at the Benbow Inn. It was an upscale hotel on the Eel River that had an old English Tudor look to it.

During the writing of *In the Peace Zone* in the 1960s, teacher Peggy Rice asked her fourth grade class how many of them would like to live in Scotia as an adult. Almost all the boys and half the girls said that they would. It was the only life they had ever known. Scotia was definitely a working-class town, and the author of *In the Peace Zone* noted that it had never produced a famous scientist, inventor, philosopher, or composer. The one dominant fact of life in Scotia were the forests and lumber.

Of course the reason for the town's existence were the mills, and in John and James's day as kids, a large redwood tree that eventually became lumber would be found on PL property, cut on PL property, trucked to the mills by PL vehicles, and sawed, graded, and cut into boards at the PL mills.

The process began when a PL worker on a D-8 Cat built a bed in the forest for the fallen redwood tree to land. The "faller" directed where he wanted the tree to end up. The faller was the highest-paid worker in the forest because his judgement could mean the difference between thousands of dollars when a tree fell "true," or shattered badly on impact.

After determining the direction of the fall, the chopper would make his undercut, factoring in wind, slope, and other factors. Suddenly there would be a sharp crack that would break the silence, followed by a splintering sound and breaking foliage. Then the huge redwood would hit the ground with an earthshaking thud, followed by a plume of branches, dust, and debris.

Before the dust even settled, the faller would walk the log in caulk boots, measuring the board feet. One good-sized old redwood might have enough lumber in it to build two average-sized houses. The log would be trucked down to the mill pond near one of the large PL mills, and await its turn to be sawn.

In Mill A, for instance, a huge log would be dragged up to the sawyer who would analyze the log for the initial cut. In his control booth, the sawyer would decide where to make a thick cut for siding, and a thin cut for beams, studs, and paneling. A misstep could result in a broken saw, a thousand feet of ruined wood, or in the worst case scenario, automatic machinery running wild and debris and chunks of metal flying everywhere.

On a good cut, the head rig would inch forward and slice off a two-inch-thick section like meat being hacked off a turkey.

All of these cuts were called "money cuts." The cut wood would go down the line to a man operating a machine that edged the slabs of wood into recognizable lengths of lumber. By the end of the line, the wood that had once been a log would be cut into various shapes and sizes, depending upon its quality.

Growing up, John and James didn't live in the town of Scotia proper, but in the nearby town of Fortuna that was still very closely associated with PL. Most of the townspeople there worked for or were associated in some fashion with the mill. James recalled, "When we were kids growing up in Fortuna, John was just a normal kid. He wasn't mean or cruel in anyway. Our parents were good people who taught us good manners and respect for our elders. We didn't have a lot of money, but we had a great childhood. Fortuna was a good place to grow up in."

The town had Rohner Park to play in, and the surrounding hills and forests were a pleasure to explore. John and James liked going fishing and hunting with their dad in the surrounding area. James, in particular, was a good hunter from a young age, especially as a spotter. His future wife Pam Smith, Sherry's sister, would say, "James can spot wildlife from a mile away. He is often a guide for people who go hunting. Even if he has a tag, he won't bag a deer until everyone else has theirs. James is really considerate. He's always putting other people before himself."

One of the places that their father took James and John hunting was up on Redwood House Road. It was a winding, twisting little road, dirt most of the way, that wound up the hills from the Van Duzen River valley. In its backcountry was an area that would one day become the eco-battleground of the Headwaters Forest, pitting environmental activists against PL. It would also have a dark and indelible link to John as well—one that he could never quite escape.

More than any other place, though, it was the Eel River along the margin of Fortuna that was a great place for the boys to ride their bikes to and enjoy, especially in summertime. By midsummer the Eel was only a few feet deep, perfect for swimming or riding on air mattresses or inner tubes. The river was a refreshing way to beat the heat on a hot summer's day. There was an idyllic quality about it, with its smoothly flowing waters and towering groves of redwood trees along its banks.

The Eel River was a sleeping giant, however, and in December 1964 it awoke with a vengeance, turning the Annibel family's world upside down. Near Branscomb at the headwaters of the South Fork of the Eel, it rained more than twenty-seven inches in six days. Near Island Mountain, where the North Fork of the Eel met the main fork, the water rose to an astonishing hundred feet in a few days, as it churned through the narrow canyon.

To make matters even worse, there had been a heavy snowfall up in the Trinity Mountains, which fed streams into the Van Duzen River, which emptied into the Eel. By December 21 the small towns of Alton, Pepperwood, Weott, Myers Flat, and Miranda were all flooded. On December 23, another fierce rainstorm hit the area and Humboldt County became cut off from the rest of the world.

The headlines in the *Humboldt Times*, announced: "PEPPERWOOD WIPED OUT, OTHER TOWNS CRUSHED! Thirty million board feet of logs escaped from the Pacific Lumber Mill ponds at Scotia and became battering rams, raging down the Eel and destroying bridges along the way. Thousands of dead cattle joined the logs in the maelstrom. Roads and railroad tracks were washed away, bridges collapsed, and a wall of muddy, dirty water raged towards the ocean.

The only way into Humboldt County was by air or sea. A U.S. Navy destroyer was sent to Humboldt Bay with relief supplies and aircraft flew off the deck of the carrier USS *Bennington*. Air operations were not without risks. A helicopter attempting to rescue trapped residents at Ferndale crashed, killing all seven people aboard.

Finally on Christmas eve, the rains began to cease and the waters recede. Towns everywhere along the Eel were flooded and half-destroyed. Pepperwood never did recover. Even Forutna was hard hit, with debris, uprooted trees, junked cars, and flotsam everywhere. It was a scene that looked more like a European city in World War II that had been bombed, instead of a quiet lumber town.

It was an interesting and exciting scene, however, for young John and James and their classmates to explore during the clean-up process. Many familiar landmarks had been swept away or severely damaged. Earthmovers, cranes, and bulldozers were at work all over the area. Near town, the main Highway 101 bridge over the Eel had to be reconstructed.

At the age of twelve, John and James had to tell their classmates in Fortuna goodbye when their family moved south into the wild country at Fruitland Ridge above Myers Flat. By comparison Fortuna was an outpost of civilization. "The Ridge" was a backcountry wild area with tangles of oak, redwood trees, manzanita, and poison oak that had always given the area a rough reputation. Some of the people in the area even referred to themselves as "Poison Oakers." It was a badge of pride to note what a rugged and wild area they inhabited. The countryside had once been the haunt of cattle rustlers, bushwhackers, and some people living on the edge of the law. There were still some residents back in there who lived the same way their ancestors had, except now the preferred illegal activity was growing pot instead of rustling cattle. There was a roughhewn quality of rugged individualism that permeated life in the area, and in some cases, a disregard for the law.

Something happened to John Annibel up on the Ridge. Perhaps it was the onset of puberty. Perhaps it was missing his friends in Fortuna. Or even the fact that each boy now had his own cabin, separated from the main house. John would later brag that by the age of twelve, he had his own cabin, his own horse, and his own motorcycle. It was paradise for a boy, but one that had dangers for a boy with limited self-control, especially for the type of boy that John was becoming.

James would recall later, "I started hanging out with the older kids. Ted and I hung out together and started excluding John from everything we did. John was turning into a tattletale and always running to Mom to tell her what Ted and I did. He was becoming very weird.

"Some of Ted and my friends would belittle John right to his face. One girl named Sherry Nordgren particularly made fun of John. He really hated her. One night when John was about fourteen, he got ahold of some alcohol and got really drunk. Somehow he got Sherry to walk up to the horse corral with him. He said he had something to show her. When they got there, John got behind her and swung an ax handle into the back of her head. She was bleeding a lot, but managed to escape. She came down and told us what John had done. She said he tried to kill her.

"Ted was going to beat John up real bad for this. But then he saw that John was so drunk that he probably didn't even know what he was doing. Afterward Ted and I felt a little responsible for John being so violent. Maybe if we hadn't shunned him so much, he might not have been so violent. But he was so weird by this time, we didn't want to be around him."

Sherry Nordgren would later have a slightly different variation of the story. She said that on New Year's Eve, 1973, John had asked her to walk up the trail toward the horses. She walked in front and on the way up there he suddenly hit her in the head with an ax handle. Her head started bleeding and she grabbed the ax handle away from him and asked why he had done it. Amazingly, John said that he hadn't hit her. He said a tree branch had fallen on her head. The bloody ax handle obviously told a different story. Sherry later claimed that John did not hate her, but she did admit to a friend that "John is becoming really weird."

At South Fork High School, Pam Smith began riding to basketball games in the same car with John and James. Initially she sat in the backseat and talked with John. She didn't know at the time that it was James who had a crush on her. She would say later, "James was very shy."

As time went on, however, James got up his nerve and began asking Pam out on dates. Before long they were boyfriend and girlfriend. Pam said, "John would say later that I was his girlfriend, but that just wasn't true. I was nice to him and that was all. John lived in a fantasy world a lot of the time."

Pam also said, "My sister Sherry knew John. She would have been comfortable being around him."

The one girl that John really liked up on the Ridge was a girl named Vicki. James would recall, "Everyone liked Vicki. She was real friendly and sweet. She treated everyone well, even John. He had a bad crush on her. I think he had this crush all his life, even when he got married later. Vicki was the one girl he really wanted, but she didn't like him back in the same way."

Vicki would later say that she liked John to pal around with, and they went out and did things together, but it was never a boyfriend/girlfriend kind of relationship. She said he would get angry when she dated other guys. At those times he would be verbally abusive towards her. She also noted that he was never physically abusive toward her.

It's hard to know what demons were scratching on the inside of John's mind as he went through his teenage years up at Fruitland Ridge. Shunned by his brothers and longing for Vicki, but according to James and Pam, unable to have her, and belittled by Ted and James's friends, in James's words, "He just became weirder and weirder. We didn't want to be around him."

Like the other Annibel men, John took a job with the Pacific Lumber Company after graduating from high school. He worked on the Green Chain, and he grew to be tough and strong. James later said that John had incredibly fit and powerful arms. He recounted, "I was pretty strong myself, but John was even stronger. It was almost unreal. He could bale hay all afternoon and it wouldn't hurt his arms at all. Kids at school originally tried making fun of us because of our last name. I'd sometimes get into fights and win. They wouldn't even mess with John, because they knew how strong I was, and they knew he was even stronger. If they couldn't whip me, they knew they sure couldn't whip John."

All John's frustrations were now seething right below the surface. On April 30, 1976, Sherry Lynn Smith asked him for a ride at the Garberville dance. Years later, Pam said, "I learned that John was mad at Sherry at the dance, because he wanted to go home and she wanted to stay and talk to her friends. I think when he gave her a ride back up the hill, he was thinking that she owed him. She'd have to put out for him. That was his thinking. I think when John turned south at the junction, and not toward the Annibel place, Sherry knew something was wrong. I think he attacked her and she fought back. Then he raped her and killed her. But I didn't think this at the time. I only came to this conclusion much later. There was a good reason I began to think about things in this way."

CHAPTER 3

"No Sign of Dead Woman"

By 1979, the furor over the Sherry Lynn Smith case had died down and was definitely on the back burner, as far as law enforcement in Humboldt County was concerned. There were plenty of other cases to address. John Annibel was no longer being questioned about her death, although DOJ Special Agent John Lilly had said that John was the primary suspect in the case. John settled down to a routine of work at the Scotia Mill, and later the Carlotta Mill for Pacific Lumber, working on the Green Chain. He was a good worker, according to his foreman, and brought home a steady paycheck, but the one thing he did not have was a steady girlfriend. All of that changed in the summer of 1979.

Mike Cortopassi was a young man in the Eureka area who was going with an eighteen-year-old girl named Lisa LaDe-Route. Lisa had an eighteen-year-old sister named Andrea, who was called Anghs most of the time by her family and especially Lisa. Andrea had been going with a guy named Billy Ryan for a number of years. By the summer of 1979, however, Billy had left her and she took it hard. To try and cheer her up, Lisa asked

Mike if he knew anyone that Andrea could go out with. He said yes, he had a friend. The friend's name was John Annibel.

Andrea and Lisa's young lives had not been easy ones. Their father was a decorated World War II veteran, who had taken on a young wife, Camille, more than twenty years his junior. Camille was only sixteen at the time, and he was thirty-seven years old. Lisa's father had been courageous in the war, but he had a tough time adjusting to civilian life. He became addicted to alcohol and his marriage to Camille was a stormy one. Eventually she left him and got a divorce when Lisa and Andrea were still very young.

Camille had a live-in boyfriend later, but things weren't much better with him. Lisa recalled one incident from when she was young when the boyfriend was trying to beat her mother's head on a bathroom sink. Lisa jumped on his back, yelling and screaming, trying to make him stop. Lisa was hysterical, but Andrea very calmly called the police and reported the trouble. That was Andrea's style. She seemed to be calm and collected no matter how extreme the situation.

Lisa wrote later, "After Mom and Dad divorced, she eventually remarried [not to the abusive boyfriend]. It was a new life I'll never forget. Mom was so happy. She baked cookies and was always decorating the house and taking pictures of us kids. We seemed like a real family.

"We moved into a small cabin across the street from the ocean near Eureka, California. Every night we could hear the sweet sounds of the ocean singing us to sleep. We would all go for a walk on the beach and have a bonfire. I don't think there has ever been happier memories of me and my sister Andrea."

On one occasion her step-dad, built Andrea and Lisa a playhouse over at their grandmother's house. It was a big surprise and he wouldn't let either one of them see what was going on until it was finished. When it was finally done, Andrea and Lisa were nearly speechless. Lisa said later, "He did it just to see the big smiles on our faces. He did it for no other reason than to make us happy. We could fit six kids in there. It was like our own little house.

"Dad was always like that," Lisa said. [They called their step-dad Dad.] "He drove a truck and often drove out of state. He asked us if we had ever seen elk and bears up close. He said some time he'd take us on a trip up to Washington State and it would be our job to count all the elk and bears along the road to keep him awake. It was really just his way of saying that he liked us very much."

Yet tragedy always seemed to be lurking just around the corner for Lisa and Andrea. One day when Andrea was nine years old, she, Lisa, and their younger sisters were over their grandmother's house on a Sunday afternoon, when the phone rang. Their grandmother answered the phone and became very quiet. After a while she started to cry. Andrea and Lisa didn't know what it meant, and they quietly crept away into a bedroom.

Lisa said later, "Anghs left the bedroom to sit with Grandma at the living-room table. She started rubbing Grandma's back and asked her what was wrong. And Grandma just shook her head. A few minutes later she took Anghs into the small kitchen. I tried to overhear them, but they were whispering.

"Later Anghs took me back to the bedroom. With a blank look on her face she said, 'Dad is dead.'

"I didn't really understand. I asked Anghs, 'What is death? What is it really?'

"She said, 'Lisa, you know. When something dies, it never comes back.'

"I asked, 'Does everyone die?'

"A little exasperated, Anghs answered, 'Yes, Lisa!'

"I asked, 'What happens when you die?'

"Anghs answered, 'I don't know. Some people say you just go into the black unknown. Others say that you go to be with God. But no one knows for sure until they die.'"

Their mom never had much money to begin with, and the stress of losing her husband was too much. All of the children were taken away to foster homes for a while, but later Andrea and Lisa were reunited with their mom. The two youngest daughters, Donna and Corinna, were not. Lisa grew to be very dependent upon her big sister. Andrea was her rock in a rough and dangerous world.

In junior high school, Lisa related, "The richer kids looked down on us poor kids. They made fun of the way we looked and dressed. Andrea didn't let it get her down. She told me that when those kids were talking about us, it was because they didn't have anything better to do. Then Anghs said, 'Who the heck do they think they are, anyway? They're not anybody I care to know.'

"Anghs became really excited about fashions in junior-high school. Our great grandmother was a seamstress, and Anghs would take her ideas to her. One day Andrea excitedly told me about what she planned to make and made me promise that we would both wear her new design to school. I think she really wanted to give the rich kids something to talk about. The pants she had in mind were to be taken in at the knees; in other words, cut the pant legs just above the knees, and hem them as you would a pair of cutoffs. For the lower section she would have Gramms insert an elastic band into both knees so that the lower half could be pulled on. The end product would be the same pair of pants, but with the knees showing.

"Later on I said, 'Anghs, I can't wear those to school! They already think we're nuts!'

"But Anghs got me to promise to wear them to school the next day. Anyway, a little later on, a couple of Anghs's guy friends showed up and saw our new pants. One of them said, 'Wow, where did you get those?' He was really impressed. He thought they were cool.

"The words just popped out of my mouth. 'Anghs designed them and Gramms made them.' I realized as soon as I said it, I was proud of Anghs and I was proud of Gramms. Anghs was very confident and never let peer pressure stop her."

After high school, Andrea lived for a while with her boyfriend Billy Ryan, and Lisa was out on her own by the age of seventeen. It was breaking up from Billy that brought Andrea into John Annibel's orbit. Lisa said later, "Andrea really loved Billy. I know they had a lot of things in common, but they were just too young at the time."

John Annibel could be good to Andrea at times, and awful at others. He had a strong jealous streak, something to which Vicki could attest, and he seemed to becoming increasingly paranoid and edgy. According to Lisa, there was one incident where she arrived home to find Andrea naked and crying. Lisa said, "I came home in the middle of the day and found both Andrea and John at home, which was unusual. Andrea was in the hallway at the top of the stairs, crying so hard she could hardly catch her breath. She was standing there completely naked.

"John was standing just a few feet away with his arms crossed. I went up the stairs to find out what was wrong, and Andrea shouted, 'Lisa, John tried to kill me! He tried to suffocate me with a pillow!'

"I could tell that they had both been drinking and I didn't know what to do. I walked past John and went to comfort Anghs, all the while keeping an eye on John. He slowly walked down the stairs, and out the front door, not saying a word.

"I said to Andrea, 'You're not going back to him are you?' She replied that she didn't know. She thought she still loved him, and besides, she didn't know where else to go. Without a job, she really didn't have anyplace to live."

Later, Andrea would relate another story to Lisa. She told her of when she and John were up at his cabin near the main Annibel house. Whether because of drugs, alcohol, or just plain psychosis, John started screaming at her that she had killed his cats. Andrea had done nothing of the sort, and told him so. John became enraged, however, and tried choking her. Andrea was sure he was trying to kill her. The yelling from John was so loud that his father came to investigate. He found John choking Andrea and had to pull him off of her. Andrea did not call the police on this incident, but she did tell Lisa much later. Lisa recalled, "She probably didn't tell me at the time because she knew I would go ape."

In 1979, Andrea was determined to better her life by going to college. It would give her the means to be self-sufficient and not have to depend upon John. She started attending day classes at College of the Redwoods near Eureka. About this time, Lisa remembered, "I had encouraged Andrea to go to college. I walked her through the admissions process. I just couldn't go to school during the day because I had a full-time job. So I went to school full-time at night and had a full-time job during the day. Anghs didn't have any real means of support, but because our dad had a veteran's benefit, it allowed her and I to attend school. The benefit paid for all the tuition fees and books, as well as about $340 a month for living expenses. But you had to keep up a B grade-point average."

Andrea was very proud of the steps she took to further her education. All of it was a struggle, but one she persisted in doing. She wrote about what she had accomplished in her diary.

"In the winter of '79, I enrolled in College of the Redwoods. I wanted to be a psychiatrist, so I majored in sociology. I had seen a counselor and he said it looks fine to me [about her plans]. He said, 'I don't even know why they sent you here to me.'

"In the spring of '79, I accomplished what I set out to do, and that was to get pretty good grades. During the summer I moved to quiet Myers Flat. [This was when she had moved in with John up at the Annibels' home on the hill. She and John lived in his cabin.]

"Fall of '79, I continued back in school, still without a counselor. I knew I had to improve my grades from the winter and spring quarters. So I enrolled in sociology again, but this time I was going to play it smart and get a tutor. I went there and she took down my name and told me to come back the next day and I did, only to find out that she was sick. After going there for over a month, I decided to give up on it.

"In my English class, 'Romance of Words,' our instructor Mr. Koad told us that he was going to improve our memories by having us write down words we didn't know and have us look up the definitions. Then later on that week we would have a test on them. I decided to use terms and concepts from my soc[iology] 1 book, and I thought it was the next best thing to a tutor. But it didn't turn out that way.

"At the same time, I was also enrolled in Math 171A and 171B. My teacher said in the first meeting of class that if you are signed up for 171A, finish chapters one, two, and three, in your math book and correct them. The answers are in the back of the book. After you finish that, go to Room 116 and ask for Pat and tell her you want to test for 171A. And then sign up for 171B, and repeat the same process over.

"So I did just that. I asked for Pat, and told her I was there for my math class, and I wanted a test for 171A. After I took it, I said, *is that all?* And she said yes. So I went to the administration office and signed up for 171B. When I received my report card in the mail, I knew I had to take my math classes over again.

"So for the winter of '80, I did take them over, and my instructor informed me that I was to take a test for chapters 1, 2, and 3. One thing is for sure: if you want a good counselor, you have to take some time out to find them. And I have. On-campus I have Marina Oliver and Mary Z. Off-campus from Humboldt State University, I have Dr. Cunnigham.

"I am finally getting the help and support I need to fulfill my career and goals for being a successful student, and taking the classes that will help me strengthen my weak points for a better future and a much better life in the long run."

There was a very strange notation on page two of this paper, however. Off to the side in the margin was one word. The word was "afraid." It had no connection to anything else she had written. She didn't explain why she was afraid or who she was afraid of.

Andrea knew that she needed a routine in her life if she was going to be a good student. She took this so much to heart that she made a daytime planner near the end of February 1980 to help her accomplish her goal. The schedule was built around her Monday, Wednesday, Friday classes, and Tuesday, Thursday classes.

Monday—7–8 AM: Riding bus
   8–9: Business 11
   9–10: English 177A
   10–11: Guid 52 [no notation of what that was]
   11–12: Math 171B
   12–1: Catch bus
   1–2: Home
   2–3: Housework
   3–4: Homework
   4–5: Snack, groom
   5–6: Study
   6–7: Free time, dinner
   7–8: Get ready for next day
   8–9: Read, bed

Wednesday was just the same as Monday, but Friday she had English 69, and English 177A, and quit the routine at 4 PM. Tuesdays and Thursdays were similar to Mondays and Wednesdays, except she had Business 10 and 11 on those days. Her weekends were free.

One of Andrea's classes was called "On Death and Dying." Considering what would soon transpire, it was ironic to say the least. Lisa recalled later, "At the time, I was going to night school at College of the Redwoods, and Anghs was taking the class during the day. We had the same instructor, who knew that we were related. It was the first time that Anghs and I went to college at the same time.

"I remember during the class about death and dying that we studied about the dying process and steps that lead to our ultimate demise. After watching several videos of people in their death process, and listening to individuals talk about their feelings and fears about dying, I started having nightmares. I remember the last assignment that we were given. We were supposed to make a collage on what death and dying meant to us, using anything we could find out of old magazines. I was really stuck and had no idea what to use to symbolize my feelings. I wanted to turn in just a black collage.

"Anghs, on the other hand didn't have any problems with

her collage. Most of her poster was filled with birds, flowers, and people. All kinds of things."

In the fall of 1979, John and Andrea took a trip to Colorado, where his twin brother James and his wife Pam lived. Something happened while John and Andrea were back there, and the details are no longer clear. For some reason John became very upset with Andrea. According to Lisa, "John and Andrea were back in Colorado at a residence with Tom Smith's [a friend of John's] mom and brother. Then when John and Andrea were on the road, he opened the car door and told her to get out. They were in the middle of nowhere in winter, and she didn't even have a coat on. He drove off without her. Tom Smith's mom and brother went out to the highway and brought her home.

"When Andrea got back to Humboldt County she didn't feel comfortable staying with John's mom and dad up on the ridge. So she stayed with me in a small two-bedroom mobile home owned by an elderly couple. We both slept on separate couches in the living room for about three days.

"It was around then that Andrea told me about the incident with the cats, and other times that John had verbally and physically abused her. I talked to people who had known both me and Andrea since we were very young about a place to stay. But they said there wasn't enough room. Then I told Anghs she could find a job and I'd help her type up a résumé. I said, 'As soon as you can, you need to get away from him.'

"A few days later, John returned from Colorado and picked Andrea up. Shortly afterward he and Andrea moved into a small cabin in Fortuna."

Whatever had happened in Colorado, John and Andrea rented a small "cabin" on Ninth Street in Fortuna. It was more like a cottage that sat next to another small cottage behind a larger home in front. There was a storage unit for the cottage nearby. [Later, people would refer to their residence as a cabin, a cottage, and an apartment. All the terms were for the same place on Ninth Street.]

Around Valentine's Day, Andrea sent her mother a card, but it was not your usual Valentine's Day card. On the front of the card was a depiction of a young girl standing amidst a sea of tall grass and flowers that towered over her head. The girl wore a Tam hat, held her arms out as if asking for help, and a single tear drop fell from her wide eyes. There were only two words on the front of the card—"I'm lost." It was a strange and disturbing card in light of what was soon to happen.

Lisa recalled, "On February 23, 1980, Andrea got a storage unit in Eureka to keep most of her things in. She didn't want John to know about it, and she gave a different address than where she lived on the forms. She listed a friend's address instead of her own. The storage unit held her things in case she had to leave John in a hurry."

On a Friday in early March 1980, Lisa LaDeRoute was getting ready to go to the Hoopa Indian Reservation with her friend Terry McCloskey. Just as they were about to leave, Andrea arrived in a car driven by a man named Max. As Lisa later explained, "Max had always been like a grandfather to Andrea and me. He was sixtysomething at the time and semiretired. Every summer we would spend at least one month with Max and his wife, Doris, on their dairy ranch in Ferndale."

Lisa and Andrea spoke for only a little while that day, and then Lisa drove away. She would remember ever afterward looking back and seeing Andrea waving good-bye to her for what seemed a long, long time. Lisa then turned the corner and Andrea disappeared from view.

Lisa noted later, "On the following Monday, Max called me at work. I could tell in his voice that he was worried and something was wrong. He said he was worried about Anghs. He said Anghs had asked him to take her shopping. She had just received a $340 check from her school grant, and she didn't have a driver's license. So Max had planned to take her shopping. He said he tried to call her all day, but he couldn't get an answer. I tried not to panic, and reassured him she was probably all right."

In the meantime, John Annibel had done something very suspicious. On March 18, 1980, he filed a missing person's report on Andrea at the Fortuna Police Department. The statement said that she'd left to go to college before he left for work on March 17, and that she was not at the apartment when he returned home from work. Nor had she returned that night or into the eithteenth. He wrote down that when he'd last seen her she had been wearing blue denim pants, boots, and a rust-colored jacket.

John went down to the Fortuna PD again on the nineteenth and was met at the counter by Detective Mike Losey. Losey recalled later, "I contacted him [Annibel] at the counter. He was inquiring, asking questions and that type of thing. He said that the last time he'd seen her was when she'd left for school from the apartment that they shared in the morning hours."

Lisa picked up the narrative about her and Max. "A couple of days later, Max called me again. He said John had just called him, and told him that he had filed a missing person's report on Anghs. I told Max I wanted to see John, and I asked him if he would go with me. I wondered why John didn't call me instead of Max.

"My boss was very understanding. She gave me all of the time off that I needed to look for my sister. She didn't complain about all the phone calls, and she even helped me with a poster about her disappearance. Most employers would have fired me."

The poster was of a recent photo of Andrea. She wore a baseball cap and looked directly at the camera. In large block letters near the top, Lisa wrote, HAVE YOU SEEN THIS WOMAN? In the middle portion Lisa noted, "She was last seen in Fortuna on March seventeenth. No one has seen her since." Then near the bottom Lisa wrote, "Family and friends are extremely concerned. *Please* call if you have *any* information to help locate her." Lisa then listed a phone number to call.

Lisa continued, "The next day, after work, Max and I went to the apartment that Andrea and John shared. It was the first time I had been there. We took a poster with us to give to John. When we got there John didn't answer the door. Just as we were about to leave, John pulled up with another guy in a pickup truck. John and the other guy were carrying large garbage bags—about three of them.

"John walked up to the door and said, 'I'll be right with you.'

He unlocked the front door and told us to go in. We went inside, and Max sat down. The first thing I did was look in the bathroom to see if any of Andrea's makeup was missing or if her toothbrush was gone. Anghs was a very beautiful girl, and she was very meticulous about her appearance. If she had planned on leaving John for good, she would have taken her makeup, toothbrush and clothes.

"I was frightened to find her makeup brushes, fingernail polishes, and toothbrush still sitting in the bathroom. I also noticed her wristwatch hanging on a nail next to the bed. It was something she would have taken if she had gone to school.

"While waiting for John to return from the storage room, I also found a chart that Andrea had written up about her current classes, as well as her personal schedule. I folded it quickly and stuck it in my purse before John came in.

"Meanwhile, John was putting the large garbage bags into a storage room outside the studio apartment. When he came back into the apartment, he explained that he had just finished doing Andrea and his laundry after he had let it pile up. This struck me as odd. Anghs used to always complain how she would have to do everything, and how John wouldn't help with anything, including the laundry. So why would he be washing her dirty laundry if he thought she had left him?

"While we were there, I asked John what had happened, and if he had made a missing person's report. He said he didn't know what to think. He had gone to work that day as usual, and when he got home she was gone and there wasn't a note. He said it was unusual for her not to be there when he got home from work, especially without leaving a note, even if she just went to the store.

"I asked him if he had noticed any of her clothes missing. He said nothing that was obvious. Then I told him that while Anghs was visiting me for a few days, she had borrowed one of my dresses and a slip. I asked if I could have them back. He said he put all of her clothes and things in the storage room because he felt that she had just abandoned him. But then I wondered why, if he thought she wasn't coming back, he just didn't give me all her stuff. It was more likely that she would see me than him.

"I told him I would go look for the dress and slip if it was going to bother him, and if he didn't mind. He insisted on getting them himself. So he had me describe what the dress and slip looked like. He left for a short time. When he returned, he said he couldn't find the dress, but he did find the slip. I remember thinking that something wasn't right. Not too many men that I know are aware of the kind of slips a woman wears, and I knew Anghs must have had several slips. Yet he picked my slip right out.

"Max and I left the apartment shortly afterward. I still couldn't figure out why John hadn't contacted me or my mother to let us know Anghs was missing. So when I was leaving I gave John my home phone number and my number at work. I told him to call if he heard anything. I also reassured him that I would let him know that at least she was okay if I heard from her. We gave him some posters to pin up and left.

"The next day, I called the community college that Anghs was attending. I had the class schedule that I had found in her apartment, and I wanted to find out if she was still going to school. Andrea was very serious about her education. I had also found a paper she had written explaining how she felt about her education. It was a very positive thing in her life. I contacted the administration office, and they referred me to her English instructor. This way, I thought, I could find out if she ever made it to the college on the seventeenth, when she was last seen by John. I spoke with the instructor on the phone. The instructor said she did attend class on the seventeenth of March. I was so relieved, thinking that maybe she was still just hiding from John. But then the instructor called back and said that he had mixed up the dates. Andrea had not shown up for class on March seventeenth. There was no class that day because it was finals week. Now I was more scared than ever."

Lisa recalled, "I hadn't seen anything on the news about the police asking people to help locate her. I was angry now, but mostly worried. First I tried the Eureka Police Department, and was told to contact the sheriff's office. They referred me to the Fortuna Police Department, since it was in their jurisdiction. I made an appointment to see Chief of Police Bill Terry in Fortuna.

"When I saw the chief of police, I asked why nothing was being done, and what were they planning to do. He said they were doing everything that they would normally do for a missing person's report. He said it wasn't as though it was a child missing. It appeared to him that Andrea and her boyfriend were not getting along, and she left him. I told him that it didn't appear that way to me—not from what John had told me. I told him John had said he'd gone to work, come home, and didn't even find a note. I also told him that Anghs not only didn't make it to class that day, but it was finals week and she didn't have a final that day. She didn't need to be going to the college as John had said. The chief of police seemed puzzled. He said that John had told him that he hadn't gone to work that day. The chief of police reassured me he would follow through on my statements.

"After my meeting with the chief of police, I decided to go to the bus stop where Anghs met the bus every morning to leave a poster. I asked the bus driver if he recognized her, of if he could remember the last time he had seen her. The driver said he didn't recognize her and that he didn't know if he was allowed to put up a poster like the one I had.

On March 27, Detective Losey had another meeting with John. Losey recalled, "The next contact I had with Annibel was at his apartment. The apartment itself was a single-story wood, mostly studio-type of an apartment. It had a small kitchenette with a bath and washroom that was attached but had a separate entrance.

"I did go inside the residence. I ended up going into the kitchen area as well as the main living-room/sleeping area. I observed Mr. Annibel to be extremely nervous at the meeting. The entire meeting lasted about fifteen minutes. I asked Mr. Annibel if I could meet with him the following Monday, March thirty-first. There were some concerns that I had and I just wanted to speak with him again. He said okay."

Lisa remembered, "A few days earlier, I had received a

phone call from an older woman who didn't want to give me her name. She said she knew the Annibel family and didn't want to get involved. She said she saw the posters, and she wanted to give me some information about John. She said she thought I should know that John had been involved in a murder case not long before. It was about John's sister-in-law's sister. The police had found her body [Sherry Lynn Smith] in a ravine near Garberville. John was a suspect because he had picked her up from a dance to take her home. He was the last one to see her alive. The woman said she didn't know where my sister was, but she hoped that I would find her. I later thought this anonymous woman might be Mike Cortopassi's grandmother.

"I became frightened after the phone call. I started to think the worst had happened. I asked Max to go with me to see John again. When we got there, John's parents were there. John was acting like he thought I had called the cops on him. He gave me hard, mean looks and glares. Then he said nastily that the cops had just been there with him. He said they wanted to look at his gun. He didn't have it registered, he said, but the cops didn't care about that. Then he glared at me again. He said they even found a roach of marijuana in an ashtray, but the cops just laughed. He asked his parents, 'Hey, didn't they do that?' His mom said yeah, and his dad didn't say anything.

"His mom said they looked around the apartment and everything. John said the police knew him pretty well, and had even said, 'Oh, it's you!' to him. As soon as they realized who he was, they left. I felt really uncomfortable, so Max and I left. We both felt the same way—John knew something about Anghs.

"That same night, I was feeling really scared and angry. My friends Terry Lynn McCloskey, Ethel Reed, and Dave Cross tried to cheer me up, so we went drinking. During our evening, I had been talking about how worried I was about Anghs, and how I felt like John knew something. My friends encouraged me to go back and talk to John. I was hesitant. I didn't want to see John alone, especially when I had been drinking.

"My friends were convinced that John had done something

to Anghs, but I thought they were just judging him from the past incident with his sister-in-law. Anyway, after we had been drinking a while, we went to see John. It was late, around midnight. When I knocked on the door, he answered it, and I asked if I could talk to him. He let us in, since my friends didn't want me to go in there alone. After we walked in, he wouldn't turn on the lights. He just sat in the dark. Before long, my eyes adjusted to the darkness. I couldn't see his face, but I could see him.

"I told John I knew about his sister-in-law being murdered, and I could understand how he must feel that others might think that he had done the same to Anghs. But I told him if he didn't talk to me and if we didn't work together, we would never find her. About the time I was giving him this sincere talk, my girlfriend Ethel Reed, who was so drunk she could barely stand up, yelled at him, 'John, we know you killed her! You might as well admit it!'

"She kept saying it over and over. I felt really uncomfortable. Finally I said, 'We'd better go.' I begged John to call me and talk more about this when it was more appropriate. I really felt like I had made a connection with him."

Apparently the friend yelling, "John, we know you killed her! You might as well admit it!" had made more of a connection with John. Later there would be several versions of when and why John suddenly left the Fortuna area. The most reliable one came from John's friend Rick Malcomb.

Rick had known John ever since they were kids. They had been friends, but had lost touch over the years. Suddenly, on March 27, the very same day Mike Losey had shown up at John's apartment where he seemed very nervous, John made contact with Malcomb again. John and Rick went out drinking at Fortuna's Town Club. They did so for the next four days, according to Rick. John kept pushing an idea toward Rick to come with him to Colorado. Finally Rick agreed. He said later that he had nothing holding him down at the time, and a trip to Colorado might be an adventure. On Sunday, March 30, John packed items into his Camaro until the backseat and trunk were crammed, and Rick took a few items of his own. Then they took off for Denver, Colorado, where John's twin brother now lived with his wife Pam. The trip was so sudden, John didn't even call work to say that he wouldn't be coming in on Monday morning.

Whatever had occurred, John was on his way to Colorado, and when Fortuna PD Detective Mike Losey showed up at John's door in Fortuna on Monday March 31, John was nowhere to be found. Losey was so concerned about John not being there that he phoned Pacific Lumber and found out from John's foreman that he hadn't come into work or even called. This was very unusual, the foreman said.

Detective Losey then contacted John's mother, Lyla. He learned from her that John had suddenly left the area and gone to Denver, Colorado, ostensibly to visit his twin brother James. Lyla told Losey that John had not even told her that he was going. She had learned about it from Randy Malcomb, Rick Malcomb's brother. John had given Rick a key to the apartment and told him to clean it up. (Later, Lisa would say that Losey first learned about John being gone from her. Whatever the timing, Mike Losey knew that John had gone to Colorado in a big hurry.)

Because of all this new information, Lisa was contacted by Humboldt County Deputy District Attorney Rick Moench. Lisa said later, "I received a phone call from the district attorney's office in Eureka. They wanted to see me. When I arrived in their office, I could feel tension, but I didn't know why. They asked me the last time I saw Andrea, and I asked if they had talked to her boyfriend, John. I told them he knew more about her personal life and habits than I did since they had moved in together. I can remember the investigators looking at each other kind of funny. Then one of them said that when they went to talk with John [on March 31], they found out that he had left the area. I was stunned."

Moench later related that Lisa had told him that in the past she and Andrea had phoned each other almost every day. This was not like her. Lisa said that even if Andrea was hiding from John, she would contact her. Then Lisa told Moench about the incident when John attacked Andrea over his cats, and the time he tried smothering her with a pillow. Lisa said that Andrea had spoken of leaving John, but she had no means of support and no place to go.

On April 1, Detective Losey spoke with the landlord of the apartment that John and Andrea shared. The landlord said that April's rent was now past due, and if John had just taken off, he would forfeit a one-hundred-dollar cleaning deposit. Because of all these factors, a search warrant for the apartment was asked for by Detective Losey and granted by Judge Howard Neville.

Detective Losey also spoke with the sheriff of Humboldt County and discovered that John Annibel had been the primary suspect in a murder back in 1976. At that time a young woman named Sherry Lynn Smith had been sexually assaulted and strangled to death.

Various law-enforcement officers and tech people descended on the apartment on Ninth Street in Fortuna, including Mike Losey; Sergeant Silvers, FPD; Investigator Floyd Stokes; DDA Rick Moench; Jack Morrison; and ID Evidence Tech Bud Thompson. Later, ID Tech Joe Rynearson also arrived. Stains that appeared to be blood were noticed on the bedding, the mattress, a wall, and a mirror.

Rynearson collected several pieces of evidence, while Thompson photographed the apartment and Losey took measurements and drew a sketch of the layout. Floyd Stokes also took photographs and videotaped the scene.

It was noted that the following items were removed for analysis from the apartment.

1. Complete bed, mattress, box springs, and frame

2. Mirror on the south wall above the bed

3. A metal garbage can from the outside

4. A black buck knife found on a nightstand

5. A calendar hanging on the north wall with all the days through March 17, X'd out

6. A baggie of marijuana found in a kitchen cabinet

Detective Losey later wrote, "After the warrant was served, an amount of evidence was discovered which would substantiate the probability of a violent act having occurred in the residence."

On April 2, 1980, local radio and television stations were contacted about Andrea's disappearance, as were local newspapers. The next day Losey contacted Lisa LaDeRoute and showed her a wallet that was removed from the apartment. Lisa told him that she had last seen Andrea with that wallet on March 2. Lisa said Andrea always carried that wallet in her purse. At that time it had not been empty. Losey told her that he'd found the wallet on the back of the toilet. Lisa responded that it hadn't been there when John let her into the apartment on March 19.

Meanwhile, John and Rick Malcomb had arrived in Denver, Colorado. Pam Annibel clearly remembered the day he arrived. She recalled, "It was in the evening and snow was on the ground. I looked out the front window and saw John getting out of his Camaro with another guy. I thought to myself, 'What is John doing here?' He just came by unannounced."

When John came inside the house, he explained that his girlfriend Andrea was missing, and that he thought he would come out to Colorado for a while. Later when Pam asked John questions about Andrea, he didn't seem very concerned about her.

One person who was concerned was Mike Cortopassi, Lisa's boyfriend. Apparently he and John hooked up at some point in the Denver area, and John seemed to be very angry with Lisa. John blamed her for calling the cops on him for the disappearance of Andrea.

Lisa remembered, "I called my boyfriend, Mike, in Colorado. He told me that John Annibel was in Colorado. The next day I called the district attorney's office and gave them John's address in Colorado. It was during the day, though it all seemed like a blue haze to me. The DA's office wanted to know how to reach my mom. They wanted to make sure she hadn't seen

Andrea. They also told me they had obtained a warrant to search John and Andrea's apartment. During their search they found blood all over the apartment, but nothing that could be seen with the naked eye. And they found a weapon which they would not disclose.

"Deputy District Attorney Rick Moench told me they would study the blood type, but needed to know who Andrea's dentist or doctor was so that they might have her blood type. I gave them Dr. Wolven, her dentist's phone number." (Interestingly enough, Dr. Wolven had been Sherry Lynn Smith's dentist. It was his findings about dental work that proved the victim up on Eel Rock Road in 1976 was Sherry Lynn Smith.)

"I called Mom that night. I hadn't told her anything about Anghs's disappearance. She had just married a man a few months before, and was the happiest I could ever remember her being. But now I had to call her before the police did and tell her that Anghs had been missing for almost two weeks. I remember the day I had to phone her—April 2, 1980, the day before her birthday.

"When I called her, I apologized for waiting so long in between calls, and for waiting to tell her about Anghs. But I had thought Anghs would come back before two weeks had gone by. I could tell Mom was worried, but she didn't say much. The only thing I remember her saying was, 'I think Anghs can take care of herself.' I know Mom wasn't willing to accept what I had just told her."

The DOJ lab tested the articles removed from the apartment and definitely typed the blood on the mattress to be Type A, the same type as Andrea.

Lisa recalled, "The district attorney called and asked if he could talk to my boss. I was curious as to why he would want to do that, so I asked. He told me the blood found matched Anghs's blood. They needed me to go to the Superior Court judge and request extradition papers on John. He wanted to talk to my boss so he could ask her to walk across the street to the courthouse with me. She did, and when we got to the front door, there were four or five men waiting to walk with us.

"One of them was the deputy district attorney, the rest of them were investigators. Mr. Moench, the Deputy DA, asked me if I felt like someone had just kicked me in the stomach. I said, 'Yeah.' Then he said, 'Well, when this is all over, I'll let you hit me in the stomach.'

"We all walked down the corridors to the judge's chambers, where we could find Judge Buffington. Inside there was a long table with a dozen people sitting around it with a stenographer. The judge asked me simple questions like when I last saw my sister. Did I know where she might be? And that was it. He authorized the extradition on one John Arthur Annibel."

Judge John Buffington also signed Detective Losey's Affidavit for Arrest. In part, the affidavit stated, "Based on the above evidence and information, probable cause exists to believe that LaDeRoute has been murdered. Further, the available physical evidence, as well as circumstantial evidence, indicates that John Annibel murdered Andrea LaDeRoute."

Lisa said later, "I got home later that night; I called my boyfriend in Colorado and told him the news. My boyfriend was Mike Cortopassi. He was a friend of John Annibel's. He was the one who had introduced Andrea to John in the first place. Mike had moved to Colorado a few months before. He wanted me to move with him, but we decided that I would wait for him until he became established with a job and a place to live. Mike had called for me sometime in late March. He said he had gotten a job, and he wanted me to move to Aurora, Colorado. I told him that Anghs was missing, and I had to stay until I could find her. I also told him that I thought John might have done something to her. Mike scared me when he told me he thought John did something to her, too.

"Mike started crying. That was something he never did. He said, 'Lisa, John already knows the police are coming. He's already bought tickets to fly back to Eureka. Whatever you do, don't go anywhere he knows you will be. I'm afraid he's coming home to hurt you.' Mike spent the next ten minutes of our conversation scaring me to death."

* * *

On April 5, 1980, Detective Losey and DDA Rick Moench flew to Denver, Colorado. They were picked up at the airport by Denver PD Detectives Peter Diaz and Charles Secord, and driven to James Annibel's house. Other uniformed policemen met them there. It just so happened that Rick Malcomb was over James's home as well that evening, though he was staying elsewhere in Denver.

Detective Losey recalled, "It was about 7:30 PM in the evening when we arrived. There were up to ten officers present and DDA Moench. They immediately put John under arrest, handcuffed him, and placed him on a couch."

Pam later said that the raid that netted John came as a total surprise. She said there were at least ten officers present, some in uniform, some in plain clothes, and some dressed like SWAT team members. She recalled people from Humboldt County being there (Losey and Moench). They would tell her very little about why John was being arrested, but she surmised it had something to do with Andrea being missing. It also brought back all the terrible memories of her sister Sherry's murder, although she did not make a connection at the time that John might have killed Sherry. After all, John was her husband's twin brother. The idea that he really could have killed her sister was almost inconceivable.

James gave the officers the right to search the residence, and they gathered up bags of John's clothing, a TV set, and a stereo receiver. Then they took John to the Detective Homicide Division Interview Room.

In the interview room, John was Mirandized and he began talking about the events of March 17, when he said he had first realized that Andrea was missing. He said that she had left for College of the Redwoods at 6:30 AM, and he had left for work at 6:45 AM. (Later he would change this statement and say he had not gone to work at all that day.)

John spoke of wanting to leave Humboldt County because Andrea had left him and because he wanted to skip out on paying a loan to Pacific Finance. He related that he got Lisa LaDeRoute's phone number when his father had asked Max for it. John said he did phone Lisa (she said that he never did).

Asked if he ever told his employer, Pacific Lumber, that he was leaving the area, John said that he hadn't. Then he added that he was sure that he could get his job back because his dad had been a longtime employee there and had already talked to the president of the company.

Then John most likely made up a story that his sister-in-law Carla, who was married to his brother Ted, told him that she had seen Andrea after March 17 and that Andrea was fine. Supposedly for that reason, John had not helped Lisa look for Andrea.

The detectives asked him why he had recently bought a hoe and shovel. John said that he wanted to do some planting in the yard. Asked why he suddenly bought a hose and garbage can, he answered that those items had recently been stolen from the cabin. Later, neither Lisa nor Pam could ever remember John doing any gardening, much less doing it around a place that he was only renting.

John persisted in saying that he and Andrea never had a fight at the cabin in Fortuna, especially one where she might have lost any blood. He said if she had lost any blood there, it had to have been from accidentally cutting herself.

A detective asked John about any disparaging remarks Andrea might have made toward him. John said that at one time she had said that his mom, Lyla, liked Pam and Carla more than her. Andrea supposedly added, "You're a mama's boy. You're not a man."

Asked if this made him angry, John replied, "I was a little mad. Not a whole lot."

John detailed the last day, March 16, that he and Andrea had been together. He said they spent about three hours in Rohner Park in the afternoon, and then went by a Safeway where they bought steaks for dinner. He denied that Andrea had been at the Town Club in Fortuna later that evening with him, even though Billy Ryan, Andrea's ex-boyfriend, said he saw both John and Andrea coming out of there.

Mike Losey said, "John, you seem awfully nervous."

John shrugged off the comment.

Then Losey added, "Things just aren't adding up, John."

John tried to make light of the situation by saying that he and Andrea had planned to get married in July.

Losey replied, "You gave up on her awfully quick. So why did you come out to Colorado?"

John answered that he was bummed out about Andrea leaving him and he wanted to talk to his twin brother. He said, "I can talk to my twin brother better than most of the family." [James would deny this and say that they were not close.]

John was asked about Andrea's wallet being found with no money in it. He said that she had bought a new wallet and wasn't using that one anymore. He seemed to have an answer for everything.

A detective asked John about his Camaro and some damage on the passenger side. John said that on the day before he left, he had sideswiped a Jeep near his cabin. It hadn't been bad enough for him to get it fixed.

A detective spoke up and said, "We have evidence that Andrea has been killed. She's dead."

In a very soft voice, John said, "Yes, sir."

It is impossible from the tone of voice to know whether he meant, "Yes, sir, I agree she is dead" or "Yes, sir, I understand what you're saying."

A detective piped up and added, "You tried to hide the body."

John replied, "No, that's not it. I'm not even sure she's dead."

Then John added, "I shouldn't say much more."

The interview ended at 9:08 PM. It had lasted for more than an hour.

Rick Malcomb was also questioned by Moench and Losey in Colorado. He told them that on Sunday, March 30, he and John had been drinking most of the day and talking about going to Colorado. Finally Malcomb decided to go with John because he wasn't working at the time and there was nothing holding him down in Humboldt County. They drove to John's cousin in Grass Valley, and spent the night there. Then they took off cross-country to Colorado.

Rick said he had left his Jeep Wagoneer near John's place

in Fortuna, and agreed that it had been sideswiped by John's Camaro. Rick said he left the keys to the Jeep with his brother Randy. It was his understanding that Randy was going to clean up John's apartment after they left.

Rick said that the ride to Colorado had been uneventful, even though John did seem to be concerned about Andrea. Rick also said that John's car had been stuffed with items in the backseat, and there were garbage bags full of John's clothes. Rick said on the drive to Denver, he didn't notice anything suspicious about John's manner.

On April 6, John's Camaro was searched at a Denver PD facility. Present for this was Detective Losey and Denver techs J.F. McKinney and J.D. Warren. A rust-colored petite-sized jacket was found in the trunk of the car wrapped up in a blanket. The blanket had leaves and twigs on it. There were also leaves and twigs in the trunk. Also described and noted were:

- One green/gray/black throw rug
- One gray/red/black throw rug
- One Tam hat
- Three socks
- One trunk mat
- One hand-drawn map with information on the back (just what the map displayed, or what the information was, was not noted on the report).
- One hacksaw

John waived extradition, and on April 7 he was flown back to San Francisco and then Humboldt County. Accompanying him on the flight were Mike Losey and Rick Moench.

There were a couple of short articles in the Humboldt County newspapers about the arrest. The *Humboldt Beacon* reported, "John Annibel was arrested in Denver, Colo. last weekend by Fortuna Detective Mike Losey and Deputy District

Attorney Rick Moench following a three-week investigation into a missing person's report filed by Annibel on March eighteenth."

Another article stated, "According to the missing person's report, filed on March eighteenth, Annibel last saw LaDeRoute early the previous day as she left for College of the Redwoods, where she attended classes." Then it picked up on a falsehood John kept perpetuating. The article said she was going to finals, but in truth, she didn't have any that day, and it is most likely she had never gone to College of the Redwoods on the bus as he claimed.

Fortuna Police Chief Bill Terry told the reporters the arrest was based on circumstantial evidence and blood found in the residence shared by LaDeRoute and Annibel. A short press release from the Fortuna PD stated, "Investigators have found evidence which indicates LaDeRoute has met with foul play."

The *Eureka Times-Standard*'s article was headlined: MYERS FLAT MAN CHARGED WITH MURDER. Perhaps they didn't know that John had been living in Fortuna for about a month by the time of his arrest. The reporter spoke with DA Bernard De-Paoli, who stated what had already been said to the *Humboldt Beacon.* DePaoli added, "Investigators learned that the suspect has relatives in the Denver area, and tracked him down there. Mike Losey and Deputy DA Rick Moench flew to Colorado Saturday, and returned with Annibel in custody on Monday."

Another article reported, "Investigators discovered bloodstains on bedclothes in the cabin, and found fine splatters of blood on a mirror, the court document said. The blood was the same type as the missing woman, but it was also the same type as the defendant, DePaoli said."

Lisa said later, "When the DA's office called me again, they told me they had located John and brought him back." Later an investigator, Floyd Stokes, came to her office. He told her he had spent only a short amount of time with John and he was convinced "the guy was a sociopath."

John Annibel had a bail review on April 9, 1980. The count against him was PC 187—homicide. His attorney once again was William Ferroggiaro, just as he had been during John's questioning in the death of Sherry Lynn Smith in 1976. John's bail was set at $100,000. He apparently did not get out on bail, because the custody status at his preliminary hearing on April 23 was "in custody."

On April 16 the *Eureka Times-Standard* ran an article with the headline: NO SIGN OF "DEAD" WOMAN. The article said in part, "Investigators are still searching for some sign of a missing twenty-year-old Fortuna woman whose boyfriend has been accused of killing her. With a preliminary hearing date for John A. Annibel rapidly approaching, so far nothing new has turned up in the search for Andrea LaDeRoute." This article upset Lisa badly. She wanted to know why the newspaper was now referring to Andrea as dead, not merely missing.

DDA Rick Moench told reporters, "Investigators have devoted some time to combing the brush in some parts of the county, but right now we're waiting for some reports from the FBI." Moench added that all of northern California was a potential dump site for the body, and he had informed police agencies and the California Missing Person's Bureau. One place mentioned later that was searched was the cemetery around Myers Flat. Just why this location was searched was not noted at the time.

By now, however, there was one notable change in the newspapers. Bloody bedclothes were no longer being mentioned. Instead it was noted that blood was present on the bedding, a wall, and a mirror.

Judge John E. Buffington, the same man who had been district attorney during the Sherry Lynn Smith case, was the presiding judge at John's preliminary hearing at 10 AM on April 23, 1980. The paperwork on this is slim at best. In the column about constitutional and statutory time, the box is marked "no." In the section marked "Orders of the Court" was written, "People unable to proceed. Case dismissed pursuant to PC 859b. Defendant ordered discharged from custody."

The case was dismissed for lack of evidence, the fact that John and Andrea's blood types were the same (at least that was one contention at the time), and some blood evidence having not yet come back from the FBI lab. More than anything else, however, it was the fact that Andrea's body had not been found.

The *Times-Standard* reported the next day that charges had

been dropped because of the law which grants a defendant a speedy preliminary hearing. Under California law, both the defendant and prosecution have the right for a preliminary hearing within ten court days of the arraignment.

Rick Moench told the reporter, "The charge will be refiled, but not immediately." Then he said they were unable to proceed because tests on physical evidence, which had been sent to the FBI Forensic Laboratory in Washington, D.C., had not yet been completed. He added, "The case will continue on the completion of these tests and the testing of other items which were initially processed by the Denver authorities before being transported to California."

That was it. Lisa didn't even know that John had been released that morning. She thought he was still in custody when she was shocked by an incident in Eureka. Lisa was in her car stopped at a light when, by chance, a car pulled up next to her and in the passenger seat was John Annibel. When she happened to glance over, John gave her an evil smile, and the car pulled away. Lisa was so shaken she could barely drive home.

She said later, "I wasn't ever told officially, but after John was released, I can remember for several weeks that I had undercover cops following me everywhere. Mr. Stokes told me that I should never find myself going anywhere alone, and I should always let someone know where I was headed.

"I found out later that when they traced John to Colorado, they discovered in his car trunk the clothes he described Andrea wearing the last time he had seen her. A rust-colored coat, and boots. They only found one boot, not both. Later when I tried calling my boyfriend Mike in Colorado, his number had been disconnected. When I wrote to him, I never got a response. I don't know what or who he was afraid of, but I guessed it might be because John was now free.

"I don' know the real reason John was released. I was told by the DA's office that John had the same blood type as my sister [this was not correct information, according to Lisa]. That all the information they had was circumstantial. But primarily the reason they didn't pursue the case was because he had possibly been involved in six other murders. Investigator Floyd

Stokes told me, 'This is the closest we're ever going to come to charging him. We believe he has been involved in several other cases. He knows what he's doing.'

"I was told that they wanted to be sure that he didn't go free on Andrea's case or lose the case because of lack of evidence. That even though there was strong evidence, they needed to find her body. They said that in the entire history of Humboldt County, there had only been one case where they had convicted a murderer before they found the body." Interestingly enough, it was under DA Bernard DePaoli's watch that this had happened.

The case on Andrea LaDeRoute was not quite closed yet. The Fortuna Police Department received a strange phone call from an anonymous person. Lisa said later, "They tape-recorded the call. The person seemed to be disguising her voice. As far as I can remember the call went like this:

Caller: "I don't want to get involved."

Officer: "That's fine. Which girl are you talking about?"

Caller: "The one they've been looking for in Fortuna."

Officer: "Andrea LaDeRoute?"

Caller: "Yeah, I found a note in my mailbox that said that her body was behind a rock on Table Bluff."

Officer: "Where was the letter postmarked from?"

A long silence.

Caller: "It wasn't mailed."

Officer: "Then how did you get it?"

Another long silence.

Caller: "I found it in my mailbox. I only live a few blocks from where she disappeared."

Officer: "Okay. I understand you don't want to be involved. Would you mind sending us the note?"

Very long silence.

Caller: "I can't."

Officer: "Why not?"

Caller: "Because I don't have it any longer."

Officer: "What happened to the note?"

Caller: "I burnt it. I didn't want to be involved."

Then the caller hung up.

No body was found at Table Bluff, but something else intriguing was. According to one official report, "A driver located a black purse off the south jetty [of Humboldt Bay] in the water with a rock inside of it. The purse was identified as belonging to Andrea LaDeRoute. A leather key ring with the letter "A" was also recovered."

Yet a small article in the local paper said that the purse had been discovered by a diver, not a driver. In a third scenario, Lisa LaDeRoute was certain that Mike Losey had told her that the purse had been found in the parking lot near the south jetty. In yet a fourth report it had been a pleasure diver who had found the purse in the bay.

Whatever the circumstances, the purse seemed to be a key bit of evidence. A sheriff's diver scoured the bay and investigators probed the nearby land area with acid-sensitive probes. If the probes struck an area where a body was decomposing, they would signal to the investigators to search more thoroughly. A decomposing body would turn the soil more acidic than normal.

Of the search, the *Eureka Times-Standard* wrote, "Teams of searchers equipped with body probes scoured the area between Table Bluff and the south jetty. Members of the search teams walking in rows inserted the tips of the specially constructed, tubular-metal body probes into the ground every ten or fifteen feet."

In an even more radical departure from the usual law-enforcement investigations, DA Bernard DePaoli said he would not rule out the use of an established psychic. He told

reporters, "Certain law-enforcement agencies have had vary-
ing degrees of relatively high success by using such persons,
and should one who is already established contact the office,
we would not deny his or her participation in the case. But such
persons will not be paid for their services. We're talking about
volunteer services."

Asked whether charges would be refiled against John Annibel, DePaoli said, "We're still gathering evidence."

A few days later the *Eureka Times-Standard* wrote an article about a "psychic super sleuth" named Carole Lynn Grant
who was visiting the Eureka area. She told the reporter that
she headed the Psychic Crime Squad of the Florida State
Police. Often visions would come to her at night.

Grant said, "I can put myself [mentally] in the [murdered]
person's place and see what she saw before she was killed. It helps
having something that belonged to the person, or a picture."

Lisa would not talk very much about the hypnosis later,
except that it had been traumatic for her. One thing she really
wondered about was why she was not asked about Andrea's rust-
colored jacket. She knew she could identify that. She wondered
why, if Andrea's blood was really on that jacket and it was
found in the trunk of John's car in Denver, was it not being considered an important piece of evidence. After all, John had
said that when he last saw Andrea on the morning of April 17,
she had been wearing that jacket as she walked toward the bus
stop. Now the evidence proved she couldn't have, since it was
found in his car.

Despite search teams, acidic ground probes, and psychics,
no new evidence surfaced as to the whereabouts of Andrea
LaDeRoute, and John Annibel continued to enjoy his freedom.
As time went on, clues about Andrea faded away as they had
done for Janet Bowman, Karen Fisher, and Sherry Lynn Smith.

CHAPTER 4

Death of a Festa Queen

Only a year after Andrea "disappeared," John Annibel met a young woman named Beth. He was twenty-three years old at the time, and she was fifteen. Beth was living in Garberville in 1981, having moved with her mother from a Sierra foothills town east of Sacramento. According to Beth, she had met John through her brother. And according to John, Beth's father was a retired police sergeant from one of the cities in the Sierra foothills.

Pam said that Beth was basically a sweet young girl, who was fairly naïve. Beth was soon pregnant by John, but they were unlucky and lost the baby, who was a boy. John definitely wanted a son. Pam said later, "John always resented the fact that James and I had a boy and girl, though he eventually had two daughters. He wanted a boy. There were times when John just didn't treat Beth very well. He seemed to get into a lot of arguments with her and was pretty dominating."

John and Beth went to live up on the Ridge on Eel Rock Road, and John continued to work for Pacific Lumber. Every so often Beth would hear stories about Andrea and her disappearance, according to a later police report. Once when she asked John about the stories, he told her that he had hired a private detective to search for Andrea and the detective had found her. (This was not true. Andrea was already dead, and later evidence would prove that to be the case.) John assured Beth that Andrea was alive and well, though he did not say where she was living.

John and Beth had a daughter, Heather, and continued to live up in the rough country along the Ridge. Just how rough it was can be ascertained by a story that John would later tell police. He said that one day he was riding his horse on a favorite local trail when a man wielding a shotgun stepped in front of him and said, "You're not going any farther."

John was sure the man was guarding a marijuana patch. John backed out of there and never returned. He also told the detective of hearing at various times about bodies that were discovered in the backcountry. He attributed their deaths to be connected to marijuana patches and dope deals gone bad, as well as meth labs.

John decided to move his family away from the Ridge in 1984. It may have been for the reason he stated later, that he didn't want to raise a daughter in such a dangerous place, or it may have been for some other reason, such as his past. Whatever the reason, the city he chose to move to was Fort Bragg on the Mendocino Coast. John quit Pacific Lumber and started working for another timber industry, Louisiana Pacific, at its Fort Bragg mill.

Fort Bragg was founded in 1857 as an actual fort to oversee the local Indians. Later, when the fort was abandoned, it became a lumber town and fishing port. By 1984, those were still its main industries, along with tourism along the beautiful, rugged coast. There were miles of beaches, sylvan forests and rocky headlands in the area, along with quaint Victorian architecture. The nearby town of Mendocino was constantly being used as a location for Hollywood movies, including *East of Eden*, *The Summer of '42*, and the locale for the television series *Murder, She Wrote*.

The town of Mendocino had one more item of interest that would become emblematic of all the lost girls—Sherry, Andrea, and others. It was a large wooden carving atop the Mendocino Masonic Lodge. Erick Albertson was a member of the lodge, and in the late nineteenth century he spent his spare time at a Big River beach carving mythical figures to adorn the pedestal atop the building. His carving portrayed the Angel of Death, the Hourglass of Transience, the Weeping Maiden, the Anointment of Her Hair, the Acacia Branch, the Sacred Um, the Sundered Column, and the Book of Light. All of these were symbolic within the Masonic Order.

Only four years after John, Beth and their daughter moved to Fort Bragg, a murder would take place on the road leading to the town of Mendocino. It would involve a girl who had come a long way to reach her final resting place. Her name was Georgina Fatima Pacheco, and her story began in the faraway Azores Islands of the Atlantic Ocean.

Born in 1968 on the island of Santa Maria, Georgina's family included father Jose and mother Maria. She had an older sister, Laudalina, affectionately known as Laud; a brother, Jose; and a sister Zenalia, known as Zee. Georgina was the fourth and last child born to the Pachecos in the Azores. Daughter Julie would be born later in the United States.

Life on Santa Maria could hardly have been more different than Fort Bragg. Steeped in the Old World ways of Portugal, Santa Maria was tied to the fishing industry and some cattle raising. The island had been discovered by Portuguese explorers in 1427 and became a key position in the Atlantic on the way to the Americas and the Orient. There were rugged hills and mountains in the interior, and beautiful bays and inlets along the coast. Festas were a big part of the social life on the islands.

The family moved to the United States, settling in Fort Bragg in 1969. There was a large Portuguese community on the coast, most of them working as fishermen or in some aspect of the fishing industry. Often they traveled out to the dangerous waters of the Pacific on their fishing expeditions. They were a hardy and resourceful bunch.

Jose Pacheco was very Old World in his outlook, and he raised his children in a strict manner that was more in line with the ancient ways of the Azores than modern America. According to Laud, "Georgina, or as we knew her, 'George,' was her own person from a very young age. She was very headstrong and wanted to do things her own way. She would stand her ground, even with Dad. They got into a lot of arguments, but they loved each other. Georgina was just very outspoken."

Even though Georgina was continually declaring her independence, she was not rude or mean-spirited. In fact, she had lots of friends in school and around town. Laud said, "Georgina was friendly with everyone. . . . Everyone around Fort Bragg seemed to know her. She wasn't shy at all. We could be driving down Main Street and people would constantly be waving and saying, 'Hi, George.' It seemed like she knew just about everybody."

Laud recalled, "She did have a big mouth, but George was also kind and always sticking up for the underdog. That went for animals as well as people. She was always taking in some poor stray mutt. She felt sorry for them. People, too. She hated it when somebody bullied somebody weaker."

Zee added, "Georgina had big heart. She liked a lot of people and treated them well. Georgina was very loyal to her friends. She was someone they could count on. That went for her sisters, too. Our youngest sister, Julie, really loved her."

Georgina was flamboyant, spirited, and always butting heads with her father. In his eyes, she was not growing up as a good Azorean Portuguese girl should, but then Georgina, she was not a Azorean Portuguese girl—she was an American girl. While Jose tried to draw the line, Georgina was always stepping over the line.

"Georgina was kind of the black sheep in the family," Laud said, "but we all liked her. I was so much older than her, that I almost felt like she was my daughter. It was funny, I was proud of her like she was my own daughter. To Julie, the youngest, George was a big sister. Georgina really stuck up for Julie."

When Georgina was fifteen, she bought herself a diary and began to write in it. On the front page she wrote about a horoscope she'd seen for her birth sign, and it fit her to a tee. The horoscope stated: "You are proud, aggressive, self-willed, original, and a good conversationalist."

In March 1984, Georgina wrote in the diary, "I went to the dance at the hall. It was a lot of fun." A few days later she wrote, "Well, me and Lupe broke up from seeing each other. I have never told this to anyone, but I do love [she crossed out love and wrote like], like him a lot. I guess this is all for the best."

In June of that same year, Georgina was sixteen years old and wrote, "Well, my life has been great until my parents came back. [They were apparently out of town.] I met this guy named Andy and another named Blackie. Andy is really cute and so is his brother. Andy is eighteen. I wish to get out more often. I would love to go with Andy. At home I'm surprised they don't have bars on the windows."

Then in December she wrote, "Life has been great for me. Me and Lupe got together and made up. It was great. We talked, then made out. I got to know him better. Maybe he got to know me better, too. He wants something more than just making out. He wants to go farther. I don't."

Georgina became the Portuguese Festa Queen for Fort Bragg in the mid-1980s. It was a special time for the large Portuguese community in the area. Wearing an elegant outfit and cape, she was crowned with a tiara and flanked by two "ladies in waiting" who accompanied her down the street in a parade. Georgina wore a big smile on her face and greeted her numerous friends in town as she walked down the streets. It was her shining moment. Later on, there was a large banquet in a reception hall.

Zee said, "Georgina was always laughing with friends and having fun. She enjoyed her friends a lot." And Laud added, "Sometimes they did silly practical jokes—like 'Yogi bearing.' That's where they would go out to the state park and hide people's picnic baskets. Like they were Yogi the Bear. These were stupid things, but harmless."

Georgina had plenty of part-time jobs in her later teen years. She worked for the Noyo Bowl as a waitress, at Great Burgers as a cook and waitress, and as a maid at the Best Western motel. She even worked for awhile at the Sherwood Oaks Convalescent Home where she may have met Beth Annibel, who had a job there. She certainly knew a young woman and fellow employee there named Robin Johnson. Robin would later say that she and Georgina were friends, but later events would stretch the reliability of that comment.

The practical jokes and fooling around town may have been harmless fun, but by 1987 a more sinister aspect was creeping into Georgina's life. She began doing drugs, first marijuana, and later turned on to cocaine and meth. One of her main haunts became the parking lot of the Sprouse Reitz store on Main Street in Fort Bragg where a lot of drug activity among young people took place.

Meth was not a good choice for Georgina. She was already full of energy and meth made her hyperactive and unstable. A few of the people around the parking lot weren't just stoners, they were dangerous as well. Some had already done jail time or prison time for violent crimes. Georgina found herself in a volatile mix of characters.

In 1988, she was working at the Sea Pal restaurant at Noyo Harbor, just south of Fort Bragg on Highway 1. Noyo Harbor is one of the most scenic landscapes on the California coast. Little more than a deep cleft in the cliffs, between the harbor itself and the open ocean, a tall highway bridge of Route 1 spanned the dramatic harbor entrance. Waves crashed against the seawall, and fishing boats lined the dock area near the place Georgina worked.

In late August 1988, Georgina's car had problems and she had to put it into a shop. That meant she had to walk about a mile to work from her Stewart Street residence in Fort Bragg. Georgina's route took her directly down Highway 1. On September 1, 1988, Labor Day weekend, Georgina was waiting for a ride from a friend after work, but the girl didn't show up. Georgina was about to start walking when she spotted Robert Parks, her brother-in-law (Laud's husband), driving by in his vehicle. She flagged him down and he gave her a ride back towards town.

Georgina had Robert let her off at the Sprouse Reitz parking lot. It was around 9 PM. He looked out the window and saw her walking toward the parking lot. Then he left.

Georgina did not show up for work on September 2, nor on the third. By September 4, her family was getting worried. It was not like Georgina to just disappear and not let anyone know where she was. On the fourth, the family filed a missing person's report with the Fort Bragg Police Department. Then Laud and Zee and Julie began going around town, asking Georgina's friends if they knew where she was. None of them seemed to. At the park near Noyo Harbor they even questioned Georgina's ex-boyfriend, Victor Gray, if he'd seen her. He said that he hadn't.

The missing person's report described Georgina as 5' 4" tall, weighing 140 pounds, and having dark brown hair. She had been last seen wearing gray sweatpants and a black jacket with the word "George" stenciled on it.

As the days passed and no word came in about Georgina, her family became more and more worried. On September 8, Laud went by the Fort Bragg Police Department and picked up a dental chart form to be filled out. She was already preparing herself for the worst. That same day, policeman J. Grant went by the Noyo Harbor trailer park and talked to Victor Gray. Gray was cooperative and agreed to help look for Georgina.

September 9 came and went, with no signs of Georgina. Cars cruised up and down Main Street, the last of the summer vacationers camped and picnicked at the state parks along the coast. People everywhere went about their routines, except in the Pacheco home. There was fear, hope, anxiety, and dread in that family.

Rodney James Elam lived in the forested area south of the Noyo River. He was a truck driver who worked long hours all week long. The weekend was his time to party, however, and Elam didn't arrive home from the bars until the early-morning hours of September 10. Elam found that he couldn't sleep, so he went over to his brother-in-law's residence and later took the dog out for a walk around 6:20 AM on Pearl Drive and the surrounding dirt roads in the forest. Everything was still dark and quiet at this early hour.

The dog was not on the leash, and as it ran ahead of Elam it suddenly darted into the brush alongside an isolated dirt road and began growling. Elam called for the dog, but it would not come. It kept growling and barking and Elam walked into the brush to get it. Suddenly he spied something pale and unnatural beneath a pile of brush and branches that resembled a deadfall. Underneath the deadfall was the shape of a human body.

Elam was so rattled by the sight that he didn't stick around to check if it really was a dead person. He hurried back to his brother-in-law's home nearby to call the police. Once there, however, Elam thought that maybe his imagination had gotten the better of him. It was still dark outside under the trees, and he had been out drinking most of the night. What if it wasn't a human body at all? What if it was a mannequin, or even some woman passed out and not really dead? He'd look pretty foolish calling the cops.

Elam walked back to where he had seen the strange sight. Building up his nerve he moved some brush aside, reached down, and squeezed the person's arm. There was no doubt about it now—it was indeed the body of a nude young woman and she was clearly dead.

Rushing back to his brother-in-law's house, Elam called the Fort Bragg Police Department. It was 6:40 AM. A short time later, Officer R.J. Shipley arrived to question Elam. Elam told him that he'd been out drinking in a bar with friends on the evening of Saturday the ninth. He'd been at the bowling alley for a while, and then at the Golden West Bar until 2:30 AM. He got home around 3:30 AM and tried to sleep, but he was too wound up. He drank a few more beers and walked over to his brother-in-law's home, where he watched television until the sun came up.

"That's when I took the dog out," he said. "It went into the bushes and I saw a body. I grabbed her arm. It was ice cold."

Since this might be a homicide, and it appeared to be on county land, not in the city of Fort Bragg, Officer Shipley called for Mendocino County Sheriff's (MCSO) Detectives. At around 8:30 AM, Detective Tim Kiely and Sergeant Pintane were summoned. They arrived out on Pearl Drive at around 10:15 AM, since they had to drive in all the way from Ukiah, the county seat about fifty miles away over a twisting two-lane road. These officers, along with ID tech Don Trouette, went to the scene of the body.

The young woman's body was lying in a very brushy area along a tree-lined dirt road, about ten to fifteen feet off the roadway. There were no houses in the immediate area, and it was pretty secluded in general. A crime-scene perimeter was established and secured. Elam, who was also there, spoke to the officers about his own shoe prints being in the vicinity. He said they'd been made when he went to look at the body on two occasions. A pile of loose brush had been placed over the young female's body, and he said he had touched that. The brush was collected by the officers and bagged.

It was noted that the young female was nude and her right arm was bent at the elbow and rested across her head and forehead. Whether it rested that way naturally, or had been placed that way, could not be determined.

At 11:50 AM, Detective D.J. Miller of the Sheriff's office arrived and taped a statement from Elam and he got permission to take Elam's boots in as evidence. Then Miller talked to Elam's brother-in-law, Larry Goeker. Detective Miller asked Goeker about Elam's habits for the previous week. Goeker said that Elam drank five or six beers a day on workdays, but on weekends it was not unusual for him to go on a binge at the bars. Afterward he might be wandering around half the night, unable to sleep. Then Goeker said he recalled a white utility van out on Pearl Drive around 7 PM on Saturday night. The van had sped by at a high speed, followed by a beat-up, oxidized-red Toyota pickup truck.

It was noted by the tech that the female's body had a tattoo. The tattoo was inscribed on one breast and said "George." There were no injuries on her fingers or hands, a sign that she probably hadn't put them up in a defensive struggle.

The female's body was taken to a mortuary in Fort Bragg at 2:20 PM. At the autopsy several important things were noted. Some of the things were not released for public consumption, but what was listed was that the victim had been murdered by strangulation with a hemorrhage on the right sternohyoid muscle. A ligature was listed as having been used.

The autopsy report told of the detectives finding her body in a wooded area, and added one more telling thing—"She apparently had been dead about two days by the time her body was discovered."

Autopsies are not totally accurate, but if this one was even close, then Georgina had dropped out of sight from her family members and job from September 1 until September 6, 7 or 8. What had she been doing all that time? Where had she stayed? And whom had she been staying with?

Earlier that day, police officers had asked Laudalina what shoe size Georgina wore. When Laud heard that question, she knew the worst was probably coming. The worst did arrive when Detective Tim Kiely showed up at her door at 3:50 PM. Detective Kiely informed her about the death of her sister. Laud was devastated, but she wanted to be the one who broke the news to her parents and siblings. Always feeling like she was almost "George's Mom," she took on the role once again.

Sometime after 4 PM, Detective Kiely conducted interviews with the Pacheco family members. And around 5:30 PM, Detectives Miller and Kiely contacted Colleen Caukwell, an acquaintance of Georgina and Julie Pacheco. Caukwell had known Georgina for three or four years and said she had seen her at the Pentecost Festa in August. Caukwell did, however, have a visit with Julie on September 7 and they discussed Georgina's disappearance. Caukwell told detectives to talk to Georgina's best friends, Heather Moore and Robin Johnson. (According to Laud, Robin Johnson was Colleen's half sister.) Robin Johnson also happened to work at the Sherwood Oaks Care Center where both Georgina and Beth Annibel worked at one time. If she had ever seen John Annibel there, she didn't divulge such at the time.

Before the detectives met these two, they contacted a young woman named Daniella Hogan, a friend of Georgina and Heather Moore. Hogan told the detectives that both Heather and Georgina had been using large amounts of cocaine and meth in the previous months. Then Hogan added one more bit of interesting information—she said that she'd seen Georgina walking past the Gray Whale Inn at 6 PM on September third.

This was two days after Robert Parks had dropped Georgina off at Sprouse Reitz and claimed to be the last one to see her alive. According to Hogan, Georgina had been walking south, wearing black jeans, a gray sweatshirt, white high-top socks, and tennis shoes. Hogan also gave the detectives the name of two more friends of Georgina—Noelle Wooden and Amy Beckman.

Hogan said that since Georgina didn't have a car that was working, a girl that she knew only as "Midnight," had given Georgina a ride in a dark brown sedan sometime in early September. This "Midnight" was one of Georgina's acquaintances from the Sprouse Reitz parking lot. The detectives already knew that the parking lot was a hangout for young people and drug activity.

The family were in a complete daze after learning of Georgina's death. Laud would break into tears at the least provocation. Zee was more often in a haze and angry. She recalled at the memorial service for Georgina, "The service was packed. Just about everyone was crying, but I was drained. One woman came up to me and hugged me and said, 'I know how you feel.'

"I wanted to scream at her, 'No, you don't!'

"I was in a bubble. It was like I was watching everything without really being there. It was all unreal.

"Later on, my brother took Georgina's dog. It was just a mutt. He never particularly liked the dog before. I think he took it because it reminded him of Georgina. It was a connection to her."

Laud recalled an eerie premonition Georgina had only a week before she was missing. Laud said, "About a week before her murder, Georgina had a nightmare. It was about being choked. The nightmare was so bad, she even told my mom about it.

"And many years ago, just when Georgina was about to be born in the Azores, and before we moved to America, my mom had her palm read by a woman. The woman told her that she would have a son that died at the age of twenty. Well, we all called Georgina "George." That's a boy's name. And she was murdered at the age of twenty."

An article in the *Santa Rosa Press Democrat* stated, "Georgina Pacheco had been killed by ligature strangulation." And the *Ukiah Daily Journal* noted, "The twenty-year-old was strangled with some type of binding material or cord."

These mentions of binding material and cord were more than the police wanted to reveal, but Lieutenant James Tusso of the Mendocino County Sheriff's Office explained, "We know what weapon was used to kill Pacheco, but we will not release all this information for fear of jeopardizing the investigation." Then he added that there had been a flood of phone calls to the sheriff's office about more than one body being discovered in the woods off the dirt road. He said these rumors were not true.

Detective Miller spoke with Robin Johnson about Georgina, and Robin added that she'd seen Georgina as late as September 7 at 2:30 PM at the Cummings Trailer Park, down by Noyo Harbor, when Georgina had stepped out of an older Datsun pickup. Robin said Georgina had gotten out of the pickup near Captain Flint's Café. Robin stated that she'd talked to Georgina for about five minutes near the pickup, and she gave the detectives her impression of the driver. Robin said he was a white male with dark curly hair, was wearing a lime-green plaid shirt and a white T-shirt, and that there was a "peace sign" on the back of his pickup.

Robin said she had been friends with Georgina for thirteen years, and that a few months previously, she and Georgina had been to Todd's Point, drinking beers and snorting cocaine. Georgina had spoken of family problems and how tough it was to still be living at home. Johnson added that Georgina owed some dealer money for cocaine. Robin mentioned a party that Georgina had attended on September 3. Georgina hadn't really been a part of the party, but had shown up and was on its fringes, according to Robin.

Detective Miller received a letter from Laud that had been written to Georgina from the Vacaville State Prison, because Georgina had been writing to a prison inmate there. The letter from the inmate was written on September 7. Just what the letter contained wasn't noted in the files.

Robert Parks told Detective Miller that he knew Georgina had been at a carnival in Fort Bragg at the end of August. He thought she had been there on August 28 or 29.

Detectives contacted Jim Meredith, who lived at a trailer park near Noyo Harbor. Meredith said that he had arrived at Nog Johnson's residence for a party on Boice Lane around 1 AM on September 4. The detectives wondered if this was the party to which Robin Johnson had referred. Meredith admitted that he worked on a fishing boat, the *Saint Bernadette*. The detectives found out that Meredith also owned a van. They got permission to check it out, but found nothing suspicious, either on the boat or in the van.

Pete Dunnigan, who worked at the Gas and Grub Self Service station, told detectives he had seen Georgina as late as September 6. She had been in a Camaro with a white male driver who he estimated was in his late twenties and that the driver was about 5'8" tall.

Detective Miller spoke with Cindy Becks, a good friend of Georgina. Becks knew Georgina's ex-boyfriend, Victor Gray, and Becks stated that on September 2, Georgina related that she thought she was pregnant and that Victor was the father. Then Becks said that Georgina had not returned home when she thought she was pregnant because she was afraid to do so. (Later tests would prove that Georgina was not pregnant at the time she was murdered.)

The tale of Georgina possibly being pregnant, also had another adherent. According to Dawn Laiche, Georgina had spoken with her on August 31. Georgina had told her that she might be pregnant, according to Laiche.

Detective Miller contacted Linda Moody, another acquaintance of Georgina's. Moody said that her mother lived on the East Coast and had experienced a strange premonition. According to Miller, "On Sunday, September fourth, 1988, at about 10 AM, her mother told her [Moody] she had a vision that a person would kill Linda or someone else. But since Linda had telephoned, her mother was sure the danger had passed. In her mother's vision, the perp was thirty to forty years old; had long brown hair, a mustache and a beard; and was wearing a red plaid shirt."

Detective Miller later showed several photos to Robin Johnson. One of the photos was of a man named John Henley, and Henley had a police record. Miller discovered around this time as well that a guy named Lenny Richardson had been an ex-boyfriend of Georgina. Richardson now worked at a sea-urchin processing plant south of Fort Bragg. Richardson had supposedly gone with Georgina for two to two-and-a-half years and according to some, he was the one who had turned her on to cocaine. Then their relationship supposedly ended badly.

Mellisa Figueirado told Detective Miller that she definitely saw Georgina at the carnival on August 26, and according to Figueirado, Georgina had been there with her friend Heather Moore.

Detective Tim Kiely was busy as well as Miller. He went to Nog Johnson's residence on Boice Lane, where the party had supposedly taken place on September 3 and the early-morning hours of September 4. Kiely found some interesting items in a bucket that were similar, though not quite the same, as some items found at the crime scene. Kiely also learned more about Georgina's association with the Sprouse Reitz parking lot crowd, and some of the individuals who hung out there.

One very interesting piece of information turned up for Detective Kiely via Detective Les Pierce of the Fort Bragg Police Department. It was an anonymous letter that had been mailed in Fort Bragg. The letter declared, "You should question James Ballantine about the Pacheco girl. The college girl found in Westport. He is supposed to be involved in a satanic cult. Also, where is his ex-girlfriend Laurie Pettit? Maybe even Bobby Jenkins and Ed Brown."

There were a couple of things wrong with this letter. Georgina was not a college girl, and her body had not been found in Westport, north of Fort Bragg. It had been found south of the city. Yet this unsigned letter was strange, because in some respects it mirrored the anonymous letter that Lisa had been told about concerning her sister, Andrea, and the Table Bluff area. Certain specifics were wrong; others were correct.

Detective Pierce also passed along to Detective Kiely information from Heather Moore. The info was about carnival workers who had been in the Fort Bragg area in late August. These carnival workers had supposedly partied in the woods on September 3, although Moore did not say if she and Georgina had partied with them, the implication was that they had.

Cynthia Bennett told Detective Kiely that she was afraid of an associate of Georgina named John Cash Henley. Henley had been convicted of battering Bennett and she thought he might be responsible for Georgina's murder. This was the second time Henley's name came up.

More stories also drifted in about the party at Nog Johnson's residence on Boice Lane. Neighbors said it had gone on until 2:30 in the morning of September 4. The party was thrown by son Carl Johnson, who was home from Sacramento State University. Boice Lane was not that far from where Georgina's body had been discovered, and it was easily within walking distance.

Lyle Koski told Kiely that he had dated Georgina for about two-and-a-half months, up until June 1988. He knew she hung out at the Sprouse Reitz parking lot. Koski added that Georgina dealt with a dealer named John. He didn't know John's last name, but this John supposedly conducted deals near Angelo's Pizza Parlor.

On September 15, Detective Kiely discovered that Fort Bragg Police had arrested one of the carnival workers on the previous day. The man was being held for supposedly having stolen items in his possession. The carnival worker was named Anthony Johnson (no relation to Nog Johnson, Carl Johnson, or Robin Johnson), and two other carnival workers that Johnson had been palling around with had been let go. One of these men was named Roger Wayne Loveless, and he, it was learned later, was wanted on an assault charge in a different state.

John Henley by now was definitely a "person of interest" to the detectives, but his whereabouts on September 16 were still unknown. Henley's name kept popping up among friends of Georgina's, and many of them spoke of Henley as a dangerous person. Detectives learned that he did have a record.

On the sixteenth, the detectives spoke with a woman named Jamie Keener who had been living at the Crest Motel during 1988. Keener spoke of a strange encounter she had with Georgina and a guy named Michael Todd Rose two weeks before Georgina disappeared. Rose had supposedly told her, "It would be easy to hide a body in the woods." Then she added he had told her three days after Georgina's body had been found, "She was strangled with panty hose." Even though the panty hose was not correct, his comments were suspicious.

Keener described Rose as "scary and a predator." She alleged that he had attempted to strangle her in the past and that Rose's grandmother had died under suspicious circumstances in Texas.

Since John Henley was wanted on a parole violation, the detectives went to check his house, and they found an old Datsun pickup in the yard. Henley worked at Mighty Might Truck Service in Willits, and Detective Kiely eventually was able to contact Henley in San Jose, where he was arrested on the parole violation.

Detectives Kiely and Miller were following leads in all directions by this time. Miller spoke with Heather Moore and asked if she had ever dated any commercial fishermen. There was an item of interest at the crime scene that would relate to this occupation. Moore said that she had dated a fisherman named James McGraw. This was one more lead that went nowhere.

Miller also interviewed a carnival worker who had been in the Fort Bragg area for a couple of weeks. The worker admitted he had been around the Sprouse Reitz parking lot, but when shown a photo of Georgina, he said he didn't know her. He did say, however, that he'd slept with a girl who lived on Nameless Lane (the actual name of the lane). This had occurred in late August.

After his stint in the Fort Bragg area, the worker quit the carnival and went to Lake County. He was back in Fort Bragg, however, by September 14. A person named Boyer came to see the carnival worker at the Fort Bragg Police Department, and this Boyer lived with a female minor named Michelle Comer, who lived on Boice Lane.

Michelle knew Georgina and said that Georgina had been to a party on Boice Lane in July. Whether Georgina had been to the party at Nog Johnson's residence on September 3, she didn't know, but she knew that Georgina was familiar with the surrounding area.

On September 17, Detective Miller took Robin Johnson to a sketch artist down in Santa Rosa. The sketch artist listened to Robin's description of the driver she said she'd seen in the Datsun pickup truck at Captain Flints—the one person Georgina had supposedly been with on September 7. The sketch artist drew up his interpretation of Robin's description of the young man with dark, curly hair, and she said that it was a good likeness. After this was done, Detective Miller gave the sketch to Lieutenant Tusso of the Mendocino County Sheriff's Office.

Miller didn't get much sleep that night. At around 2 AM, a young woman named Sandra Terry called him and said that John Henley had told her that he'd killed Georgina—or at least that's what she said he had told her. She also said she heard that Henley had raped Georgina before killing her. According to the autopsy, there was a possible rape involved.

Terry had been dating John Henley since July 1988. She knew he had been in jail, but didn't know the reason why. She described Henley as having dark hair combed straight back and a mustache.

That same night at 2:45 AM, Detective Miller contacted Robin Johnson at a Noyo Harbor trailer park, because she had apparently been trying to call him. She seemed frightened and said, "I can't talk to you anymore. They won't let me!"

When he asked who "they" were, she wouldn't say.

Miller advised her that for her own safety she should come to the police station in Fort Bragg, and around 3 AM he went and picked her up. Once at the station, Robin related that earlier that night she had taken a trail cutoff to her house after work. While walking along the trail she said she'd seen two young males sitting on stumps. When she started to walk by them, one of them got up and punched her in the mouth.

Then he said, "Don't talk to cops anymore about the Pacheco murder or you'll never see your baby again!"

After that Robin said she was allowed to pass. She had gone to the phone booth and called D.J. Miller at 2:40 AM.

Miller noticed that Robin did have a swollen upper lip and an abrasion, but there was no fresh blood on her face and the wound looked more than a couple of hours old. This was not consistent with her story of the males along the trail, and doubts about Robin started creeping into Miller's mind.

On September 20, Miller contacted the Fort Bragg PD and asked Detective Pierce to take a battery statement from Robin Johnson. Then Miller discovered that Johnson worked at the Sherwood Oaks Convalescent Home and got off work at 11 PM, not at 2 AM as she had claimed. She seemed to be lying about a lot of things now. He asked her about the discrepancies, but she swore that everything she had told him was true.

George Cole, an inmate in the Fort Bragg jail, came forward and told the detectives he might have some information on the Pacheco's girl's killing. He looked at the sketch put together after Robin Johnson's statements, and said the sketch looked a lot like a guy who worked out at the sea urchin plant. He may have been alluding to Lenny Richardson or another person with the last name of Whicker.

At noon that same day, Miller spoke with Ralph Umbris, owner of Captain Flint's Café. Shown a photo of Georgina, Umbris said he didn't recognize her or remember any incident in the parking lot involving the girl and a Datsun pickup truck.

Forty minutes later, Miller contacted Yvette Schnaubelt who was a manager at the Sea Pal Restaurant. Yvette said that Georgina had always been a good employee and was well liked. Miller talked to one of Georgina's fellow employees there, John Crawford. He said that on September 1, Georgina had phoned a friend named Melissa for a ride home, since her car was in the shop. Melissa didn't come, and Georgina was ready to walk home. Then she spotted her brother-in-law Robert Parks driving by, and flagged him down. He gave her a ride. Crawford added that Georgina didn't look well that day.

Someone from the Sprouse Reitz parking lot told Miller that

Georgina wanted to score some meth. Perhaps the date was September 1. The person then told Detective Miller that on September 17, he had run into Sandra Terry at Sprouse Reitz and she was sure that John Henley had killed Georgina. According to Sandra Terry, Henley had done a similar crime before.

On the twenty-third, Detectives Miller and Kiely drove to the sea urchin processing plant south of Fort Bragg. They were going to check on someone Robin Johnson had said was named Jack Winkler, but they soon found out that his name was really Jack Whicker and that he knew both Georgina and Robin. Just what they found out there is not recorded, other than the fact that Whicker became a "person of interest."

Finally, on September 27, Miller and Kiely interviewed the elusive John Henley who had supposedly exclaimed to Sandra Terry that he had killed Georgina. Now in front of the detectives, Henley categorically denied this. Henley said that on September 6, he had stopped by his cousin Richard Frey's house with his new girlfriend Dana Kennerly. When he drove up he didn't notice Sandra Terry, his old girlfriend's car was there. Terry was very upset with him and handed him some of his clothing, then drove off. A short while later she returned and threw some more of his clothing at him. She had an ax to grind as far as Henley was concerned, and he believed that inspired her claim that he'd killed Georgina. According to Henley, he hadn't done it, and added that he spent the night of September 6 at Frey's home. Just why he indicated September 6 was an important date was not recorded, though it may have been because he thought Georgina was still alive up to that time, and the autopsy report seemed to confirm this.

Josef Gavette, an acquaintance of Georgina and a fellow employee, didn't show up for work around the time of her disappearance, and in fact his sudden departure seemed strange. He was just one more puzzling character in all of this and someone who needed to be contacted.

New strange evidence came from a man named Ed Valadao. Valadao told Detective Kiely that on August 31, he'd seen Georgina with a white young male who had blond hair. They had been on Franklin Street. According to Valadao, the male had pulled a knife on Georgina and yelled, "I'll stick it up your cunt!"

"They argued for a while after this, but then made up and walked away hand in hand," Valadao said.

The detectives wondered if Valadao was speaking about Victor Gray, Georgina's ex-boyfriend. He was a blond and known to have knives. When they got to Gray's residence once again, Kiely asked about a knife hanging on the bedpost. Gray said it was his, but denied ever making any threats toward Georgina, and he gave the detectives permission to search his residence. They came up with no evidence.

With all the stories going around in circles in the Fort Bragg area, Detectives Miller and Kiely decided to try and track down the employees from the carnival that had been in the area. The rides for the carnival were run by Butler Amusements and the detectives found that they had to travel clear down to southern California, where the carnival workers were now located. It was about a 500-mile drive.

In southern California they contacted a man named John Holland who was a carnival worker who fit the description of Robin Johnson's sketch of the man in the Datsun pickup truck. Holland said he didn't own a Datsun pickup, but he did tell them that a friend of his, Richard Miller, owned one. The detectives contacted Richard Miller, and found that he worked in the kiddie-ride area. When they got there, however, he proved to them that he owned a big Ford pickup truck, not a small Datsun. And Miller looked nothing like Robin Johnson's sketch.

The detectives talked with carnival manager Manuel Martinez. Martinez said that after the Fort Bragg stay, the carnival workers had split up into several groups. Most of the workers were now in southern California, but some, including a person of interest, were with a contingent up in the Central Valley near Fresno.

After another long day of driving, the detectives were able to track down the carnival worker. They spoke with him, but he was able to prove an alibi for his time in Fort Bragg. It didn't look like he was the killer of Georgina.

A lot of time and energy was wasted trying to track down these carnival individuals. After the wild goose chase down to southern California, the leads in the Georgina Pacheco case started drying up. It wasn't until October 14, that another substantial lead surfaced. On that date a Fort Bragg high-school girl told her teacher, Thomas Blackwell, that a friend of hers was at a party when Lenny Richardson threatened her friend for talking about the Pacheco homicide. This friend was worried about retaliation from Richardson if she went to the police. The detectives were eventually able to get the name of the girl, and spoke with her.

A few days later, Detective Miller contacted Candi Gibney. Ten days before the murder, Candi and her mother had gone down to the sea urchin place where Lenny Richardson worked. According to Candi at that time she asked Richardson, "Why aren't you going out with Georgina anymore?"

Richardson supposedly told her, "She's a bitch! She slept with my brother when she was going out with me. I'm so mad I could kill her!"

Detective Miller spoke with Heather Moore again, and she recalled a dinner she'd had with Lenny Richardson at Noyo Harbor, where he told her he really hated Georgina.

These Lenny Richardson comments kept popping up, and an "Angela" (no last name) said she'd had a dinner at Captain Flint's three days after Georgina's body was found. According to Angela, she'd been sitting in a booth when she overheard a person say to Lenny Richardson in another booth, "I hope the cops don't come after you."

Supposedly Lenny replied, "Shut up! Someone might hear you!"

Soon thereafter, this Angela said she got a phone call from someone she thought was Lenny. According to her, he said, "If you tell anyone, I'll kill you too!"

Since Georgina's ex-boyfriend, Victor Gray, was still under suspicion, he agreed to take a polygraph test at the sheriff's office in Ukiah. Part of his polygraph test went as follows:

Q. Do you know for sure who strangled Georgina Pacheco between August thirty-first and September tenth, 1988?

A. No.

Q. Did you strangle Georgina Pacheco between August thirty-first and September tenth, 1988?

A. No.

Q. Were you physically present with Georgina Pacheco at the time she was strangled?

A. No.

Q. Did you see Georgina on the morning of August thirtieth, 1988?

A. Yes.

Q. Between August thirty-first and September tenth, did you injure Georgina Pacheco with any kind of object?

A. No.

After the analysis of the charts, produced during the examination, it was noted: "It is the opinion of this examiner that Victor Gray was truthful."

As for Robin Johnson, who also went in for a polygraph test, her questions went as follows:

Q. "Do you know for sure who strangled Georgina Pacheco between August thirty-first and September tenth, 1988?

A. No.

Q. Did you strangle Georgina Pacheco between August thirty-first and September tenth, 1988?

A. No.

Q. Did you see Georgina Pacheco on September seventh, 1988 in a pickup with an unknown person you described to police?

A. Yes.

Q. Were you physically present with Georgina at the time she was strangled?

A. No.

Q. Has anyone specifically told you they caused the death of Georgina?

A. No.

The examiner then stated, "It is the opinion of the examiner that Johnson was deceptive on her answer to the question— "Did you see Georgina Pacheco on September seventh, 1988 in a pickup with an unknown person you described to police?"

The detectives wrote afterward, "During that part of the test phase, Johnson stated she purposefully distorted the composition she furnished the authorities, as the individual would know she had furnished the information. She said the person did drive a gray pickup, but not like the one she described. She said she was not accosted, but was told by a friend of J.J.'s [Jay Sallien] not to talk. She said the person associates with Danny Zeeman."

Jerome Thomas Sallien, known as J.J., took a polygraph test on November 21, 1988 and passed. Just who his friend was that also knew Danny Zeeman didn't come to light at the time in a document.

Robin Johnson's admission that she had lied in her description of the person in the pickup, and lied about the pickup itself, really hurt the case. A lot of time and effort had been spent running down these false leads. Georgina's sister, Julie, was particularly upset about Robin. She said that without Robin's lying, the culprit or culprits might have been caught early on. Once Robin lied about the mystery man in the pickup, however, the detectives had gone searching in the wrong direction looking for a person who didn't exist. "I blame her a lot for what happened," Julie said later.

In fact, it became plain to the detectives that a lot of people who knew Georgina were lying to them. Many of them were pointing their fingers at certain individuals in attempts to take the heat off others close to them. The "witnesses" seemed to be breaking down into factions, and the truth was the last thing on these people's minds.

It wasn't until January 20, 1989, that another interesting bit of evidence surfaced. On that date, Randy Sherwood told Detective Kiely about how he had used alcohol, marijuana, cocaine, and meth with Georgina. The interesting thing was that he said he'd seen her alive on September 5 or 6—four days after Robert Parks left her off at Sprouse Reitz. Sherwood said that on the fifth or sixth, Georgina was with another young woman at the Sprouse Reitz parking lot, and he said he knew it had to be those dates because he got a traffic ticket on the sixth, and he saw Georgina right around then.

Another friend of Georgina was Ernest Linebaugh. He was sure he'd seen Georgina on September 7 with Colleen Caukwell on Chestnut Street. When Caukwell was asked about this by detectives, she said her memory wasn't good and she couldn't remember the date or the incident. What was evident, though, was that a number of people said they saw Georgina alive around September 6 or 7—a date that John Henley found to be important.

In January 1989, Russell Frey was at the Mendocino County jail in Ukiah, and he indicated that he wanted to talk about Georgina's murder. At 2:56 PM, Detective Miller spoke with Frey, and Frey said that while he and Victor Gray were sharing a cell, Vic supposedly admitted to him that he had killed Georgina in 1988. According to Frey, Victor had said he had choked Georgina to death with his hands. (Evidence showed something else involved.) What was interesting, however, was that Frey said he had heard that Georgina had been raped and found wearing only one particular item. This item had not been mentioned in the newspapers, and he was correct about what it was.

Because of this bit of information, Frey agreed to wear a wire and went back into a cell with Victor to see if he would say anything more about Georgina. While Frey was wired, Gray did not say anything about her.

Because of all the inconsistencies and discrepancies in Frey's statements, he was asked to take a polygraph test on April 25, 1989. He failed the test. It was noted that Russell Frey was a cousin of John Henley and Henley would benefit if someone else took the blame for the murder of Georgina.

The next day Detective Miller interviewed Victor Gray. During the conversation Gray didn't say he had killed Georgina—what he said was that he felt responsible for her death. Victor declared, "Georgina died because I didn't love her enough. I didn't physically kill her."

During more investigation, the names of Deanna O'Neal, Jack Whicker, and James Ballantine came up once again. Ballantine, of course, had been mentioned in the anonymous letter that had a Fort Bragg postmark on the envelope. Anonymous letters were an ingredient of the Janet Lee Bowman murder, Andrea LaDeRoute disappearance, and now Georgina Pacheco murder case.

On January 18, 1990, Deanna O'Neal was back in the Fort Bragg area and she told Detective Miller that she'd first met Jack Whicker in 1987. By March 1988, she said they were lovers, and she moved in with him at his apartment. They were together for five weeks, but she was not enthused about the drug scene into which she was falling and she moved away to southern California, where her grandmother lived, to get away from the scene.

In May 1988, however, she was right back living with Jack Whicker. By this time, he was also seeing a fifteen-year-old girl named Trish. Some of the girls who knew her named her "Trashy" or "Trish-Trash."

Fed up with Whicker, Deanna moved in with James Ballantine sometime in July 1988. While at Ballantine's place, Deanna met Georgina. One evening, according to Deanna, she and Ballantine were in his kitchen when she heard Georgina get into a heated argument with Jack Whicker in another part of the residence. A few sentences that Deanna said she heard from Georgina to Jack were: "Let me explain! Just listen! Don't jump off the handle. If you want her back, this is what you're going to have to do!"

Deanna said she thought Georgina was talking about her, but others thought Georgina might have been talking about

Robin Johnson. According to them, Whicker had a thing going with Trish, and possibly Johnson as well.

After the argument, Georgina said to Whicker, "I'll see you at Sprouse."

All of them met again twenty minutes later at the parking lot of Sprouse Reitz. Before Whicker showed up, Deanna related that Georgina said to her that she didn't use drugs, but that Whicker was her supplier of drugs. This seemed to indicate that Georgina was dealing some, but not using. (Many people who knew her would say that she did use drugs.)

Deanna left shortly there after, for southern California once again. When she returned to Fort Bragg, Georgina's body had just been discovered, and according to Deanna, "Jack and Trish left town in a hurry."

Detective Miller was able to interview Trish Whicker on January 19, 1990. Detective Rick Shipley was there as well. Trish told them that she had first met Jack Whicker at the Sprouse Reitz parking lot. He was already in his twenties and she was only fifteen years old. She said, "I left home and got messed up on drugs. Then I married Jack on July 18, 1988. There were nights during that time when he didn't come home. We lived on South McPherson Street."

She and Jack Whicker did leave town in a hurry on September 3, 1988 for Ohio, but the reason Trish gave for the move had nothing to do with Georgina Pacheco. She said Jack wanted to leave the area to avoid a drunk-driving warrant. (If some statements and the autopsy report are correct, Georgina was not yet dead on September 3.)

Jack did drive an older Datsun pickup, however, which closely resembled Robin Johnson's statement, and they loaded it up and took off for Ohio, where Jack had relatives. One more thing was suspicious to the detectives—Jack Whicker was a good friend of John Henley.

Whicker's Datsun was not up for the trip. Near Corning in California's Central Valley, on I-5, it broke down. Whicker's grandfather, who was following behind them in another vehicle, pulled over and they loaded up all the items into the grandfather's vehicle and kept going, leaving the Datsun abandoned beside the road.

Once in Ohio, Trish learned of Georgina's death, when Trish's mother contacted her. Trish asked for more details, and her mother sent her some newspaper clippings. When Trish told Jack about Georgina's death, he showed very little emotion. Then, when Trish read Robin Johnson's description of the Datsun pickup, it seemed a pretty good match to Whicker's vehicle. A cloud of doubt about Jack Whicker began to creep into her thoughts.

Jack Whicker and Trish had a daughter on June 2, 1989, but Trish was no longer happy with him. She left Jack in July of that year and traveled back to Fort Bragg. Jack supposedly called her, and according to Trish, threatened to kill her if she didn't return to him. While Trish was talking to Detective Miller and Shipley, she said that Jack had deposited a lot of stuff from his Datsun pickup before they left. According to her, he'd dumped it out on forested Company Ranch Road sometime on September 2, 1988. This spot was about seven or eight miles outside of Fort Bragg.

On January 19, 1990, Detectives Kiely and Miller found Jack Whicker's Datsun pickup at a Redding storage yard. Meanwhile, a search-and-rescue squad combed the area out on Company Ranch Road. They found some Datsun items there, but no incriminating evidence that could be tied to Georgina Pacheco's murder.

In Redding, Detective Miller and Department of Justice criminalist Donna Mambretti went through Whicker's 1978 brown and primer-colored Datsun pickup. They found one torn paper bag, one pink comb, one David Lee Roth cassette tape, and one Bon Jovi cassette tape. Two things of interest they did spot were one broken taillight and carpet. Some bits of carpet were found near Georgina's body, as well as pieces of taillight.

While all of this was going on, Miller discussed the fact that Jack Whicker's pickup had been at Robert Rayburn's Auto Body Shop near Fort Bragg in 1988. Rayburn just happened to be John Henley's uncle. Both Henley and Whicker worked late nights there during the summer of 1988. Henley had owned a primer-colored Datsun pickup and Rayburn told Detective Miller that Georgina had been to his auto body shop early in 1988. Now it seemed even less likely that Henley did not know Georgina, as he had previously stated.

It took until September 1990 for any more important evidence to come in. On September 18, 1990, Victor Gray told Detective Miller about a girl named Marilee. This Marilee had known Trish Whicker; and Trish, according to Victor Gray, had told Marilee that Jack Whicker and John Henley had killed Georgina.

On September 24, Detective Miller was able to track down Marilee and talk to her. She told him that in the early part of 1990, she and Trish had been drinking in a bar, even though Trish was still underage. Marilee stated that, "Trish told me that Whicker and Henley did it."

Then Marilee added that at the time, her own boyfriend was Jay Sallinen (J.J.). When he was in jail in January 1990, she had written him a letter. It stated in part, "Now do you remember Jack Whicker? He split to Milwaukee [actually Ohio] because of his roommate [Henley] and him were the ones who did George. They [the cops] got his roommate, John Henley. He is in Vacaville Prison, but they can't find Jack." (If Henley was in Vacaville Prison, it wasn't for murdering Georgina Pacheco.)

All of these stories from people swirled around and around in a vicious circle. Some of the things they said were true, some were half-truths, some were conjectures, and some were outright lies. What became evident was that certain people spoke of things they had heard to throw suspicion onto someone other than their friends or boyfriends. The last thing some of the informants wanted to surface was the truth.

In June 1991, Detectives Miller and Kiely once again contacted Robin Johnson because of all the inconsistent and contradictory statements she had made. When the detectives talked to her, Johnson changed her statements once again. She said that Georgina made drug deals with Jack Whicker. Robin added that after the murder, everybody hanging around Sprouse Reitz said that Jack had killed Georgina. It supposedly had happened in a white van, and all of Georgina's clothes were missing and never found. When her body was discovered, all that was left on her person were a couple of items. How Robin knew these things, she didn't say, but she was correct about the items.

After 1991, new evidence about the murder of Georgina Pacheco dwindled down to almost zero. It wasn't until 1998 that a new name popped up on the list of suspects. The man's name was John Annibel, and he had lived in Fort Bragg since 1984. He was a man who had hit a girl in the head with an ax handle. He was a man who had been questioned in the murder of his own twin brother's wife's sister. According to Andrea's sister, Lisa, he was a man who had tried strangling his girlfriend, Andrea LaDeRoute. The same Andrea who had disappeared off the face of the Earth. Above all, he was a man about to get into more trouble than he could handle right in Mendocino County.

CHAPTER 5

Rendezvous in Laytonville

In 1994 and 1995, a young couple in Fort Bragg knew John and Beth Annibel. The man worked with John out at the Louisiana Pacific Lumber Mill. The couple said that Beth had a lot more friends than John and he seemed to be kind of a loner. They also knew that Beth worked at Sherwood Oaks Convalescent Home. The couple went to a couple of barbecues at John and Beth's home in 1995. The residence was north of town on a small road in the woods. The man thought John was "mental." He said that John was paranoid and aggressive.

According to the man, John liked war movies and action movies—movies with a lot of violence in them. "John was always drinking and when he did, he got belligerent. He spoke a lot about people he either had beat up or was going to beat up. It seemed like he always wanted to fight if he'd been drinking a lot. He was real paranoid. He talked about people out in the trees watching him. I thought he was kind of nuts. I wouldn't have even gone to the barbecue, except I worked with him.

"John had a pickup that was old and kind of beat up. There

was always stuff in the vehicle and stuff all over the house. There was stuff everywhere."

"John didn't treat Beth well, as far as I could see. He'd yell at her and tell her to go to her room. I don't think he treated the kids very well, either. He was pretty belligerent."

In fact, John's belligerence had grown to such a degree by 1997, that it got him into trouble with the law. He was arrested for threatening to kill a man and his family, and Beth. [Even John would admit later that Beth was having an affair with the man in Fort Bragg.] John went out to his work place and threatened to kill him and his family.

John was arrested on two counts, making a terrorist threat (Section 422) and trespassing at the man's work place (601). He was ordered to stay away from Hensley, his family and Beth Annibel.

In response to this order, however, Beth wrote Judge Luhan a letter. It stated, "I, Beth Annibel, request a meeting with you to discuss the stay-away order against John Annibel. . . . I do not feel a threat from John, only against my friend. I do not feel a threat to myself from John. I would like to see this one count removed, as I did not request a stay-away order." She gave as a reason for rescinding the stay-away order the fact that both she and John took care of the girls, since Beth worked nights at the convalescent home. She also said that she and John were trying to patch things up.

On June 28, 1997, John had to make an appearance at Ten Mile Court in Fort Bragg. Deputy DA Mark Kalina was the prosecutor who brought the case against John, and John had to pay a fine and stay away from the man and his friends. He did not have to stay away from Beth, however, so her letter to the judge seemed to have the desired effect.

John was soon in trouble with the police again—he was arrested for intoxication in public at the corner of the 500 block of North Whipple Street in Fort Bragg. The police report said his eyes were red and watery and he was fairly incoherent when an officer spoke with him. When asked by the officer what he was doing there, John said he was looking for someone named Cindy. He told the officer he was homeless because his wife had kicked him out of the house. John was arrested and placed in the drunk tank to sober up. At the time it was noted that he was 5' 11" tall and weighed 185 pounds.

John just couldn't stay out of trouble, however. On July 15, 1998, the owner of the residence where John and Beth lived, wanted to kick him out. The owner cited the reasons as "loud quarreling, obscene language, intoxication, and domestic violence." The landlord also said that Beth let homeless people stay at the residence and that John had once chased her down the driveway in a threatening manner. Beth seemed to have let homeless people stay at their place because she was kindhearted. No one other than John had a bad word to say about Beth. Even she would later admit to the police that he was verbally abusive to her, but not physically abusive.

Miles away, down in the small town of Laytonville, on Highway 101, another deadly encounter was about to take place. It concerned a woman who had grown up in the region named Deborah (Debbie) Sanderson, whose married name was Debbie Sloan.

Debbie had been a smart girl in elementary and junior-high school. She was good at spelling and liked to read. At some point she picked up a knack for knitting, crocheting, and quilting. Even though she enjoyed these crafts, she was not just a stay-inside type of girl. One of her favorite activities was fishing. Her mom, Pauline Sanderson, said that Debbie could spend hours just fishing and be happy. "Debbie loved sitting out by a stream or lake. She liked the outdoors in general, but she really loved fishing. I think she found it relaxing."

Beside fishing, young Debbie played basketball and was in the home-economics club at Geyserville High School. The high school she attended was small, and there were only twenty-four other students in her junior year. She got her GED, and at seventeen married a man named Albert Miller. The marriage did not last, however, and she got a divorce.

Later, once Debbie had moved up to the Laytonville area, she met a man named Alan Sloan. Alan was a full-blooded

Cahto Indian who lived on the reservation near Laytonville and worked at the Harwood Lumber Mill. Alan was also a friend of Debbie's brother, who too worked at the mill.

Alan was proud of his land and his tribe. The Cahtos had formerly lived in the Cahto and Long Valleys of Mendocino County. In the nineteenth century they were resettled near Laytonville. Related to the Wailaki tribe, they were more culturally tied to their neighbors the Pomo Native Americans.

By 1998, the Cahtos had a small casino on their land which in part helped fund projects such as the Medicine Wheel Garden, which had been planted in front of the cultural center. A brochure on the garden explained that students from the tribe and outlying areas could learn lessons about "sacred space and symbols associated with the four cardinal directions. Students can focus on the Native American approaches to healing though the making of remedies such as teas, healing creams, and syrups."

Alan and Debbie were married and started a family together. She seemed to like cooking for everyone, and her mom said she made excellent soups, stews, and roasts. "Nothing fancy, just good home cooking," her mom recalled. The Sloans lived near Laytonville, in the hills with a mix of pines, redwoods, and oaks. Deer and other wild game wandered through the yard in the evening. Small streams wound along through the sylvan landscape and emptied into Long Creek that flowed southward. It was an idyllic life in the rolling hills of Mendocino County. This was a landscape of cattle grazing in the hills, horses in corrals, and hawks soaring high overhead. It was a northern California lifestyle that many only dreamed about.

The Sloan family eventually had three children. Alan worked at the Harwood Lumber Mill out on Branscomb Road and Debbie raised the kids. Once in a while she would still participate in her favorite hobbies—fishing and playing bingo at the Red Fox Casino.

Eventually Alan and Debbie had problems and split up, but it was fairly amicable for the sake of the kids. They both loved their children and didn't want a lot of bitterness to mar the relationship. They both stayed in the area of Laytonville.

At some point Debbie got a butterfly tattoo. Miles away, up Highway 101, there was another world-famous butterfly—Julia "Butterfly" Hill, and by that autumn of 1998 she had been sitting in a redwood tree she had named Luna for nearly a year.

There may never have been a Julia Butterfly Hill story or "eco-wars" in the redwood region if the old Pacific Lumber Company of John Annibel's youth had stayed under its original management. It was a sustainable operation that husbanded the redwood trees on its vast properties. In the fall of 1985, Texas billionaire Charles Hurwitz, with the financial help of such junk-bond kings as Michael Milken and Ivan Boesky, used high-interest junk bonds in a leveraged buyout of Pacific Lumber.

Hurwitz incurred an eight-hundred-million-dollar debt in his takeover of Pacific Lumber. To pay down the debt he sold off company assets and stepped up the rate of redwood cutting, which included clear-cutting. These clear-cuts eroded hillsides and sent mud and debris down into creeks and rivers, on one occasion nearly wiping out the small town of Stafford. The eco-wars took off full blast in Humboldt County.

Ecology activists came from everywhere to filter out amongst the woods on PALCO property, especially in the Headwaters region near Eureka. This was the same area where John Annibel had once gone hunting with his dad and twin brother along the margins of Yager Creek and Allen Creek. In her book *From the Redwood Forest*, Joan Dunning described the area and one of its hidden secrets. "A waterfall, as tall as a five-story building, and unique perhaps in the entire world. I have asked people if they knew any other falls of this size entirely surrounded by ancient redwoods, and no one has."

In time, detectives discovered that John Annibel knew another secret about the area—something also hidden, and a lot more foreboding. But in 1998, according to police, he was keeping that secret to himself.

* * *

Tree-sitting became a popular tool amongst the protestors to protect large old growth redwoods. The protestors would pull themselves up into high branches of the trees by means of ropes and clamping hooks, and there they would perch, defying loggers. The most famous tree-sitter was Julia Hill. Since tree-sitters masked their identities by picking pseudonyms, such as "Slo-mo," "Treetop," and "Felony," Julia chose the name "Butterfly" because as a child she had been entranced when a butterfly had landed on her arm.

Julia's living area, on the tree she named Luna, was a tiny platform perched 180 feet above the ground. Her epic tree-sit began on December 10, 1997. At first terrified by being so far off the ground in a tree that swayed with every breeze, over time she learned to scramble around the uppermost branches without any ropes or safety devices at all.

One of her most memorable and terrifying moments came during a storm in early 1998 that threatened to fling her out of the branches of Luna to her death, or send the whole tree crashing to the ground. Later she would write of the experience, "I was trying to hold onto life so hard that my teeth were clenched, my jaws were clenched, my muscles were clenched, my fists were clenched, everything in my body was clenched completely and totally tight. I knew I was going to die." But she didn't die, and Luna did not come crashing to the ground. Instead, Julia became a media darling with various news agencies around the world. Julia was bright, good-looking, and very articulate.

Another activist, David "Gypsy" Chain, was not so lucky several months later. On September 17, 1998, Gypsy, along with several other activists, headed out from Grizzly Creek Redwoods State Park up onto PALCO land to try and stop timber cutting in an area they said would cause stream erosion. One of the timber-cutters for PALCO that day was a man with the nickname of "Big A," and he was not having a good day, especially when protestors showed up. Big A was sawing into a 130-foot tall redwood tree that held about $7,000 worth of timber in it. Big A yelled and cussed at the activists to get the hell out of there, but they hung around the margins of the area. Big A made his final cuts during a strong wind, and according to one activist, Mike Avcollie, he suddenly heard, "the tree stem crack like a string of firecrackers popping on the Fourth of July."

All the protestors ran except for David Chain. Maybe he froze, or maybe he slipped and fell. Whatever the circumstances, a 130-foot heavy-branched redwood came crashing down, killing him almost instantly.

It was Big A who first found David's body. Big A yelled, "Holy fuck! His brains are falling out!"

Madness seemed to have descended upon the redwood forest that autumn. It also seemed to infect certain individuals, one of them being John Annibel, who now just happened to work at the Harwood Lumber Mill along with Alan Sloan and Debbie Sloan's brother.

John's household had been in turmoil for years, with him threatening to kill Beth and her "boyfriend," his public drunkenness, and their looming bankruptcy. It all came to a head on Thanksgiving morning, November 26, 1998, when John got into an argument with Beth. Beth grabbed the kids and took off. For the next two days and nights, she and the kids hid out in a local motel. What really spooked her was that on the first night away from John, she saw his car at a motel next to where they were staying. She was sure that John was following her.

Doing so or not, John had not found Beth or the kids by Saturday morning, November 28. In a fit of anger he drove to Laytonville over Branscomb Road and stopped by a coworker's house owned by Gordon Watts. While there, John told Gordon's wife Cathy and her friend Vickie Bronson that his wife was a whore. He said that he had searched for his wife and kids for two days and couldn't find them anywhere.

According to Cathy Watts, John was an angry person in general. She later said, "He was always saying he was going to harm someone. He was upset that day because his wife had been gone, and his daughters, and he couldn't find them. He was going to get a motel. He was trying to find another place to live, he said. He said he was tired dealing with his home.

"John said he wanted to find a woman and asked to know where could he find one. He wanted to visit a bar. I said there were only two in Laytonville. Boomer's, but they were too elite and old a crowd for him. The Crossroads would be the best bet. And he said, 'Well, I'll look there.'

"My husband and best friend Vicky were there [at home]. John just stood in the kitchen. He was always making comments about women. He called them whores, especially his wife. He also talked about killing my dog. He always made comments about the dog."

Sometime before noon, John checked into a motel called the Cottage Motel, in Laytonville. Most of the rooms were just that, separate small cottages. Since his room had a refrigerator, John went to a store and bought some Lunchables (lunch meat, cheese, and crackers), a half gallon of white milk, a quart of chocolate milk, and some cigarettes. He put the food in the refrigerator and walked down the street to a hamburger place where he ran into Gordon and Cathy Watts once again. They were ordering some food to go.

John talked to the Wattses for a while and then they left. He sat at a table and ate his burger and had a milkshake and some fries. After lunch, he walked on down the road to the Crossroads Bar.

The bartender would recall later that he served John for a while, and then a woman came in and sat down near John. The woman was Debbie Sloan. Whatever anger was seething within John, he kept it hidden and began chatting with her. The bartender recalled John buying her four or five drinks over a two-hour period. They seemed to be getting along well.

By late afternoon, John and Debbie discussed having dinner at Boomer's, a restaurant and bar that was about a block away. When they got there they had some food and Debbie played a bingo-type video game while John drank Schnapps. They stayed at Boomer's until dusk.

From Boomer's, John and Debbie both walked back to the Cottage Motel, but apparently decided to have a few more drinks. They went to a small liquor store where John bought some more Schnapps. Unexpectedly, they ran into Debbie's ex-husband, Alan Sloan, at the store. John related later that Debbie was uncomfortable to be seen with him by her ex-husband.

John and Debbie headed off to the Red Fox Casino, where they gambled for a while. John would recall later losing about twenty dollars, but what happened next is only recorded by John. He said, "She was gonna give me a blow job in my car. There wasn't anybody there in the parking lot. I think the only one in the parking lot was the chick that was working there.

"We got in the backseat, but it just wasn't working. The car wasn't big enough. We were in the backseat maybe ten minutes. Not very long. My pants were down. She might have had her pants down, but it wasn't working. We went back to the motel.

"I didn't have to be anywhere til Monday morning. I never really looked at the clock. Time really didn't matter and I didn't care. At the motel I had some more Schnapps, and she had a shot. Then, well, she gave me a blow job. I didn't cum in her mouth. She wouldn't do that."

According to John, their sexual encounter lasted anywhere from fifteen to twenty minutes. He said that he "finger banged" her while she gave him a blow job. According to John, they were both naked.

Afterward, according to John, Debbie wanted to get something to eat. He said, "I didn't want to do that. I was pretty well hammered. I didn't want to go anywhere. I had food there."

Up to that point, John's recollection of events had probably been fairly accurate and truthful, but what happened next would only come to light by the collection of evidence and the winnowing of truth from what John said. The events that occurred had to be reconstructed from Debbie Sloan's dead body and the memories of others.

The weekend of November 28 and 29, 1998 was incredibly stormy in Mendocino County. Rain lashed down through the trees, creeks overflowed, and branches and debris washed over the roadways. It became a real mess on several roads in the area and Branscomb Road was no exception. On Monday morning, November 30, County Road employees, George Ferguson and Linda Mitchell, were out on Branscomb Road checking for storm damage. Near mile marker 5.45, Linda Mitchell looked down off the side of the road into a ravine and thought she spotted a human body. Shocked and not wanting to go down to look any farther, she called her supervisor, Carl Meckling, and described what she had witnessed. Meckling in turn phoned the Mendocino County Sheriff's Office and reported the incident.

Deputy Phillip Center arrived at the scene on Branscomb Road at 11:30 AM. He said later, "I saw a nude female adult, I would estimate thirty feet down the embankment, lying on her back. [Other estimates would range from ten feet to twenty-five feet down the embankment.] I made sure no one went down there until detectives arrived."

One of the detectives who did arrive was Mendocino County Sheriff's Office (MCSO) Detective Christy Stefani. She was suffering from a bad cold at the time and it was not a good day to be outdoors. It was ice cold, the rain was falling down in buckets, and the wind howled through the tree tops. But she had a job to do and got on with the business at hand.

Her fellow detective Kurt Smallcomb was also sick that day, and the bad weather added to his misery. Detective Stefani remembered, "We spent all day collecting evidence from that area—everything that might be important. It was slippery and the mud was slick on that steep bank. We were walking up and down that road and embankment all day long. We found some women's panties, but they turned out not to belong to the victim.

"It was freezing cold. We were stumbling all over the place on the embankment and I was on medication and had a fever. Kurt was just as sick. It was exhausting, miserable work, but we didn't give up. We knew the clock was ticking and every minute was important. The rain and weather was degrading evidence, and the more time that passed, the less likely it was that we would catch our killer."

The detectives spent all day on Branscomb Road, scouring

the area, even though they were both on the verge of catching pneumonia. When their investigation expanded in scope, one of the first people Detective Smallcomb spoke to was Alan Sloan. Ex-husbands of murdered wives always come in for scrutiny, especially when they still live in the area. Detective Smallcomb spoke with Alan, and bit by bit Alan became less of a suspect. There was one thing, Alan said however, that really piqued Detective Smallcomb's interest. Alan told him that on November 28, he had gone to a store in Laytonville and saw his ex-wife with John Annibel. Alan knew Annibel from work. He had no idea why John Annibel would be with Debbie, since he knew John was married and lived in Fort Bragg.

The name John Annibel rang a small bell with Detective Smallcomb. It was a name connected to a couple of unsolved murders up in Humboldt County years before. They had happened some time back in the 1970s or 1980s. Smallcomb wasn't sure about the exact dates, but this Annibel character was worth checking out.

Questioning at the convenience store where John Annibel and Debbie Sloan had been led back to Boomer's. One of the waitresses said the description fit a customer she had served and the woman that was with him. It's not apparent if the waitress knew Debbie Sloan by sight. From Boomer's, the trail led backward to the Crossroads Bar, and the bartender there definitely recalled the male and female at his bar. He thought they had been there around 2 PM on Saturday the twenty-eighth and that he had served them several drinks.

From the Crossroads, a link was made to the Cottage Motel, where a receipt proved that John Annibel had stayed there. No one recalled seeing Debbie Sloan, but one guest had something very interesting to say. Barbara Allard said she had stepped out of her cottage at 2 AM on the morning of Sunday, November 29, to smoke a cigarette. While she did, she saw a man carrying a large bundle wrapped in a blanket, walking toward a vehicle. The bundle seemed to be heavy.

More leads kept popping up concerning Annibel. It was discovered that he not only worked with Alan Sloan at Harwood, but John also worked there with Debbie's brother. It turned out that John had gone to work on Monday, November 30, but then went home sick and stayed away from work on Tuesday. John's arrest records in Fort Bragg were checked out, as well as the route he generally took from home to work. That route was on Branscomb Road to Highway 1.

On December 1, an autopsy was performed on the body of Deborah K. Sloan by pathologist Jason Trent. He noted, "The body is presented in the nude state. The body is that of a well-developed, well-nourished, slightly overweight Caucasian female who appears older than her recorded age of forty-one years. She is completely wet and covered by brown pine needles. The hair is reddish-brown, slightly curly, and measures approximately seven inches in length."

Trent noted that Debbie's forehead had a reddish contusion above the left eyebrow, and a slightly larger contusion below the left eyelid. There was a small amount of saliva in her mouth, and some reddish marks on the right side of her neck. Trent dissected the neck organs, and there was no evidence of anterior neck trauma. There was however, a moderate amount of hemorrhaging around the right horn of the hyoid bone. Mucosa in the larynx and trachea was reddish-pink in color, and her lungs had a moderate amount of congestion.

Trent made a diagnosis that noted petechial hemorrhaging of the mucosa of the lower eyelids, acute, hemorrhaging of soft tissue at the right horn of the hyoid bone, and moderate congestion of her lungs. He wrote as cause of death—"Asphyxia due to strangulation." He also noted the bruises on her eye and on the scalp, which was consistent with blunt force trauma.

Because of all the people saying that John Annibel had been in Laytonville, probably with Debbie Sloan, and because of questions concerning the murder and disappearance of his girlfriend in Humboldt County, detectives sought and got a search warrant for John's home in Fort Bragg.

On December 4, 1998, John's forty-first birthday, law-enforcement officers staked out the Annibel residence on McPherson Street in Fort Bragg. Officers were directed to watch the residence and contact Detective Smallcomb if John Annibel tried to leave. Very early on the morning of the fourth, the officers informed Detective Smallcomb that John was near his vehicle in the carport and ready to depart. The officers were instructed to contact him at his car and detain him until the detectives arrived.

Detectives Smallcomb and Stefani and Andy Cash arrived on the scene at 4:30 AM and served a search warrant that covered John's car and residence. When they arrived, John was sitting behind the steering wheel of his vehicle. He couldn't go anywhere because Fort Bragg Police Officers Naulty and Walker had him blocked in.

Kurt Smallcomb began a conversation with John out at the carport.

Smallcomb: "John, Kurt Smallcomb, Sheriff's Office."

Annibel: "Hi."

Smallcomb: "Sorry about the inconvenience. I know you're on your way to work and everything. We thought maybe we could talk to you for a little bit."

Annibel: "Sure."

Smallcomb: "Okay. Any problem with going upstairs?"

Annibel: "No. Not at all."

Smallcomb: "All right. Man, it's chilly."

Annibel: "It's colder in Branscomb."

Smallcomb: "Oh, yeah. I bet. A little shadier, too."

Annibel: "Come on in."

Smallcomb: "All right. [To another officer] Hey, Brad. Can you pat him down real quick. Just for our safety and your safety, too. You're not under arrest or anything."

Annibel is patted down.

Smallcomb: "John, is there anyone else in the apartment?"

Annibel: "Yeah, I got my daughters and my wife."

Smallcomb: "Your daughters and your wife are up there? How old's your daughter?"

Annibel: "I've got a thirteen-year-old and an eight-year-old."

Smallcomb: "And your wife's up there too? They all sleep in the same bedroom?"

Annibel: "My wife's in one room and my daughters are in another room."

Smallcomb: [To other officers.] "Yeah, he said we could come inside. We don't want to startle anybody."

Annibel: "May I ask you what this is about?"

Smallcomb: "Sure. Sure. No problem. Maybe you don't want to hear it in front of your wife? Um, any problem about coming down and I'll tell you what's going on at the office?"

Annibel: "Sure."

Smallcomb: "Okay. We don't want to inconvenience anybody here. So is there any problem with us taking a quick look around?"

Annibel: "No."

Smallcomb: "Would you guys do that? Tim. [Tim Kiely]. Christy. Why don't you go out so it's not an inconvenience. I've got a search warrant for the house, too, okay John. Just to let you know what's going on."

Annibel: "What are you looking for? Um, this has to do with the . . ."

Smallcomb: "Yeah. Situation over there near Branscomb."

Annibel: "I heard about that."

Smallcomb: "We're basically talking to anybody and everybody that drives that road. Or anybody and everybody that might have had contact with that gal. We're talking to everybody."

Annibel: "I'll do what I can to help you."

Smallcomb: "Great. Great."

Annibel: "Can I take my coffee with me?"

Smallcomb: "You betcha. Sorry about the birthday present this morning."

Annibel: "Where are we going?"

Smallcomb: "Oh, we're just going down to the substation down here in Fort Bragg. We gotta stop by and get some keys to get inside there. Let's get over to this Jimmy here. Sit in front."

Annibel: [Getting in the GMC police vehicle:] "Not much legroom."

Smallcomb: "Pretty tight confines. What time do you get to work?"

Annibel: "In an hour."

Smallcomb: "When we get to the office, you can call somebody and let them know you might be late."

Annibel: "I might be able to phone Dennis Lynn. He's my foreman."

Smallcomb: "Oh, here's your license back. I have a habit of hanging on to those, once in a while. You might get stopped for something and not have your license with you. Today's your birthday?"

Annibel: "Yep."

Smallcomb: "I'm going to take off my sheriff shit."

Kiely: "Get that cop stuff off. You look funny."

Smallcomb: "No shit, huh. If I can get it off."

Detective Smallcomb, Stefani, and District Attorney Inspector Tim Kiely went with John to the substation while the search warrant for the residence was served by Detective Frank Rakes and Detective Andy Cash. They would be there for most of the rest of the day, looking for evidence and talking to Beth Annibel.

At 5 AM, at the substation in Fort Bragg, John had his first interview with Detectives Smallcomb and Stefani. Initially, Kurt Smallcomb did most of the talking.

Smallcomb: "You're not under arrest, okay? We needed to talk to you. The situation here is, maybe you were seen in Laytonville. So we needed to find out. We needed to touch bases with anybody that may have been with her, or talked to this gal. We're hopin' you can help us out a little bit."

Annibel: "I'll do whatever I can."

Smallcomb: "What do you know? Let me start off with that."

Annibel: "I just know that you found a body on Branscomb Road."

Smallcomb: "What did you hear about the body?"

Annibel: "I just heard they found one. That's all I heard from the guys at work."

Smallcomb: "Just talking around the mill stuff?"

Annibel: "Yeah."

Smallcomb: "Tell me about your route when you go back and forth."

Annibel: "Well, I just drive straight there and straight back. Do you have any leads?"

Smallcomb: "Yeah, we have some. What were your usual days off?"

Annibel: "Sundays."

Smallcomb: "You're usually workin' Saturdays?"

Annibel: "Yeah."

Smallcomb: "Okay, we're talkin' to a lot of people. But there is a reason we're talking to some people. I want you to know that the only way you can burn yourself is not being up front. We're not serving a search warrant on everybody's house. There's a reason we came to your place. And you're married?"

Annibel: "Yeah. We've been together seventeen years. We had to wait until she was eighteen to get married."

Smallcomb: "So, when you travel and stuff, she's with you on your days off."

Annibel: "Usually."

Smallcomb: "Okay. So last weekend, did you work the full week, or what?"

Annibel: "No, I had a four day week last week."

Smallcomb: "Okay. The thing I'd like to say is, John, if you know a little bit more about this, well, we're trying to figure it out ourselves. Like I say, not everybody's getting a search warrant. And I think maybe you might know a little bit more about what's goin' on. And, in no way am I sayin' that you had somethin' to do with it. But your name has been mentioned as far as being in Laytonville over the weekend."

Annibel: "Yeah. I was."

Smallcomb: "Okay. Well can you tell me about that?"

Annibel: "I went there to stay with friends."

Smallcomb: "Did you hear anything about this over the weekend?"

Annibel: "No, on Tuesday."

Smallcomb: "That was just mill talk, or what?"

Annibel: "Yeah. But I went home sick, early on Monday. From the mill. It must have been around ten o'clock. So Tuesday's the first time I heard about it."

Smallcomb: "What did you do on Saturday when you were in Laytonville?"

Annibel: "I just saw some friends, went to the bar, got a motel room, spent the night, and came home."

Smallcomb: "You just hung out?"

Annibel: "Yeah. I did a little bit of gambling at the reservation. First time I been gambling since I got married. There at the Red Fox Casino."

Smallcomb: "Do any good?"

Annibel: "I lost twenty bucks."

Smallcomb: "Okay. People were talking. I need to ask you some questions. Either to clear you and get you on your way, okay? And I want to ask you some specific questions to either get you on your way or to ask you more questions. Before I get to that, we came to your house, went with a bunch of cops and guns and shit."

Annibel: "Yeah. You had me a little nervous, you know."

Smallcomb: "I want to tell you everything, okay. We came to your house with a search warrant. And I want to advise you of your rights. So I'm going to advise you of your rights."

Detective Smallcomb read John the Miranda warnings and asked him if he understood them. John said that he did understand his rights.

Smallcomb: "Can I ask you some questions? Will you talk to us?"

Annibel: "I'll talk to you alone."

John did not like Detective Christy Stefani in the room. She made him nervous and he kept glaring at her. There was a six-minute break while they got new cups of coffee.

Smallcomb: "Let's see. It was Saturday. What happened then?"

Annibel: "Well, I drove over there, stopped and saw Gordon Watts. Him and his wife for a while at their house. I got a motel room and then walked down to a burger place. The Burger Station, I think it's called. I sat there at the picnic tables. It was a sunny day. I ate there and walked over to Geigers. I bought some food. I had a little refrigerator in my room. So I bought some stuff to eat, milk and cheeses. Took 'em back there and I went to the bar. It's right across from Boomer's. I went in there and I had a beer. And then I walked over to Boomer's and had a couple of drinks there."

Smallcomb: "Did you talk to anybody at the bar? Meet anybody there?"

Annibel: "Yep. That same chick that was at Boomer's."

Smallcomb: "You said you had a room or something. Where was that at?"

Annibel: "At the motel. I don't know the name of it. The one, it's right by Geigers. I didn't even want to shower in the morning when I got up. I just came home instead."

Smallcomb: "What time did you check in?"

Annibel: "I don't know. It must have been about one o'clock. Two o'clock. Somewhere in there. A little after lunch. I went to Geigers first. And then I stopped by my friends, then went to the Crossroads. Is that what that bar's named?"

Smallcomb: "Yeah. How long were you in there?"

Annibel: "Long enough to have a beer. A half hour maybe."

Smallcomb: "Okay, and you said earlier that Patti was there [meaning Debbie]? You said her name was something like Patti?"

Annibel: "Uh-huh."

Smallcomb: "Talk to anybody else in there?"

Annibel: "At the Crossroads? No."

Smallcomb: "Okay, then you went to . . ."

Annibel: "Over to Boomer's. I had a Schnapps there."

Smallcomb: "You talk to anybody there?"

Annibel: "Yeah a couple of people. Jason, I don't know his last name. He drives a loader at the mill. And Patti, the chick who was playing Bingo or whatever it was. I talked to her."

Smallcomb: "Was that the first time you met her? You meet her anywhere before?"

Annibel: "No. First time."

Smallcomb: "How long do you think you were at Boomer's?"

Annibel: "An hour maybe. I walked to the liquor store later and saw a couple of people I knew."

Smallcomb: "You go up there by yourself?"

Annibel: "No, Patti was with me."

Smallcomb: "Patti have a last name by any chance?"

Annibel: "I don't know. I don't know if she even told me."

Smallcomb: "Did she sound like she was from Laytonville?"

Annibel: "Yeah. She was from Laytonville. She got a little paranoid because her ex-husband saw us. So she wanted to leave."

Smallcomb: "And you got caught up in the middle of that?"

Annibel: "I didn't want to get into it. I'm a married man. So we left and gambled at the Res."

Smallcomb: "How long do you think you were there?"

Annibel: "Not too long. I lost twenty dollars. I don't think it took me very long to lose it. I don't know. Forty-five minutes. Maybe an hour."

Smallcomb: "See anybody at the casino you know?"

Annibel: "I don't think so. If I did, I didn't pay any attention. I was just lookin' at the slots. Like I say, I don't usually gamble. I haven't been gambling since I got married."

Smallcomb: "Then what did you guys do?"

Annibel: "We went back to my motel. And she wanted something to eat, and didn't like what I had. All I had was cheese and crackers. Like those little Lunchables my daughters eat some time."

Smallcomb: "When you left the casino, did you go straight back to the motel?"

Annibel: "Mm-hmm."

Smallcomb: "How long do you think you were at the motel together?"

Annibel: "Half an hour maybe."

Smallcomb: "Tell me about her. Tell me about this Patti gal. How did you know she was from Laytonville?"

Annibel: "Well, I ran into a guy I work with that she said used to be her husband. I don't know his last name. I know his first name. I know what he does. His name's Alan and he's a lug-peeter at the sawmill. I've known him for a few years. I believe he grew up on the Res."

Smallcomb: "You've been working at the [Harwood] mill how long?"

Annibel: "Be three years on the twelfth of this month. I worked for LP here in town for fifteen years. I got laid off one time. A three-month layoff. They drug-tested me and found I had pot and fired me. Then they offered my job back the same day they fired me. I hired on before they broke the union, and my benefits were pretty lucrative. And they fired me just 'cause they knew I smoked pot. It had nothing to do with my job. And I wasn't even mad that they fired me 'til they offered to hire me back. And I told them, 'Fuck you. I'll never work for you again.' I had like forty thousand dollars in stocks that they owed me. And my daughter needed braces. So I said, 'Go ahead and fire me. I don't want my job back.' I figured if I was gonna start at the bottom again, I'd go somewhere else."

Smallcomb: "You go over to Pacific Lumber then?"

Annibel: "No. I worked at PALCO first. Before I went to work for Louisiana Pacific. Right out of high school. I grew up in Myers Flat."

Smallcomb: "So tell me about this gal. What's she all about?"

Annibel: "She just wanted to drink and have fun, I guess."

Stefani: "What did she look like?"

Annibel: "A little bit heavyset lady. Probably in her forties. Red hair. Glasses."

Smallcomb: "I'm going to show you a photograph, okay?"

Annibel: [Looking at the photo:] "Yeah. It looks like her."

Smallcomb: "You know, I want to be straight up with you. What's goin' on? That's the gal we found."

Annibel: "Oh, is that right?"

Smallcomb: "So, that's why we're asking this stuff. Because we didn't know you knew Alan. This Alan guy you were talking about, he told somebody that got ahold of us, that she was seen with you. She was found Monday morning about eleven o'clock between Branscomb and Westport. And anybody that had anything . . . well, was seen with her, whether it had been at the bar, the store, the motel, whatever, we got to talk to them. I need to get a kinda feeling where this gal was coming from. 'Cause I really don't know her."

Annibel: "I don't really know her either. I just, talked to her. I didn't really know her after she left. I mean, she was just somebody I met."

Smallcomb: "What was she drinking. Hard liquor?"

Annibel: "Yeah."

Smallcomb: "Bacardi? Bacardi rum and cokes? Could that be it?"

Annibel: "I'm not sure. Maybe. Like I said, I don't know what she was drinkin'."

Smallcomb: "How many drinks do you think you bought her?"

Annibel: "Two or three at the most. At Boomer's."

Smallcomb: "Did you drink anything at the Crossroads together? Or buy her any drinks at the Crossroads?"

Annibel: "A beer."

Stefani: "Would you describe her as the girl next door? Or a young lady who would go back to your motel room and engage in . . ."

Annibel: "More like a young lady who would go back to my motel and engage."

Smallcomb: "I'm not going to say this gal was an angel, okay? So, at any time did you guys have sex?"

Annibel: "No."

Smallcomb: "That's important. We need to know that."

Annibel: "No sexual intercourse. But oral sex, yeah."

Smallcomb: "Okay. Explain that. Tell us about that."

Annibel: "I don't know what to say to you . . ."

Smallcomb: "Let me ask you, did she give you a blow job?"

Annibel: "Yeah."

Smallcomb: "Did you orally copulate her?"

Annibel: "I ate her."

Smallcomb: "How about having sex?"

Annibel: "No."

Smallcomb: "Did you ejaculate?"

Annibel: "Yeah, not in her mouth. On the bed, probably."

Smallcomb: "Did she have her clothes on or off?"

Annibel: "Off."

Smallcomb: "How about you?"

Annibel: "Yeah."

Stefani: "Did she ever ask you for money for giving head?"

Annibel: "No. But she wanted me to take her to dinner. I didn't want to go out to dinner. I had already eaten. She left, and she was going to get something to eat."

Smallcomb: "Did she have any money?"

Annibel: "I don't know. I assume so. I mean, she was sittin' in a bar when I walked in there. So she must have had a little something on her. I don't know. She didn't spend any when she was with me."

Smallcomb: "What was she wearing?"

Annibel: "Blue jeans and a blue jacket. Tennis shoes. That's all I remember."

Smallcomb: "Going back to the motel . . . do you know if her pants had a button or a fly?"

Annibel: "I don't know. I didn't take 'em off."

Smallcomb: "She took 'em off?"

Annibel: "Yeah."

Smallcomb: "Did she have a purse?"

Annibel: "Yep."

Smallcomb: "Can you describe the purse to me?"

Annibel: "Um, it was like a handbag. Either black or blue."

Smallcomb: "It was like a handbag? It had a strap?"

Annibel: "Yeah. It was a handbag. It had a strap."

Smallcomb: "How about jewelry?"

Annibel: "I don't think so."

Smallcomb: "How about her shoes. Can you tell me about her shoes?"

Annibel: "Sneakers."

Smallcomb: "Do you know what color they were?"

Annibel: "White."

Smallcomb: "Any undergarments?"

Annibel: "I don't think she was wearing a bra."

Smallcomb: "You said she had glasses. Her parents said she can't see anything without her glasses."

Annibel: "Yeah. She had glasses. My wife wears glasses too, but she can see fuzzy without 'em."

Stefani: "Does your wife know anything about this night?"

Annibel [Irritated]: "No. I hope she doesn't find out. I love my wife very much. I feel guilty about just . . . this is the first time I've done this, and I just don't feel good about it."

Smallcomb: "And I appreciate that. I appreciate you're being honest with us. I know it's kinda hard . . . So it could have been longer that you were with this gal at the motel. 'Cause like I said, we talked to some people at the motel."

Annibel: "It could have been, yeah."

Smallcomb: "When I say longer, I'm talking maybe up to two or three hours."

Annibel: "Uh, not that long. Two, maybe. I'm not really sure. It wasn't like an all-nighter."

Smallcomb: "No, no. That's not what anybody's saying. I'm just getting at that it was longer than forty-five minutes. So what's going on while you're there? I know you're having oral sex. But what was she talking about?"

Annibel: "Well, she was worried that we ran into Alan. She was afraid of Alan. I don't really know what to tell you."

Smallcomb: "Did you have a conversation with Alan at all?"

Annibel: "Yeah, I talked to him. I told him I was goin' to the Res."

Smallcomb: "What did he have to say, I mean did he see his ol' lady with you?"

Annibel: "Well, I saw him in the store. She was sittin' in the car outside. I don't know if he saw her sittin' in the car or not. I don't know. She saw him. And she saw me talking to him. And when I walked out, he was still in the store. So she said, 'Let's get outta here.' He just asked me what I was doin' in Laytonville. And I said I was goin' to the casino."

Smallcomb: "Does Gordon Watts work at the mill?"

Annibel: "Yes, sir. He's one of the control . . ."

Smallcomb: "He's been there for awhile?"

Annibel: "He just hired on again about three years ago. But he used to be a foreman. So, yeah, he's worked there for years. He'll be about forty-two this month."

Smallcomb: "So this gal . . . what time do you think you checked out?"

Annibel: "It must have been around four-thirty or five."

Smallcomb: "And where did you go from there?"

Annibel: "Straight home."

Smallcomb: "Okay. What was the weather like?"

Annibel: "It was stormin'. There wasn't any place to stop. As a matter of fact, I had to pee, but I couldn't because I didn't want to get out of the car. I waited until I got home."

Smallcomb: "Did you dodge any fallen down trees or anything like that?"

Annibel: "No."

Smallcomb: "Lucky. It's a helluva road."

Annibel: "Yeah, I was there the other day, Monday, as a matter of fact. Got the flu bug or something. And on the way to work, there was a tree down. And there were three women in a Bronco stopped, looking at it. I grabbed it and tried to pull it out of the way. I managed to break off the top where you could drive around it. And then I went to work. And I started feeling bad. So I came home and they had the road blocked. I just drove through the block and went over around the power lines. I guess I was lucky I wasn't electrocuted."

Smallcomb: "What day was that?"

Annibel: "Monday."

Smallcomb: "You went home sick?"

Annibel: "Yeah. It was storming Monday morning real bad again."

Smallcomb: "Yeah. It was a son-of-a-gun. Real slick this morning, too. So, you leave, you check out of the motel room between 4:30, 5:00, and you go straight home. Then did you tell your wife where you were or anything?"

Annibel: "She knew I was in Laytonville. But I didn't mention anybody. I love my wife. I don't want to hurt her."

Smallcomb: "What did you tell her you were doin' in Laytonville?"

Annibel: "I left a note. She was gone when I left."

Smallcomb: "You left a note on Saturday?"

Annibel: "Yeah."

Smallcomb: "What time did you leave Fort Bragg on Saturday?"

Annibel: "It must have been around one o'clock, or around noon."

Smallcomb: "Is there a reason that you decided to leave a note and go to Laytonville on Saturday?"

Annibel: "I was just, I don't know. I just wanted to get away from my wife for a while. Just needed some time apart. We've been together a lot of years. It's not always easy. Especially with our views about the kids. I'm too strict. I got one daughter who is thirteen and thinks she's going on twenty. She thinks she's an adult and that I don't know anything. My wife grew up in a family full of boys. When I talk to my daughter about her boyfriends, they are all like sixteen, seventeen, and eighteen. She's just thirteen. They all have driver's licenses. I talk to her about them."

Stefani: "Was there ever a time in the past where you and your wife weren't getting along, where you'd be apart?"

Annibel: "There's a couple of times. We were separated for a while. My wife had an affair a couple of years ago. And we split up and were separated for a while. But we're working it out. I forgive her. I love her. She'd never had anybody but me in her whole life. And I can understand her. When I lost my job at LP, we ran into financial debt. I was working nights. I wasn't there to help her with the kids. And she had an affair to escape. I forgive her. I love her. It happens."

Smallcomb: "Time away is okay once in awhile. I say it's okay, as long as it's not too long. You know what I mean?"

Annibel: "Yeah."

Stefani: "What time did you get to talk to her on Sunday?"

Annibel: "Just as soon as I got home. That would have been around five in the morning."

Smallcomb: "She ask you what was up or anything?"

Annibel: "She just asked me how I was. If I was okay."

Smallcomb: "Back at the motel, did you use meth or anything?"

Annibel: "No."

Smallcomb: "How about . . . did you see her using anything while you were there?"

Annibel: "No."

Smallcomb: "There's some talk about sex in the car. How was that goin' on?"

Annibel: "I don't really remember."

Smallcomb: "Okay, then in the motel . . . there's you guys having oral sex. Where does that take place in the room?"

Annibel: "On the bed."

Smallcomb: "Okay. Oral sex. No intercourse at all?"

Annibel: "No."

Smallcomb: "It's important. If you had sexual intercourse, I don't want to see it show up on a sexual-assault exam, okay. I need to know, is there going to be semen that's going to show up anywhere that could come back to you?"

Annibel: "No, sir."

Stefani: "Better that we know now."

Smallcomb: "There's some allegations where . . . I know you don't want your wife to find out. Anybody that was with her is going to be tested. And if there's semen in her vagina, don't burn yourself. If you guys had sex, you need to let us know."

Annibel: "No, we didn't. Um, she didn't swallow. You're not going to find any of my semen."

Smallcomb: "Why no sex?"

Annibel: "I don't know. I just didn't really want it. She didn't seem to mind doin' what she was doin'."

Smallcomb: "She was a willing participant?"

Annibel: "I have a beautiful wife. And I really just don't . . . it just kinda happened. It's not something I'm proud of. I love my wife."

Smallcomb: "I understand. I'm trying to respect that. I want to believe you, okay. I just don't want to see you down the road and have it come back on you. I want to give you the benefit of the doubt. But we can't miss it on a sexual-assault kit. A full exam, pubic exam, and everything."

Annibel: "You're not going to find any semen."

Smallcomb: "This is important. We'll find fibers and stuff in the vehicle, 'cause I got a search warrant for your car. Was there sexual stuff there? Don't bury yourself. Be honest. At any time in the vehicle did she have her clothes off, because we're going to do all kinds of nifty-difty tests, and get all kinds of fibers and shit."

Annibel: "I realize what you guys can do."

Smallcomb: "Same thing goes for the motel room. Describe that to me. Were you on the bottom. Was she on the bottom?"

Annibel: "I was on the bottom."

Smallcomb: "So she was on top, giving you oral sex. At any time was she on the bottom?"

Annibel: "Yeah. Well, actually, later we were side by side. 'Cause I was just banging her and she was giving me a blow job."

Smallcomb: "You were banging her with your finger, I take it?"

Annibel: "Yeah."

Smallcomb: "Okay, we've got a blanket from the room. And it's got a bunch of what looks like human crap on top of it. We got samples from that. And we've got samples from her bowels at the autopsy. So is it gonna come back to her, or you?"

Annibel: "I don't really know anything about it. I'm sure I didn't shit myself in bed."

Smallcomb: "She wanted you to take her to dinner. And you didn't take her to dinner?"

Annibel: "No."

Smallcomb: "Anything about getting paid for what she did?"

Annibel: "I know she really wanted me to take her to dinner."

Smallcomb: "I think something happened in the motel room. She pushed the issue, or something was done to you. I don't know if she was blackmailing you, or what she was doin'. But something happened in there. Tell us exactly what transpired as far as you and her afterward. I think she started pushing the money issue and going to dinner and stuff. I want to believe what you're saying. But don't bury yourself. She is kind of forceful verbally. I've been talking to some of the patrons at the Cottage Motel. And they heard something going on inside your cottage. Tell us what happened as far as what she was doing."

Annibel: "I don't know what to say to you that I haven't already said. It looks like your saying that I did something in there."

Smallcomb: "I'm saying she might have pushed the issue. I wasn't in that hut. I'm being up front with you. I'm saying people heard shit going on inside there. What your telling me is she wasn't raising her voice for you to take her somewhere? I think she was being kinda loud. I'm not making this shit up. I'm telling you what I've been told."

Annibel: "I really don't recall her getting too upset. She wasn't happy that I wouldn't take her out to dinner. But I don't remember her making a big scene. She wasn't demanding money or anything like that. She just wanted to go out again. I couldn't drive anymore. Not safely."

Stefani: "In the past you talked about you and your wife separating, where maybe a verbal argument got a little out of hand?"

Annibel: "Uh-huh."

Stefani: "Has there ever been a problem in the past between you and your wife?"

John does not like where this is going, and he is irritated by Christy Stefani.

Annibel: "Did I ever hit my wife, do you mean? Is that what you're talking about?"

Stefani: "Have you ever gotten to that point?"

Annibel: "No, I never laid a hand on my wife."

Stefani: "And she would say the same thing?"

Annibel: "Oh, I'm sure."

Stefani: "Have there been any restraining orders?"

Annibel: "No."

Stefani: "Have there been any restraining orders against each other?"

Annibel [Getting hot]: "There was a restraining order, but my wife didn't want it. My wife left and went to Florida. I threatened the guy who was fucking my wife. I said I'd put a bullet in his head. My wife was in Florida, and somehow there was a restraining order where I couldn't see her or my kids. And my wife, as soon as she got back from Florida, tried to get the judge to . . . I've never threatened my wife. I did threaten her boyfriend. But I never threatened my wife. My wife will say that to you. My wife's never been afraid of me."

Stefani: "And if she was to find out what happened on Saturday night? How do you think she'd react?"

At this point, according to Kurt Smallcomb, it looked as if John was about ready to spring out of his seat and attack Christy Stefani.

Annibel: "It'd hurt her."

Stefani: "I'm having a hard time believing it never got to that point between you two."

Annibel [Angry]: "It never has. You can talk to my wife. You can do whatever you want! Matter of fact, I think I've said enough to you guys."

Seeing that John might be getting ready to clam up, Smallcomb tried to settle him down.

Smallcomb: "It's entirely up to you."

Annibel: "I don't know what else to say. You're accusing me of beating my wife. I've never lain a hand on her."

Smallcomb: "You remember what I said. I want to believe you."

Annibel: "Can I have a smoke?"

Smallcomb: "Absolutely."

At this point, it was decided that it might be best if Christy Stefani left the room. John clearly did not like her. Once again, here was a strong woman who would not back down to him. In her place, Inspector Tim Kiely came into the room and introduced himself. Even then, John was still trying to explain himself concerning his wife.

Annibel: "I wouldn't even think about hitting her. She's my best friend. Even when I'm mad at her, she's still my best friend."

Smallcomb: "Well the reason I've asked Tim in here, he was with us on the scene and knows a little bit about everything and what's going on. So the car . . . I asked you about the backseat. Explain what happened in the backseat."

Annibel: "There wasn't enough room for her to give me a blow job. My pants were down. She was lying on the seat and I was kinda on the floorboard. And she was bent over giving me a blow job. But there wasn't enough room. It's a little car."

Smallcomb: "At any time did you come in the car?"

Annibel: "No."

Smallcomb: "Any cars pass you or anything?"

Annibel: "No. It wasn't very busy."

Kiely: "Well, I've listened in a little bit, and talked to the guys at the scene a little bit, John. Just to let you know who I am, I work for the district attorney's office. I'm an investigator. We work cases together with the sheriff's office all the time. This is just a shoot-the-bull session right now. It's all we're doing. I'm not a bad guy. So just relax and bear with me for a minute. Number one, no one thinks you're a wife-beater. No one thinks you're a bad husband. I don't think that at all. So let's forget about that bullshit. I think you're probably a hard worker. Probably a decent guy. However, something tragically went wrong that evening. And I'm not saying that you came out of the bushes like some kind of monster or mass murderer. I just think something tragically went wrong. I don't know exactly what it was. I need to hear it from you. To get the truth on your side of what happened. Like I said, she's not a saint. She's not Mother Teresa. If a person is strong enough to tell the truth, I'll put a lot of belief in that. What I'd like you to do is tell me about it and what happened. I don't know if there was a fight, if it was an accident. There's a million things that could have happened. So I'll give you the benefit of the doubt. No one is accusing you of being some kind of monster. You're a good hardworking guy. But people drink and get fucked up and something went wrong. I know it's hard. I can tell that your nervous. You're upset and shaken. And you have the truth on your side, John. You need to get the truth out in the open. It's killing you. I can tell. You're shaking."

Smallcomb: "If we thought you were a monster, we would have put the handcuffs on you."

Kiely: "We're here to get the truth on your side, John. Let's work with this. Let's get this over with."

Annibel: "I don't know what to say . . ."

Kiely: "John, let's get this over with. Come on. What happened? What happened?"

Annibel: "Nothing."

Kiely: "Was there a fight?"

Annibel: "No."

Kiely: "Okay, John, listen to me. This is important."

Annibel: "You're saying I did this and you're going to put me under arrest."

Kiely: "Am I saying you took a butcher knife to somebody and killed them? Of course not. I'm saying something tragically went wrong and I'll listen to you. Do I think you're some kind of mass murderer? Of course not. But there's nothing pointing to anyone else being with her. We have guys checking the car. We have guys checking your house. Let's cut to the chase here. Let's get with this thing. Let's tell the truth. I know it's eatin' you up inside. What happened with her? What did she do? Tell me."

Annibel: "I got nothing else to say."

Kiely: "You want to tell the truth about this, John. I mean, come on. Listen to me. This is bothering you, or you wouldn't be nervous."

Annibel: "Well, maybe if you were sitting here and I was the one drilling you, you might be a little nervous. You know what I mean?"

Kiely: "Oh, John. Of course I would. John. John. John. I'm just telling you that something went wrong. And you know from being a small kid and telling the truth that the truth goes a long way. I'm not saying that for years you were trying to kill her. No one thinks that. I mean a lot of stuff could have happened. I don't know. We have to check all that stuff. Man to man, you've been a good guy. I have no beef with you in the world. However, something happened here, John. And I can't make it up for you. I don't know if she attacked you. I don't know if there's someone else involved. I don't know a lot of stuff. We're starting to piece it together. But the best piece is what you can tell. She screwed up. You screwed up. You both screwed up. It was an accident. It's got to come from you John. I've been doing this a long time. Tell me what happened, John."

Annibel: "I got nothing else to say that I haven't already said."

Kiely: "Did you dump her body by the side of the road? Did you panic? If I thought you were John Dillinger or Jack the Ripper. If we thought you were real, real bad we'd have you in fuckin' handcuffs. Tell us what the fuck happened in there. Nothing's ever as bad as it seems. There are two sides to every story. We'll work with you on this thing. Like I said, we don't think you came out of the bushes. I think you were with the wrong person on that night."

Annibel: "Definitely."

Kiely: "Yeah, definitely. It's unfortunate to put you in this situation, but we have to deal with it. I know something happened in that room. We know she was getting loud. You set out to have a couple of drinks, have some fun. And maybe have a little action and get the hell out of Dodge. Am I right about that?"

Annibel: "Yeah."

Kiely: "And people are doing that all over America. So that's not a big deal. That's not even an issue. You ended up with the wrong person. Wrong place, wrong time. You set out to have a few drinks, do a little gambling, get a blow job. Big deal. But something happened. She put you in some kind of position where you felt you had to respond."

Smallcomb: "I don't know her drug history. Maybe she overdosed. I don't know. She might have OD'd in your goddamn motel room."

Kiely: "There's been an autopsy. There's a toxicology report. You're not stupid. You know what happens. Panicking is one thing. If you panicked and fucked up, because she OD'd or she vomited, or she died in her vomit or crap, or whatever, we need to know about that."

Smallcomb: "I don't see you as a killer, John. But what we're saying is if there's an explanation for something happening in that motel room, fuck, now's your opportunity."

Kiely: "Panicking is one thing. I mean, we fuck up all the time. He's done it. I've done it. We all have done it."

Smallcomb: "I don't think you raped her. I don't think you beat her."

Kiely: "She was with you voluntarily, we know that. You weren't dragging her in that place, for God's sake. I believe everything you're telling me so far, everything except the fact that she died somehow. If you didn't kill her, but threw her body down there, tell me about it. There's crap in the room, there's crap on her, there will probably be crap in your car. A plus B equals C. But that doesn't make you some kind of mass murderer. I mean here's some poor guy trying to get a roll in the hay and not get caught, and now ya got this. You're not some kind of bad guy. You work, you got things going for you. If she nodded, and you panicked and tossed her, then we can work with that. If she died of a drug overdose, or banged her head, or whatever the hell happened in there, then tell us. I know she was transported in your car. But it doesn't make you the worst guy that ever lived. I don't think you'd been seeing her before. You never dated her before?"

Annibel: "I never met her before."

Kiely: "And I bet you wish you never had."

Annibel: "Yes, I do."

Kiely: "You know, guys fuck around all the time. You were with her. You transported her in your car and she was dumped off a route that you frequently use. That's pretty obviously what happened. I don't want us to get pissed off about this. We're not gonna beat it out of you, John. That's not how we work. I just want you to think for a second what's the smart thing to do."

Smallcomb: "John, she was not beaten. She was not savagely abused. I don't know what the situation was."

Kiely: "John, come on. We're all guys here. We all know what happened. Jesus Crimany, John, don't make this worse than what it is. It's not gonna go away, John. We need to deal with this."

Smallcomb: "Don't let people assume stuff, John. You're not into beatin' ladies. Shit, you're still with your wife. Don't make yourself out to look like Jack the Ripper, 'cause you're not."

Kiely: "Could she have shot up before she seen you?"

Annibel: "She could have. She could have gone into the bathroom at the motel. I mean I never saw any drug use."

Kiely: "You're not a drug user, are you?"

Annibel: "I'm a drinker."

Kiely: "Okay, so there's no reason to believe that John is some kind of crack dealer. I do know you gave her a ride down that road. And I know that's because you panicked. But that doesn't mean you killed her. Listen, John. You're actually a likable guy. You really are. But common sense is gonna take over here. I mean, you picked the wrong person to fuckin' nail that night."

Annibel: "Yes, I did. But I'm apparently going to jail, no matter what."

Kiely: "We haven't mentioned jail. We haven't mentioned jail at all, have we?"

Annibel: "It's just, I can see where this is heading with what you guys are saying."

Kiely: "No, John. I have to hear it from you first before I make any determination on who's goin' anywhere. I'm not gonna bullshit ya. You don't want me to bullshit ya, do you? Play little tricks on you. You wouldn't do it to me. And I ain't gonna do it to you. The bottom line is, she died in that motel room. She was yelling stuff in the room. She was acting like an idiot, whatever. She was freakin'. Use common sense. You haven't lied to me yet. The only thing you haven't done is tell the whole truth. Did she have an overdose, John?"

Annibel: "I don't know how she died."

Kiely: "Did she die in your motel room?"

Annibel: "Yeah."

Kiely: "Okay, then what happened?"

Annibel: "I took her out of there."

Kiely: "Took her where?"

Annibel: "Branscomb Road."

Kiely: "And dumped her?"

Annibel: "Mm-hmm."

Kiely: "Where was she dead when you woke up?"

Annibel: "On the floor."

Kiely: "Okay, you panicked."

Annibel: "Mm-hmm."

Kiely: "And you took her to Branscomb Road and threw her down the bank. Where'd you put her?"

Annibel: "Down the bank."

Kiely: "Was she clothed or not clothed?"

Annibel: "Unclothed."

Kiely: "Okay. Where can we find her clothes? That will go a long way toward getting the truth out here. Where can we find the clothes?"

Annibel: "In the ocean."

Kiely: "In the ocean? Do you feel better now?"

Annibel: "I don't want to go to jail. I love my wife."

Kiely: "I know you love your wife. I would never say that you don't love your wife. Does she even know about this?"

Annibel: "No."

Kiely: "Did she know you were seeing another woman?"

Annibel: "No."

Kiely: "Any ideas how she died?"

Annibel: "Nope."

Kiely: "Okay. I'm not going to give you any false hopes and tell you that it's going to go away. That's not how we work here. We're doing things aboveboard."

Smallcomb: "Remember, what I said before? If I thought you were some kind of animal . . ."

Annibel: "Could I see my wife before you do all your . . . is that possible? I, I, I, look, I'm not gonna run or do anything."

Kiely: "Let's do this. I can tell you this. If we decide to hold you, and you want to see your wife before hand, we can allow it."

Annibel: "Okay."

Tim Kiely went through the scenario of all the places John had been with "the gal" on Saturday, November 28 in Laytonville. Kiely asked John what he saw when he woke up and found Debbie dead in his room. Earlier he had said he found her dead on the floor. Now he had a different story.

Annibel: "She was lying on the bed. On her back. I just wake up all the time, every night. I don't ever sleep over six hours. The lights were off. I saw that she was dead. I panicked. I shook her. I felt for her pulse on her. [He showed the detectives where on her neck he felt for a pulse. Then he said something very revealing.] I felt on the carotid."

Carotid is not a term most laymen would know. It refers to a specific area within the neck. John obviously had heard this word before. He probably heard it in relation to the murders of Sherry Lynn Smith and possibly Andrea LaDeRoute.

Kiely: "So what was going on in your mind?"

Annibel: "I'm scared. I panicked. It was a bad situation. I was thinking, *I'm going to jail*. I have kids to support."

There was a short break.

Kiely: "Okay, when we stopped talking, you panicked and a couple of hours went by. What time did you leave the motel room?"

Annibel: "Around four o'clock or so."

Kiely: "What happened then?"

Annibel: "I packed her out."

Kiely: "Pretty heavy?"

Annibel: "Yeah. I put her on the backseat. Face up."

Kiely: "No one saw you?"

Annibel: "I don't think so."

Kiely: "What did you do with her clothes?

Annibel: "I put 'em in a paper bag. Shoes, pants, jacket, purse."

Kiely: "Did you look in her purse?"

Annibel: "No, I didn't."

Kiely: "Was there money in there? Did you know that or not?"

Annibel: "I have no idea."

Kiely: "In the room . . . did you look for something that might have killed her?"

Annibel: "No."

Kiely: "What's the first thing you did when you got in the car?"

Annibel: "I left the window down. And the driver's side got soaked. I got the jacket I had in the backseat and sat on it. I drove from Branscomb toward Westport."

Kiely: "Why'd you pick that spot?"

Annibel: "I was just afraid of having someone in the car with me."

Kiely: "Was there a turn out where you stopped?"

Annibel: "No. I left the car running. Lights on. I went to the back door and opened it. I grabbed her by her arms. I did it quick. Just threw her over the bank. I just kinda pushed her off. She went down on her back, I think. I didn't stop to look over the edge. I just heard the leaves rustle, and I knew she hadn't gone very far. I got back in the car and drove off."

Kiely: "Then where did you go?"

Annibel: "On the road to Fort Bragg. Right about here [he points at a map], I stopped and pulled off and got rid of the clothes. Down on the ocean side. I don't know if they hit the water. The wind was blowing real hard when I tried to throw it out. It might have blown back on the bank."

Kiely: "Did you ever take any money."

Annibel: "I'm not a thief. I'm not a robber."

Kiely: "Okay, where'd you go next?"

Annibel: "Home."

Kiely: "And what time did you get home?"

Annibel: "About five o'clock."

Kiely: "Was anyone awake?"

Annibel: "My wife was awake."

Kiely: "What was she doin'?"

Annibel: "She was talking to some friends who were over there."

Kiely: "At five in the morning?"

Annibel: "Um hmm. They work nights at Sherwood Oaks."

Kiely: "So you walk in . . . did you have blood on your clothes?"

Annibel: "No."

Kiely: "So what happened next?"

Annibel: "I took a shower, and then my wife and her friend that she works with . . . well, this friend had a taillight out. She'd left her driver's license at home. And she lived in Albion. So we followed her to Mendocino so a cop wouldn't pull her over for having a taillight out. And then we came home."

Kiely: "Were you a little nervous about having your wife in that car after all this had been going on, or anything? What were you thinking right then? What was going through your mind?"

Annibel: "I was scared. I didn't want to lose my wife."

Kiely: "What was the friend's name you followed to Albion?"

Annibel: "Sara Jacobson."

Kiely: "And your wife doesn't have any knowledge about this, right?"

Annibel: "No."

Kiely: "So then what happened when you got home?"

Annibel: "We get ready. My youngest daughter was with my mom. And my mom and my brother were bringing her back from Thanksgiving. And we cleaned the house . . ."

Kiely: "The house in Fort Bragg?"

Annibel: "Um-hmm."

Kiely: "What else did you do on Sunday?"

Annibel: "Just visited with my family."

Kiely: "Did you wash your car on Sunday?"

Annibel: "No, I washed it yesterday. On Thursday. Um, I had a lot of ash and dust and shit. Well, I didn't really wash it, I just took a washcloth and wiped the dash . . ."

Kiely: "Fingerprints?"

Annibel: "No. Just getting rid of the dust."

Kiely: "Okay. 'Cause I could understand that if you didn't want any trace of this woman in your car, regardless of what happened . . . did you try to get rid of fingerprints?"

Annibel: "No. I just wiped. Just took a washcloth and wiped down the dash."

Kiely: "I mean, I would if I was you. I wouldn't want any fingerprints in my car. So was this just something you normally do?"

Annibel: "It's something I do. Probably every two months or three months when it gets dusty."

Kiely: "Okay, so did you wash the outside of the car, too?"

Annibel: "Yes."

Kiely: "And did you vacuum the car?"

Annibel: "Yes."

Kiely: "Okay, let's back up. Did you go to work on

Monday?"

Annibel: "Yes."

Kiely: "From what time to what time?"

Annibel: "Well, I got the flu bug. I only could work . . .
well, I was getting real cold. Fluish. I worked until about
9:30 and asked the foreman if I could go home. So I went
home and went to bed."

Kiely: "Did you go to work Tuesday?"

Annibel: "No."

Kiely: "Wednesday?"

Annibel: "I went to work."

Kiely: "Okay. When did you wash your car?"

Annibel: "Thursday. After my daughter got home from
school. I asked her if she wanted to go with me to the car
wash. And the neighbors offered to take her to the beach
instead. So she went with them. I went to the car wash
by the Taco Bell."

Kiely: "And did you use the power wash to wash the outside of your car?"

Annibel: "Yeah."

Kiely: "And you used their vacuum to vacuum your
car?"

Annibel: "Um-hmm."

Kiely: "Were you worried about something from her
body stuff being in your car?"

Annibel: "Maybe her hair. I wasn't so concerned about
fingerprints. There's so many people in my car. I mean,
my wife chauffeurs all the kids around town."

Kiely: "Then Friday morning, you're met by us. They
talked to you down at the carport?"

Annibel: "Um-hmm."

Kiely: "Okay, so do you think she died of an overdose or something?"

Annibel: "I don't know."

Kiely: "If you had to make a guess, John."

Annibel: "I don't know."

Kiely: "Is it possible she wasn't murdered?"

Annibel: "Uh-huh."

Kiely: "Any evidence to show that she was murdered?"

Annibel: "I don't think so."

Kiely: "And there's no way we'll find your semen?"

Annibel: "No."

Smallcomb: "You think we can recover the clothes?"

Annibel: "I think so. Maybe. I think there's a good chance. I did it in the dark. And I'm afraid of edges. I just kinda threw it over the edge."

Kiely: "Okay. Well, let's go out."

Smallcomb: "We'll let you visit with your wife and we'll go by the house. And then we'll come back here."

Kiely: "You're going to cooperate with us on finding the clothes?"

Annibel: "Yes. Uh, if my wife found out about this, I'm gonna lose her."

Kiely: "Where did she think you were going on Saturday? I forgot to ask you that."

Annibel: "Just to Laytonville. To see friends."

Kiely: "You guys have a little bit of an argument or something. A spat or something?"

Annibel: "Just a little bit. I thought maybe we should have a day apart."

Kiely: "Okay. Let's go out and find those clothes. And then we'll come back and do a little more talking."

Kurt Smallcomb, Tim Kiely, and John Annibel got into a law-enforcement vehicle and drove up to the cliff along the ocean where John had tried throwing Debbie Sloan's clothing into the ocean. They arrived there to find that the clothing had not made it to the ocean, as John had surmised. Debbie Sloan's articles of clothing were ultimately found in vegetation on the cliffside. Kurt noted later, "The cliffside overlooked the Pacific Ocean and was very steep. I climbed down the cliff with Detective Stefani and we recovered numerous articles, including Debbie's clothing and purse."

John Annibel was being cooperative so far, but he was about to slip up.

CHAPTER 6

Masters at Work

After John and the detectives returned from retrieving Debbie Sloan's clothing, he was given a chance to talk with his wife, Beth. The conversation was recorded.

John: "I met her at the bar, and we continued in the hotel room. If anybody had intercourse with her, the autopsy would show it. She was drunk. I think I woke up in the middle of the night and she was dead. She was dead in my bed. And I panicked. I thought of phoning the cops. But I figured they'd put me in jail."

Beth: "I'm so sorry, sweetheart."

John: "I didn't have sex with her in the butt. The autopsy will show that. I was lonely. I didn't know who she was. But I'm gonna go to jail for trying to cover it up. I ruined our lives."

Beth: "I'm sorry. I'm so sorry for you."

John: "I'm so scared what's gonna happen to you and the girls."

Beth: "We're gonna be okay, sweetheart. We'll make it."

John: "I don't know how she died, Beth. She was dead when I woke up. I think the cops are not being honest. God, I miss you."

Beth: "Is there anything in the autopsy that she died of an overdose or something?"

John: "I don't know how she died. I have no idea. I'm sorry. I didn't have intercourse or anything. I just wanted someone to talk to. I picked a bad person."

Beth: "I'm sorry it happened."

John: "I wanted to be with you this weekend. Now I need to sign you up for welfare, or Medicare, or whatever."

Beth: "Oh, I'll take care of that, sweetheart. You just worry about getting out of there."

John: "I don't care what happens to me anymore."

Beth: "Do you swear on your heart that you did not do it?"

John: "I didn't do it. We did nothing, except for the high. Now we lost the car and everything. I get another paycheck out at the mill. It'll cover the total for . . . I know it ain't much. I'm so sorry, damn it. You're the best thing that ever happened to me, Beth."

Beth: "Well, we better go. We'll be here for you. I know you didn't do these things. I know you didn't do anything."

John: "I didn't do it. They're trying to make it out like . . ."

Beth: "I told them straight out that you've not hit me, ever. I was straight-up about everything."

John: "I should have phoned the cops. I guess I got scared. I mean, you're scared when you wake up and there's someone dead in your room."

Beth: "Was she on drugs when you picked her up?"

John: "I don't know. Probably. I never saw her do any."

Beth: "Did you do any?"

John: "No, my system's cleaned out. I haven't done any drugs."

Beth: "Okay. I just wanted to make sure about that."

John: "Uh . . . there's still the sock drawer." [He may have been talking about marijuana.]

Beth: "They've already found it. They tore the whole room apart. They found it all."

John: "I told the department, there's nothing in there. I didn't rob her or anything. I just wanted to come home."

Beth: "I said, I wished Thursday would have never happened." [Referring to the Thursday when she and John had the fight, and she took off with the kids.]

John: "The kids are already at school, huh?"

Beth: "Yeah. "[Someone they knew] heard they were investigating at the mill. 'Cause she didn't hear us talk about that last night. [Inaudible] this never would have . . ."

John: "I love you."

Beth: "I love you, too. (Inaudible) would that clear you?"

John: "I'm guilty of hiding a corpse. I'll go to jail. The fact that I cooperated with them. Hopefully, they'll cut me some slack."

Beth: "If they did see that, that you cooperated very well . . . well, keep up the good work, and get out of here. We'll come and see you. I'll ask Sarah to come. Because [our] car will probably be repoed after that." [She may have meant taken as evidence.]

John: "Yeah. I'm so sorry."

Beth: "It's okay, sweetheart."

John: "All I want to do is hold you."

Beth: "I know. These last few days . . . I'm so sorry. I still do love you. You're gonna get out of this okay."

John: "I don't know. What are you gonna do? I wish I could hold you forever."

Beth: "I'm so sorry."

John: "You're everybody I've ever loved. If you guys need help, it seems like some state agency or somebody will help you. I'd rather that happened than see you quit your job. I'm gonna miss you so much."

Beth: "They can't keep you forever."

John: [Inaudible—he may have said something about harming himself.]

Beth: "You will live for me and the girls, please! Please don't do that to us! The girls will understand. Please don't do that."

John: "God, I love you, Beth."

Beth: "I love you too, John. It's such a nightmare."

John [Disgusted]: "Happy Birthday! I knew I shouldn't have gone to Laytonville."

Kiely: "Hi. You guys about done?"

John: "Yep."

Kiely: "I need a couple of more minutes. So I'm gonna go talk to Kurt."

John: "Thanks."

Beth: "Here's some smokes. You need some matches? It's gonna be okay. I'm gonna help with the phone bills and do whatever I can."

John: "Beth, I love you."

Beth: "I love you, too."

John: "How about a kiss."

[She gives him a kiss.]

Beth left and the interview process continued with Annibel, Kiely, and Smallcomb.

Smallcomb: "What happened there, John? I mean, John, come on. John wakes up next to a dead gal!"

Annibel: "I don't know. I really don't."

Kiely: "I'll explain something. I want you to think hard about this. We've done some phone calls. One was to the pathologist. He's the one that does the autopsy. There's been a cause of death listed."

Annibel: "And what is that?"

Kiely: "Cause of death is . . . strangulation. She was strangled. Which could happen in a lot of ways. Someone put their hands around her neck and strangled her to death. Were you really, really drunk that night?"

Annibel: "Yeah."

Kiely: "Something happened between the time she sat next to you on the bed and the time you woke up. I know you said you put your hands on her neck, checking her pulse. We need to come up with something. So what's going on here? Are you telling the truth?"

Annibel: "Yes."

Kiely: "I mean, you know she can't breathe. I'm trying to find a way to make this right. I'm trying to find a way to make sense of this. We're just learning . . . what's the word for it, Kurt?"

Smallcomb: "Asphyxiation."

Kiely: "Any recollection of this, John?"

Annibel: "No."

Kiely: "Have you ever passed out drunk before, and done something while you were drunk? Something stupid?"

Annibel: "I've drunk and blacked out. I don't remember what I did."

Kiely: "Okay. Well, how are you gonna explain this? I mean, did she ever hit you? 'Cause we're gonna look at her whole body."

Annibel: "Sure."

Kiely: "Are there any marks on her body?"

Annibel: "No."

Kiely: "John, did you kill her?"

Annibel: "No."

Kiely: "Was there a fight or not? What happened, John? What happened? We have to account for this somehow. I mean a guy with a knife in his hands . . . he's going to do an autopsy and you can see the finger marks. The indentations. And you can gage the width of the hands. I don't know. I'm guessing, but the width of the hands is probably about the same size as your hands."

Annibel: "I don't know what to tell you."

Kiely: "You didn't intentionally choke her?"

Annibel: "Nope."

Smallcomb: "You come from a pretty rural area. Your mom probably did quite a bit of baking. And made cookies. Say you went to the cookie jar. And you took two cookies, but you were only supposed to take one. And your mom calls you, and you come out to the kitchen. So you'd better tell her the truth. Would you tell her two cookies or one cookie?"

Annibel: "I'd tell her two cookies."

Smallcomb: "Okay, same thing here, man."

Annibel: "I've been trying to be up front with you guys."

Kiely: "And I think you have been for the most part. Except this is the hardest thing to talk about. We need to deal with it John, 'cause it's not going to go away. You're a nice guy to talk to. This is nothing personal. I wish we could shake hands and call it a day. But it's not gonna go away. I know you want to do this. I know you want to do the right thing. We're almost there. I think you choked her, whether you meant to kill her or not. I mean I know the

type of guy you are. You wouldn't do something unpro-
voked without some kind of reason. I realize you're feeling bad, you want to tell the truth about this. It's bothering
you so bad today that you can hardly look at us. You want
to do the right thing. Otherwise, you wouldn't have taken
us to the clothes. We can only assume. And we don't want
to assume. It's not like you're an animal. So tell us what
happened."

Annibel: "I don't know."

Smallcomb: "You do know, though, John. You do know. I
can look at you, okay. You're sitting there shaking. Shiv-
ering. Damn you! You've been square with us the whole
time. Don't leave this thing hanging. Let the people know.
Let us know what the hell happened."

Kiely: "John, I'm a nice guy. You're a nice guy. We just
need to get the truth out. It was a disastrous evening, man.
It was a total screw-up. Let's get this over with."

Annibel: "But I don't remember."

Kiely: "You do remember!"

Smallcomb: "You're remorseful. Jesus Christ, what else this
gal did is not the case. I told you that from the beginning."

Kiely: "You were upset and crying earlier, John. I don't
think it was fake. I mean, you'd feel better. And for her
family. Everybody's got a family. They need to know what
actually happened. This was something you didn't mean
to do. Were you fucking around, playing games?"

Smallcomb: "These assumptions pile up on top of each
other. All of a sudden these assumptions come down. The
only person who's gonna be screwed by it is you. Don't
let that happen. Don't let other people dictate what is
going to happen. I've seen it hundreds and hundreds of
times. I can't make you any promises. But I can say,
'Hey, shit, man. John told us the goddamn truth. John panicked, but he's not an animal.'"

Kiely: "Let's set the record straight, John, and get this over with. We've been talking for a long time. It's not a believable account that you don't remember how she died. It's not gonna fly. We're looking for answers on this."

Annibel: "I don't know what to tell you."

Kiely: "Well if we need to talk to you in day or two, that will be okay?"

Annibel: "Sure. I'll talk to you anytime."

Kiely: "Okay, if you come up with something, you can let the jail staff know. You know that you're going to jail. You know that?"

Annibel: "Oh, yeah, I realize that."

Kiely: "Okay. Because there's no choice. It's nothing personal."

Annibel: "I don't have anything against cops. I like cops. We need them."

Kiely: "We can leave our business cards with you. We try to do things aboveboard. I mean, have we made any threats or promises?"

Annibel: "No."

Kiely: "Coerced you or anything?"

Annibel: "No. You let me see my wife. I'm real thankful for that. Thank you very much. It meant a lot to me. I love her."

Smallcomb: "I know that."

Annibel: "You've been real nice to me. Right from the very beginning. I'm so happy that you didn't disturb my family."

Kiely: "Well, no one gets a thrill out of this. Think about things. We may come to see you this weekend. We may come to see you Monday."

Annibel: "Whenever, sure."

Smallcomb: "Let me just give you a rundown on what's

gonna happen. We're going back over the hill to Ukiah. Before you get booked, we're gonna stop by the hospital. Because of the sexual stuff. They'll take some hair samples from you. They'll take pubic hair. They'll draw blood. All that stuff. We'll take photographs of you. And . . . why don't we get you something to eat. Are you hungry?"

Annibel: "Yep."

Smallcomb: "Why don't I get you some food? You can hang out a little bit longer. And I'm getting hungry myself."

Annibel: "Can I just step outside and smoke? I'm not gonna run or do anything."

Smallcomb: "No, don't worry about that. We'll get you a smoke."

Kiely: "And hopefully we'll hear from you between now and Monday."

Annibel: "You guys are very smart, or you wouldn't have the job you have."

What occurred next would become a point of contention that would involve the detectives, deputy district attorney, a judge, and John's future lawyer, Linda Thompson. Thompson later addressed this issue, and her statements, while one-sided, nonetheless provide a clear idea of John's thinking and his hopes for a line of defense. John was street smart in a way and he basically knew about his Miranda Rights.

Thompson said, "On December 4, 1998, at approximately 5 AM, Detectives Smallcomb and Stefani conducted the first interview with Mr. Annibel. During the course of the initial interview, Mr. Annibel was subjected to several hours of interrogation by a minimum of two officers at a time. It was not until page ten of the transcript that Miranda warnings were given."

Thompson added that at a point early on in this interview, when one of the interrogators became too obviously antagonistic and hostile toward Mr. Annibel, she (Detective Stefani) was asked to leave the room wherein another officer took her place.

Thompson claimed it was the defendant's contention that he had invoked his privilege and that all questioning should have ceased, and that did not occur. At some point during the interrogation, the officers allowed a brief contact between Mr. Annibel and his wife. This conversation was also recorded. During this conversation it was obvious, declared Thompson, that Mr. Annibel was emotionally distraught and concerned about the well-being of his wife and daughters. He indicated during this conversation that he felt like hurting himself because of what he had put his family through. At the conclusion of this brief meeting the interrogation continued with Detective Smallcomb and Tim Kiely.

There would be plenty of disagreements between what John Annibel said occurred during this first interview and what the detectives noted. None was more flagrant than John's contention that Detective Stefani was antagonistic and hostile toward him. In fact, it was the detectives contention that just the opposite was true—John was antagonistic and hostile toward her. He did not like the fact that a strong woman was questioning him. At one point Detective Smallcomb said, "It looked like he wanted to jump out of his chair and strangle her."

Detective Stefani agreed. "John didn't like being talked back to by a woman. He was practically coming out of his chair. He looked very angry."

Detective Stefani had left so that Detective Kiely could enter. It became apparent they weren't going to get far if John was so angry at Stefani.

Between December 4 and December 7, John was placed in a safety cell, because he had mentioned hurting himself. This was the standard precaution for a prisoner contemplating suicide. John would later complain that he didn't eat or sleep while in the cell, and that he was constantly cold from lack of clothing and adequate heating.

On December 7, 1998, Detective Smallcomb asked John to come in to the detective's office for another interview. John agreed and sat down with Detective Kurt Smallcomb, Detective

Frank Rakes, and later, Inspector Tim Kiely. After small talk about cigarettes and how tired he was, John and the detectives began talking about the events that had occurred over the previous weeks. John spoke of the argument with his wife on Thanksgiving, getting a motel room in Laytonville, and meeting Debbie Sloan at the Crossroads Bar. Whether as a mistake, or for some deliberate reason, John called her Patti. He then spoke once again of the events occurring at Boomer's, the casino, and the abortive attempt to get a "blow job" in his car at the casino. Finally he spoke of their sexual encounter at the motel.

At this point the second interview really got down to business, and it was a masterful bit of work by the detectives and inspector Kiely, worthy of a textbook in the process of interviewing suspects.

Smallcomb [Speaking about when Debbie got back to the room after going out to get something to eat]: "Were you awake when she got back?"

Annibel: "No—when she walked in the door, I was sitting on the bed."

Smallcomb: "What did she talk to you about?"

Annibel: "Well, at that point, she knew my phone number. I don't know how she got my phone number."

Smallcomb: "Where was your wallet and everything?"

Annibel: "It was in my jeans."

Smallcomb: "She know that you had a wallet?"

Annibel: "Yeah, but I don't have my phone number in it."

Smallcomb "So you told her your name and stuff?"

Annibel: "Yeah."

Smallcomb: "So she has your phone number. What'd she say?"

Annibel: "Well, that she wanted me to give her some money or she was gonna phone my wife . . ."

Smallcomb: "And what happened then, John?"

Annibel: "I got mad."

Smallcomb: "Was she baiting you? Am I right?"

Annibel: "Yeah."

Smallcomb: "What happened?"

Annibel: "I got mad and I grabbed her. And I started to choke her. I realized . . . I flashed on my wife and I let her go. She just started making a clicking sound. But I didn't mean to do it."

Smallcomb: "I know that. Remember I told you before."

Annibel: "I tried to let go. And I tried to stop. I don't know if I broke something or what I did. But, well, I'm stronger than I thought. I'm really sorry."

Smallcomb: "I know you are, man."

Annibel: "I just . . . I didn't want my wife to find out. I love my wife very much."

Smallcomb: "No doubt about that. There's no doubt about that."

Annibel: "My wife doesn't deserve what's gonna happen to her."

Smallcomb: "Okay, so when this happened, are you on top of the bed or on the floor?"

Annibel: "On top of the bed."

Smallcomb: "How long do you think this is going on for? I know it's hard."

Annibel: "I don't know. Four or five minutes."

Smallcomb: "You hear some kind of click? Some kind of clicking sound?"

Annibel: "Uh-huh."

Smallcomb: "Okay, then what happens?"

Annibel: "She just quit making any noise. I checked her

and she was dead. I seriously thought about phoning you guys. But I kept thinking about my wife and how I knew I was going to prison. I'll never see my wife again. I didn't know what to do. I sat there for a few hours, trying to figure out what I should do. Finally I decided maybe I should just try and hide it."

Smallcomb: "So, you were probably in the room for a couple of hours afterward?"

Annibel: "Oh, yeah."

Smallcomb: "All right. Then what? You put her in the car?"

Annibel: "Uh-huh."

Smallcomb: "Is she clothed or unclothed?"

Annibel: "Unclothed."

Smallcomb: "And where'd you put her in the car?"

Annibel: "I had a sleeping bag in the car. I laid the sleeping bag out and put her on top of it. In the backseat."

Smallcomb: "So you drove . . . well, I'll tell you something else. You wanted somebody to find her, didn't you?"

Annibel: "Yeah."

Smallcomb: "I can respect that. It's not like you took her and dumped her in the goddamn ocean, where somebody couldn't find her. I mean . . ."

Annibel: "I wanted her to be found."

Smallcomb: "She was hitting you up. She was basically saying that she was going to burn you. Am I right or wrong about that?"

Annibel: "She wanted me to pay her off."

Smallcomb: "Was she pushing the issue?"

Annibel: "Yeah. I made the mistake earlier in the evening of telling her how much I love my wife. And how long we've been together. I shouldn't have even been there. I mean, none of it should have happened. I'm really sorry for everything."

Smallcomb: "Twenty-twenty hindsight. Monday-morning quarterbacking."

Annibel: "I don't care what happens to me. But I'm really worried about my family. Very much."

Smallcomb: "I know that. I know that you are. It's just that . . . when my partner started talking to you about domestic violence . . . well, you never touched your wife. It was just the wrong fucking place at the wrong time. I don't need to tell you that."

Annibel: "I'm very, very aware of . . . well, I knew you guys were gonna catch me. I wasn't really sick Monday or Tuesday afternoon. I took the days off work. I just wanted to be with my wife, before you guys got there. 'Cause I knew you were coming. There's no doubt about that."

Smallcomb: "You know, I told you before, you're not Jesse James. Or the Boston Strangler. You've got remorse."

Annibel: "Well, I'm not who I wanted to be."

Smallcomb: "Okay, so you put the body there. Describe to me how you put the body there. When your car got there, did you roll her down the hill? Did you carry her down? I mean, how did she get there?"

Annibel: "I pulled her feet first out of the car. Then she was kind of . . . her butt was at the top of the bag and I started pushing her down."

Smallcomb: "Did you walk down?"

Annibel: "No, it was dark. I didn't walk down the bank at all. I just stood there. It was raining hard. It didn't sound like she went very far. I don't know, maybe six, seven, or eight feet. From the sound of the leaves rustling."

Smallcomb: "Was it raining out?"

Annibel: "Yes, it was raining hard."

Smallcomb: "When you dropped her down the side of the hill, were you standing on the shoulder of the road?"

Annibel: "Yes."

Smallcomb: "Did your feet sink in the gravel?"

Annibel: "My left foot might have."

Smallcomb: "But you didn't walk down to the body?"

Annibel: "No."

Smallcomb: "Okay, did you drop any other things, any bottles, cans, or anything down there?"

Annibel: "No."

Smallcomb: "From the time you parked till the time you got her out, how long do you think it took?"

Annibel: "Couple of minutes. Minute and a half. I was scared. Panicked. Just trying to do it quick."

Rakes: "Was she limp at that time?"

Annibel: "No. She'd been in the room a while."

Smallcomb: "She was stiffening up?"

Annibel: "Yeah."

Rakes: "What did you do with the sleeping bag?"

Annibel: "I've got it."

Rakes: "You have it?"

Annibel: "Yes, I do."

Smallcomb: "Where is that, John?"

Annibel: "It's in my storage unit."

Smallcomb: "What color is it?"

Annibel: "It's black or gray. It's rolled up, sitting on top of the ice chest."

Smallcomb: "The storage unit there at the apartment?"

Sherry Smith and her little sister, Paulette, had lots of pets to play with as children.
(Photo courtesy of Pam Smith Annibel)

Sherry Smith was well liked as a student at South Fork High School in the redwoods.
(Yearbook photo)

Sherry Smith enjoyed cheerleading and became the South Fork High School mascot in 1976. *(Photo courtesy of Pam Smith Annibel)*

Andrea LaDeRoute was very proud when she graduated from high school. *(Photo courtesy of Lisa LaDeRoute Lawler)*

Despite a tough childhood, Andrea was always upbeat and optimistic about her future. *(Photo courtesy of Lisa LaDeRoute Lawler)*

Andrea and John Annibel were girlfriend and boyfriend, and eventually they shared a place together. *(Photo courtesy of Lisa LaDeRoute Lawler)*

Andrea's mom died at the age of forty-four while her
daughter was still "missing."
(Photo courtesy of Lisa LaDeRoute Lawler)

Georgina Pacheco
loved her brother and
three sisters. They
grew up in Fort Bragg,
California on the
rugged Pacific coast.
*(Photo courtesy of
Laudalina Pacheco Parks)*

Georgina was the Portugese Festa Queen for the Fort Bragg area in the mid-1980s.
(Photo courtesy of Laudalina Pacheco Parks)

Young Debbie Sloan liked home economics and sports as a student at Geyserville High School in California's wine country.
(Yearbook photo)

John Annibel was one of a set of fraternal twins. He graduated from South Fork High School—the same school that Sherry Lynn Smith attended. *(Yearbook photo)*

John's twin brother, James, said that John was already "becoming weird" by high school. *(Yearbook photo)*

John went to work for the Pacific Lumber Company, which owned the largest redwood mill in the world. *(Author's photo)*

On March 17, 1980, John reported that his girlfriend
Andrea LaDeRoute went missing from the cabin they shared
in Fortuna. She was never seen alive again.
(Author's photo)

A Mendocino County Sheriff's deputy points to the spot
where Georgina Pacheco's body was discovered by a man
walking a dog. *(Mendocino County Sheriff's Office)*

Detectives pulled away brush to reveal Georgina Pacheco's body. *(Mendocino County Sheriff's Office)*

Pacheco's body was found not far from one of the most famous "mystery houses" in America—the Jessica Fletcher house in the village of Mendocino, featured in the television series "Murder She Wrote." *(Author's photo)*

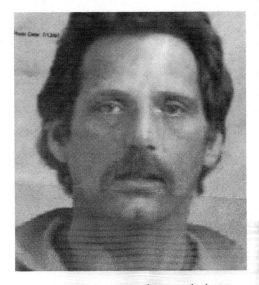

John Annibel was arrested for making a threat against his wife and others in 1997. *(Mendocino County Sheriff's Office)*

John was arrested early on the morning of his forty-first birthday, December 4, 1998, for the murder of Debbie Sloan. *(Mendocino County Sheriff's Office)*

Detectives learned that John had taken Debbie Sloan to Boomers Saloon and Restaurant in Laytonville, California, before murdering her. *(Author's photo)*

John had oral sex with Debbie at the Cottage Motel in Laytonville and then strangled her to death. *(Mendocino County Sheriff's Office)*

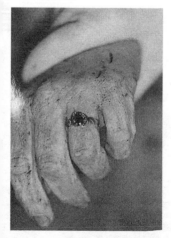

Debbie's sister indentified a ring that Debbie owned. *(Mendocino County Sheriff's Office)*

Detectives Kurt Smallcomb and Christy Stefani worked through a torrential downpour, gathering evidence at the spot where John had deposited Debbie Sloan's body in the redwoods. *(Mendocino County Sheriff's Office)*

John Annibel tried to get rid of evidence of the murder by throwing it over a cliff on the Mendocino coast into the Pacific Ocean. *(Author's photo)*

Mendocino County Evidence Technician Debbie Foster examined many items of evidence connected to Debbie Sloan's murder. *(Author's photo)*

DDA Rick Martin, Detective Christy Stefani, Detective Kurt Smallcomb and Evidence Technician Debbie Foster *(seated)* made a great team in the prosecution of John Annibel for the murder of Debbie Sloan. *(Author's photo)*

DDA Rick Martin has had a colorful career in the law, including a stint as the Attorney General of a South Seas island paradise. *(Photo courtesy of Rick Martin)*

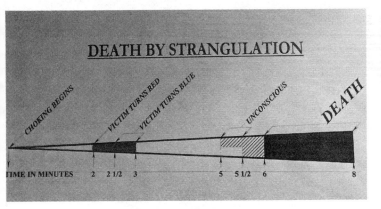

DDA Martin presented a timeline to the jury, showing just how long it took John Annibel to strangle Debbie Sloan to death. *(Author's photo)*

Investigator Harris worked with Pam Smith Annibel and Lisa LaDeRoute Lawler to bring justice for their murdered sisters, Sherry and Andrea. *(Author's photo)*

In August 2002, Andrea LaDeRoute's skull was found in the redwood forest not far from where Julia "Butterfly" Hill had made her famous tree sit. Here Julia addresses an audience. *(Author's photo)*

The number 13 had always been Andrea's lucky number. Her skull and other evidence was found not far from a tree marked with the number 13 by forestry workers. *(Author's photo)*

Lisa LaDeRoute Lawler gazed down into an area where Andrea's remains were discovered by foresters planting trees. Andrea's skull had remained hidden for twenty-two years. *(Author's photo)*

Lisa never gave up in her fight to bring justice for her murdered sister, Andrea. *(Yearbook photo)*

Sherry Lynn Smith is buried in a Eureka cemetery that faces the Pacific Ocean. *(Author's photo)*

Friends and family always put flowers and balloons on Georgina Pacheco's grave on her birthday. *(Author's photo)*

Annibel: "Yeah."

Smallcomb: "Any problems with us going back and getting it?"

Annibel: "No, not at all. I would really prefer my family wasn't there when you did it. I mean, if you got the key . . ."

Smallcomb: "Did you guys search that at all?"

Rakes: "Yeah, I saw it."

Smallcomb: "What did you guys use to get in there?"

Rakes: [Inaudible.]

Annibel: "Did you get my key ring, one of them has a Marlboro thing . . . is that the ring you have?"

Smallcomb: "No, I think it's got a blue thing on it."

Annibel: "Okay, my wife might have given you her keys. There should be a key on that too."

Smallcomb: "You still have the keys to the car?"

Rakes: "I think so."

Smallcomb: "Okay. No problem with us going back there and getting that?"

Annibel: "No, not at all."

Smallcomb "If that's what you want us to do, that's what we'll do."

Annibel: "If you can do it without . . . I mean, if you've got to talk to my wife, well, okay. But if you can do it without that, there's just no reason to upset her anymore than what's been done."

Smallcomb: "We'll do that. We can do that. I know you're trying—but what time do you think you were there at the place she was found?"

Annibel: "I know it's pretty accurate. Because I know how long it takes to drive home. And I know what time I got home. That was about four o'clock in the morning. 'Cause it's a forty-five minute drive from Branscomb to my house. I'm aware of that. It was storming. So I drove slower than usual. It was raining real hard. It was raining so hard a couple of times I almost had to stop."

Smallcomb: "It was a hard, son-of-a-gun weather for about a week."

Annibel: "And then I stopped where I showed you where the clothes were."

Smallcomb: "Right, and at any time, were there any trees falling on the road or anything like that on Sunday morning?"

Annibel: "No."

Smallcomb: "You pass anybody on Branscomb Road?"

Annibel: "No, not on Branscomb Road."

Smallcomb: "Okay, you go home. There's your wife there. You say you're vacuuming the car. When would that have been?"

Annibel: "Thursday."

Smallcomb: "The first time you cleaned the car was Thursday?"

Annibel: "Yes."

Smallcomb: "Well, you went back to work on Monday morning. Did you stop by and look at the body?"

Annibel: "No."

Smallcomb: "At any time between the time we came and talked to you and the time this happened, did you stop and look at the body?"

Annibel: "No."

Smallcomb: "Did you ever check on where the clothes were?"

Annibel: "No."

Smallcomb: "A pair of glasses. Did you ever know where her glasses were?"

Annibel: "They should have been with the clothes."

Smallcomb: "Down the side?"

Annibel: "Yeah, I'm sure they're there. I'm sure of it."

Smallcomb: "Going back to the room . . ."

Rakes: "You have enough coffee?"

Annibel: "I can use a little more. And if I can bum another cigarette from you, from the other detective, it would be great."

Smallcomb: "Bring me a smoke, too. So, when you're back in the room, when this happened, were you on the bed or on the floor?"

Annibel: "On the bed."

Smallcomb: "Did you miss any money in your wallet? What was she saying to you, John? What was she telling you?"

Annibel: "Well, she gave me my phone number and told me if I didn't give her 500 bucks, she was gonna phone my wife. I told her I wasn't gonna give her any money, and she got mad about that."

Smallcomb: "She asked for $500?"

Annibel: "Yes."

Smallcomb: "And what happened?"

Annibel: "Well, one thing, I didn't have $500, but I think she saw the Visa in my wallet and thought maybe I could get it. I had a couple of hundred on me. She got mad, and said she was gonna phone my wife and tell her that I had sex with her. Well, my wife and I have been together for seventeen years. I know we've had our ups and downs, and we've had some rocky spots, but I didn't want her to say that to my wife."

Smallcomb: "Seventeen years is a long time."

Annibel: "Yes, it is."

Smallcomb: "So, when she's asking you for the $500 and stuff and saying if you don't give her the money, she's gonna call your wife—where was she in the motel?"

Annibel: "She was sitting on the bed."

Smallcomb: "You were sitting on the bed at the same time?"

Annibel: "Yeah."

Smallcomb: "Then what happened?"

Annibel: "That's when I grabbed her."

Smallcomb: "Get her on top of the bed?"

Annibel: "Yeah."

Smallcomb: "Did you roll on top of her?"

Annibel: "We might have rolled off onto the floor. I was pretty hammered. We might of rolled off the bed. I grabbed her by the throat, and I started to choke her. And then I realized . . . I saw a flash of my wife, and I realized I'd never see her again if I did that. I let go of her. That's when she started making the clucking sound."

Smallcomb: "Well, how long do you think you had her by the throat?"

Annibel: "Just a minute or two. Not very long. I didn't think long enough to kill her. I don't know whether I broke something or not. My hands are pretty strong. I grade lumber. I flip over big shit."

Smallcomb: "You're pretty stout. Was she kicking or . . . ?"

Annibel: "No."

Smallcomb: "She doing anything?"

Annibel: "No."

Smallcomb: "No resistance?"

Annibel: "Uh-uh."

Smallcomb: "But her clothes were off?"

Annibel: "Yeah."

Smallcomb: "And your clothes were off?"

Annibel: "Uh-huh."

Smallcomb: "You grabbed her with both hands?"

Annibel: "Yeah. What's gonna happen to me?"

Smallcomb: "I can't make you any promises. I'd be lying if I told you, John, what's going to happen to you."

Annibel: "I know, I know. I mean I know . . . I'm not ignorant. I know I'm in deep shit. I knew that when everything happened. I took a couple of days off to see my wife, 'cause I knew I would never get a chance again."

Smallcomb: "Well, I'll tell you one thing. You're being honest and everything. It goes to your benefit. Because, like I told you before the only person that can help themselves out is you. You're being honest and that plays a big part as far as what happens between the judge and the district attorney's office. All I can do is register my input as 'John remorseful' and 'John told us the goddamned truth. John is not an animal.' This is a bad flicking place to be. I don't think you went looking for something like this."

In point of fact, the detective didn't believe half of what John was saying. The contention that he wanted the body to be found sounded like a bald-faced lie. It was already known that John had some domestic violence with Beth, and his claim of loving her so much rang false. The detectives didn't believe the tale that John was concocting about Debbie Sloan trying to extort money from him, either. From what they knew about her, she was not that kind of person. They seriously doubted that Debbie Sloan had not put up a struggle while being choked to death. Evidence already showed that it took a lot longer than a minute or two to kill her. Then there were the contusions on her head as if she might have been struck before being strangled to death.

Annibel: "I wasn't looking to fuck up my life. Or my wife's. That's what really sucks. I mean, if it was just my life, I could handle fucking it up. But now I just fucked up my daughters' and wife's lives, too. You know what I mean?"

John started telling them about where Beth had come from and about his early home life as well. Not once did he mention that he had a twin brother. John began expressing concern for Beth once again.

Annibel: "Her dad lives by us. He's an old drunk. He hasn't worked in thirty years. His mom died, and he thought maybe Beth would take care of him if he moved out here. 'Cause he needs somebody to take care of him. He's almost . . . well, he's gonna be destitute pretty quick. He had like $30,000 worth of certificates of deposit and a fifty-thousand-dollar house, and he hasn't worked for a while. He spends $600 a month in rent. He's pretty well spent most of what he had."

Smallcomb: "She have any brothers or sisters?"

Annibel: "She's got a brother down in L.A. Her mom lives with him."

Smallcomb: "Does she stay in contact with her mom at all?"

Annibel: "Yeah."

Smallcomb: "They get along?"

Annibel: "Yeah."

Smallcomb: "All right, it doesn't look like she's gonna be destitute or maybe on the streets. We have programs in the county which will help her."

Annibel: "The thing is, my wife really loves her job. She ain't gonna want to move. I just don't see her making it on her wages."

Smallcomb: "Well, like I said, there's some resources out there."

Annibel: "My brother [Ted] and mom both own property up at Myers Flat. And my Dad just died, and my mom's got a big house. Beth could relocate."

Smallcomb: "Well, they're not going to go out on the street. That's not gonna happen. Okay."

Annibel: "I'm really sorry."

Smallcomb: "You know, just being honest about it always . . . it's the first step in the right direction. For the long run for you, you know. I know it may not seem like it right now, and I'd be lying to you if I said it's all going to go away."

Annibel: "I'm very aware that it ain't gonna go away for years to come."

Smallcomb: "On the same hand, you know you're a like-able enough guy."

Annibel: "I wasn't looking for trouble or nothing. I just wanted to have a good time. Things just got out of hand. And she wanted money from me. My wife actually means more to me than anything."

Smallcomb: "I know that."

Annibel: "Even more than my kids, I love my wife."

Smallcomb: "I know there's some term . . . that you can kill for your wife. You hit the nail on the head."

Annibel: "Yeah, I did. And I'm sorry, too. I mean I tried to stop before I did that. Like I said, when I let go of her, she was making clucking sounds and she just . . . she wasn't coming back. I don't know. At the time, I don't know if I wanted to kill her or I just wanted to scare her. But I think maybe I just wanted her not to threaten me. You know what I mean?"

Smallcomb: "Well, she's coming at you. She's saying she's

gonna ruin your life. With a gal you've been with for eighteen years [*sic*]. So yeah, you overreacted. Way overreacted. But on the same hand, I can feel for that a little bit. Does that make sense to you?"

Annibel: "Yeah."

Smallcomb: "It's like I told you. I've been married for eighteen years myself."

Annibel: "Well, I'm really sorry I wasn't up front with you the first time we talked. I just didn't really know how to . . . it's not something you want to talk about."

Smallcomb: "I understand that. That's why we give you the benefit of the doubt to talk to us again. 'Cause I know . . . you need to take a leak or anything?"

Annibel: "I'm all right."

Rakes: "You guys have been married for seventeen years?"

Annibel: "We lived together seventeen. I got her pregnant when she was fifteen. And her parents lived out of state. Her mom was just moving. So she said [to Beth] you can move in with us. Or you can move in with him. And she moved in with me."

Rakes: "Did it work out?"

Annibel: "We've been together for seventeen years."

Rakes: "You have a seventeen year old together?"

Annibel: "We've been together seventeen years. Our son died."

Rakes: "Oh, I'm sorry about that. So when was she pregnant the first time?"

Annibel: "Yeah, he died at birth. Two years . . . three years later, we had a daughter. She's almost fourteen."

Rakes: "How long have you lived in Fort Bragg?"

Annibel: "Fourteen years."

Rakes: "Fourteen years . . . you were raised in Humboldt?"

Annibel: "Yes."

Smallcomb: "And she [Beth] lived in Grass Valley when you met her?"

Annibel: "No, she lived in Garberville. Her mom had just separated from her dad. She grew up in Grass Valley and her mom and her husband . . . the drunk, they divorced, and he moved to Florida. He hadn't worked in years. He used to be a police sergeant in Grass Valley."

Rakes: "Thirty years ago?"

Annibel: "Yeah."

Rakes: "Boy."

Annibel: "Well, anyway, her mom worked for a long time, and he just didn't work, and she finally left him, 'cause he was just a drunk. All he does is drink. In fact, he drinks probably half a gallon of vodka a day. He's been in the hospital several times. He's just eating up the money he got from his mom when she died. I feel sorry for my wife. She's had a rough life, and now this."

Rakes: "She loves her job though, huh?"

Annibel: "Yeah."

Rakes: "I'm sure she has friends there."

Annibel: "Oh yeah, she has lots of friends. My wife is a real likeable person. She's a real nice girl. She smokes pot, but she never drinks and is pretty good with old people. She likes working with them. Plus she's real good at her job. She does in-home services, too, for a couple, and that's why it sucks about the car. She can't do that now."

Smallcomb: "Yeah, we'll get the car back to her as soon as we can."

Annibel: "She can't afford not to have it."

Smallcomb: "We still have to do some testing on it and stuff."

Annibel: "Yeah."

Smallcomb: "In the meantime, when you were choking her, were you on the ground at all, John?"

Annibel: "We might have rolled off the bed."

Smallcomb: "Is it possible that she could have hit her head, or hit the side of her head on the floor, or the bedpost?"

Annibel: "It's possible. Like I said, I had just woken up out of a stupor when she came back in. And I was still kind of groggy. She pissed me off. Then she just dropped right away about the money."

Smallcomb: "She started hitting you up on the money. What was going through your mind at that time?"

The detectives were getting into very important ground. John had already confessed to killing Deborah Sloan. That was at least second-degree murder, but intent of what was going through his mind, that could make it first-degree murder.

Annibel: "Well, I'd have given her the money, except that I didn't trust her."

Smallcomb: "But she already said . . ."

Annibel: "That she was gonna call my wife and she had my phone number. She quoted my phone number to me. So some time in the past, when she left and came back, she somehow got my phone number. I never gave it to her. I don't have it in my wallet. It's not listed."

Smallcomb: "So what's going through your mind at that time when you're sitting there and she has your phone number, John?"

Annibel: "Blackmail. What's really going through my mind is losing my wife. That's what I was thinking. My wife means more to me than anything in the world."

Smallcomb: "And you're looking for options. And there's not a lot of options."

Annibel: "No, she was pretty insistent on the money."

Smallcomb: "Is that when you grabbed her?"

Annibel: "Yeah."

Smallcomb: "You're on the bed, and you could have fallen to the ground?"

Annibel: "We were on the bed when I grabbed her. As a matter of fact, I think we did topple off the bed onto the floor."

Smallcomb: "And when she fell on the ground, did you fall on top of her?"

Annibel: "Uh-huh."

Smallcomb: "You had some abrasions on your knees."

Annibel: "Uh-huh."

Smallcomb: "It looked like rug burns."

Annibel: "No, I believe that was from chasing my daughter's rat. My daughter's got three white rats, and one of them got loose. And I tried to catch it. It dove down, and I dove down after it. I couldn't catch it, and we got new carpet. And I went and bought one of those rattraps. One of those big ones. It didn't kill the rat."

Smallcomb: "Did you receive anything from the motel room?"

Annibel: "Any what?"

Smallcomb: "Injuries?"

Annibel: "No. Any scratches that I got or anything, they're all just in the line of my job. Like this right here is a rat bite. He bit the shit out of me. Matter of fact, he bit me right here on this finger. And this is a sliver. I believe it's just stuff from the mill. 'Cause I don't wear gloves on this hand. This is the one I hold my crayon in."

Smallcomb: "To grade lumber?"

Annibel: "Yeah."

Rakes: "How much of a struggle was there, John?"

Annibel: "Not very much. As a matter of fact, I tried to let go of her."

Rakes: "She didn't try to get away, though?"

Annibel: "I don't think so. I just grabbed her. And I squeezed real hard. I started choking her and realized this ain't right. And I let go. That's when it broke something. I think I killed her, but . . ."

Smallcomb: "Want to see if Tim is out there?"

Rakes: "Sure."

District Attorney Inspector Tim Kiely came in and took Frank Rakes's place.

Smallcomb: "Where'd you go to high school?"

Annibel: "South Fork."

Smallcomb: "How big was that?"

Annibel: "There was probably 350 people in the whole school when I graduated."

Smallcomb: "South Fork is in Fortuna?"

Annibel: "It's in Miranda. About twelve miles north of Garberville."

Kiely: "Anyway, I talked to these guys. I know what's going on today. There's something we didn't figure out. We talked to you on Friday and . . ."

Annibel: "Yeah, I wanted to tell you then."

Kiely: "I know you did. I know you did. You weren't ready. You probably thought about this all weekend. Try to make the thing right."

Annibel: "That's what I want to do."

Smallcomb: "Did you talk to me voluntarily this morning, John?"

Annibel: "Yes, I did."

Smallcomb: "Okay, have I threatened you or coerced you or anything? Made any promises to you?"

Annibel: "No, you haven't. You've been real nice."

Smallcomb: "And vice versa."

Kiely: "Let's cover this one more time, and then I'm gonna talk to you about something else. When you did this, the reason this happened was because . . . well, why you did do this, that's the bottom line."

Annibel: "She was gonna tell my wife."

Kiely: "She threatened to tell your wife unless you did what?"

Annibel: "Give her money. She had my phone number. I don't know how she got it."

Kiely: "Hmmm. Okay. What time of night did she tell you that?"

Annibel: "Around midnight."

Kiely: "Were you both on the bed?"

Annibel: "Yeah."

Kiely: "She was naked?"

Annibel: "Uh-huh. So was I."

Kiely: "So what was going through your mind at that point?"

Annibel: "Well, I love my wife."

Kiely: "Okay, I believe that."

Annibel: "I don't want to lose her."

Kiely: "Okay, so you're thinking about that. What else were you thinking about? Anything?"

Annibel: "No."

Kiely: "Okay, how long did you have to think about this before anything happened? I mean, did you give it a good long thought before you did this? I know you were scared about your wife. From the time she threatened you, which isn't a cool thing to do, I know that . . . from the time she threatened you until you put your hands on her neck, about how long was that?"

Annibel: "Couple of minutes, maybe."

Kiely: "Two or three minutes. That sound right?"

Annibel: "Yeah."

And there it was—John had just admitted he thought about killing her for two to three minutes before he started in on the act. It just didn't happen in a mindless rage. He took time to formulate a suitable plan. John had just moved himself from a second-degree murder charge to a first-degree murder charge. He might have thought he was clever, but he'd met his match in Detective Kurt Smallcomb and Investigator Tim Kiely.

CHAPTER 7

"I'm Gonna Be Blamed for Everybody that Got Strangled?"

With an admission that he had thought about what he was going to do for two or three minutes before strangling Debbie Sloan, John Annibel had placed himself in very hot water. The interview was far from over, however. Having elicited this much information from John, the detectives now wanted to see if they could get an admission to him murdering Sherry Lynn Smith, Andrea LaDeRoute, or Georgina Pacheco.

Even before this new line of questioning began, John gave the detectives a remarkable demonstration of just how he had killed Debbie Sloan.

Kiely: "So you got on top of her, is that right?"

Annibel: "Uh-huh."

Kiely: "Did you demonstrate to Kurt and the guys how you put your hands around her neck?"

Annibel: "No."

Smallcomb: "Show me how you did that."

Kiely: "Sometimes we want to make sure we get it just right."

Annibel: "I just grabbed her like this."

Kiely: "Okay, you lay her on her back. Is she under the covers or over the covers?"

Annibel: "Over the covers."

Kiely: "And you're naked and she's naked."

Annibel: "Yeah."

Kiely: "And where was your body in relationship to hers?"

Annibel: "This side."

Kiely: "Okay, beside her?"

Annibel: "Uh-huh."

Kiely: "Okay, to her left?"

Annibel: "Uh-huh."

Kiely: "So, you think you got on top of her, or just stayed to the side of her?"

Annibel: "I might have rolled over her."

Kiely: "Okay, if this is her neck . . . show me how you position your hands."

Annibel: "Like that."

Kiely: "And your two thumbs, are they in the middle section?"

Annibel: "Yes."

Kiely: "Where's your pressure being applied? To the middle of the neck?"

Annibel: "Uh-huh."

Kiely: "Okay, in fact . . . you can demonstrate on me, real quick. I don't want you to choke me, okay?"

Annibel: "I don't want to choke anybody."

Kiely: "I know that, but I want Kurt to be able to see. Let's scoot over here. I'm gonna be to your left."

Annibel: "Okay."

Kiely: "You stand over here. Show me the pressure."

Annibel: "Like that."

Kiely: "Right here on the windpipe?"

Annibel: "Yeah."

Kiely: "Okay, one more time."

Annibel: "Like that."

Kiely: "Okay, Kurt. Got it down?"

Smallcomb: "Yeah."

Kiely: "How long did you have your hands on her neck until something happened?"

Annibel: "I only had it on there a minute, and then . . . I didn't want to kill her. I let go. She just started making clucking noises. Kind of like, *cluck, gasp*."

Kiely: "Were her eyes open or closed when she was making this clucking noise?"

Annibel: "Open, I think."

Kiely: "Did you notice a change in her after this clucking noise?"

Annibel: "Yes."

Kiely: "What happened?"

Annibel: "She died."

During the interview and demonstration of choking Debbie Sloan to death, John had been very animated. All of that changed as soon as the detectives started asking him about the other cases. John's demeanor became very cautious and guarded.

Kiely: "No other cases in Fort Bragg you're responsible for?"

Annibel: "No, sir."

Kiely: "Humboldt County cases?"

Annibel: "Nope."

Kiely: "I'm just giving you the opportunity right now.
Soul-searching kind of thing for you. If you want to get
something off your chest."

Annibel: "No."

Kiely: "Anything else at all?"

Annibel: "Nope.

Smallcomb: "Andrea [LaDeRoute]. What's that all about?"

Annibel: "A girl I used to live with there in Fortuna."

Smallcomb: "How long ago?"

Annibel: "Twenty years ago."

Kiely: "Is she dead?'

Annibel: "I don't know . . . missing."

Kiely: "They haven't found her yet?"

Annibel: "Well, nobody's ever told me. I don't know."

Kiely: "Okay, you were accused of something that day.
Or have they talked to you about it?"

Annibel: "They just talked to me about it. I don't know
anything about it."

Kiely: "Well, if you did this homicide—if you did this,
this is the opportunity to get if off your chest. Solve a case.
Help the family."

Annibel: "This is the only thing I've ever done [killing
Debbie Sloan]. I'm sorry about it."

Kiely: "Well, we'll hang to see how this plays out. We got
the whole truth out now?"

Annibel: "Yes."

Kiely: "Nothing we're missing?"

Annibel: "Not at all."

Kiely [To Smallcomb]: "Is there anything else you can think of?"

Smallcomb: "That Pacheco case is up on the file. If you want to look at the picture, maybe help us out. I do my homework. You lived in Fort Bragg for how long?"

Annibel: "Fourteen years."

Smallcomb: "Going back to 1988 . . . you were in Fort Bragg all those years?"

Annibel: "I lived in Fort Bragg since 1984."

Smallcomb: "You know a guy by the name of Wilson?"

Annibel: "My wife knew some Freys."

Smallcomb: "You know of any other guys from Fort Bragg? You never worked for GP [Georgia Pacific], did you?"

Annibel: "No, LP [Louisiana Pacific]." PL [Pacific Lumber] is in Scotia. It's in Humboldt. That's the largest redwood mill in the world. That's the one the environmentalists are really attacking about the Headwaters."

Smallcomb: "Pictures." [Apparently Detective Smallcomb showed John a photo of Georgina Pacheco.]

Annibel: "No, who is it?"

Smallcomb: "That's the girl we were asking about in Fort Bragg."

Annibel: "Hey, yeah, I remember a little bit about that."

Smallcomb: "It was in 1988."

Annibel: "I had nothing to do with that. I don't know her."

Smallcomb: "And Andrea, was a girlfriend of yours, correct? She's missing?"

Annibel: "I don't know if she still is. She's got a sister in Eureka."

Kiely: "Okay, well, there's one more case I want to talk to you about. I just have to sit down and throw things out."

Annibel: "Sure."

Kiely: "Sherry Smith. We've been asked to talk to you about Sherry Smith. See if we can clear it up, too."

Annibel: "Fine. I don't know what happened to her."

Kiely: "Okay, what was your relationship with Sherry Smith?"

Annibel: "She's my twin brother's, wife's sister. That must have been back in '75 or '76."

Kiely: "And were you questioned in that case, too?"

Annibel: "Yeah. So was everybody."

Kiely: "What happened to her. How did she die?"

Annibel: "She was strangled, I believe."

Kiely: "And you can see why we went to a connection here."

Annibel: "Yeah, but I had nothing to do with that."

Kiely: "Okay, this is totally up to you if you want to clear some cases."

Annibel: "I would, if I could. But I'm not gonna admit to something I didn't do."

Kiely: "We don't want you to. That would be a tragedy. That's the last thing I'd want. But here is a chance to get things off your chest, and get it over with. This is the opportunity to do it."

Annibel: "Well, I liked Sherry real well. I'd be more than happy to do that."

Kiely: "But you didn't kill her?"

Annibel: "No."

Kiely [Pointing at Georgina Pacheco's photo]: "Never seen her before?"

Annibel: "No."

Kiely: "Well, I'm not going to ask you about every case

across America. Women that have been strangled, that's somewhat connected to you."

Smallcomb: "Did you hear about that, ah, woman in Fort Bragg. A seventy-two-year old woman in Fort Bragg?"

Annibel: "No."

Smallcomb: "Three or four months ago."

Annibel: "I didn't know anything about it."

Smallcomb: "She was strangled. What do you think about that one?"

Annibel: "In all honesty, I go home every night. And up until a couple of weeks ago, my wife worked nights. So I had my daughters every night. And working, I'm gone from my house thirteen hours a day. My day's pretty well taken care of by the time I get home. And I'd help my youngest one with her schoolwork and cook dinner. Believe me, when I went over there to Boomer's was the first time I've been in a bar in a couple of years."

Kiely: "You didn't know this girl [Debbie] from anywhere, is that right? I mean, not a preset meeting or anything?"

Annibel: "No."

Kiely: "I'll tell you what. Think about it. Here's John who's all dressed up, right?"

Annibel: "Well, I'm not all dressed up. It was like I normally do on my day off."

Kiely: "Okay, wearing decent clothes. Goes to a bar. And boom, just like that he's lucky. Was there any preset meeting?"

Annibel: "No. I wish it had never happened. I wish I'd never left home. I usually don't. I'm usually at home. I'm sure my wife and my daughters will verify that. Will verify I was home every night. And have been through the years."

Kiely: "Kurt . . . anything else?"

Smallcomb: "Going back to that case up in Humboldt County. This Andrea, was she your girlfriend?"

Annibel: "Yes."

Smallcomb: "You guys have sexual intercourse?"

Annibel: "Oh, yeah."

Smallcomb: "What about Sherry Smith?"

Annibel: "Never. She was a little girl to me. I mean, we were all older than her. See I used to . . . well, her sister used to be my girlfriend. And then I broke up with her, and my twin brother had her move in with him. I had a pretty fortunate childhood. My parents bought a place out in the country. We each had our own cabin. When I was twelve, I had my own horse. Motorcycle. My own house. When I broke up with Pam, she immediately moved in with my twin brother."

Kiely: "You heard Andy, he's another detective that works here. He has a lot more information on this Humboldt County case. I wonder if I bring him in here if it's okay. I want to make sure all the questions get asked. So I want to bring him in. I'll be right back."

Smallcomb: "This gal in the old case. The whole [Georgina Pacheco] case."

Annibel: "I remember when it happened. I didn't know her. At that time I think I was working nights at LP. Like I said, I've always gone home every night after work. My wife will verify that. I've never gone out without my wife til this last weekend. I'm pretty much a home person."

Cash: "Well, that's what we're trying to do. Work this thing out. Let's talk about Sherry. And tell what you know about Sherry. They [Humboldt County] want to talk to you about it. And get it all taken care of."

Annibel: "If there's any way I can help. But I've already talked to them about that."

Cash: "You were with Sherry that night at the dance?"

Annibel: "I wasn't with her. I saw her at the dance."

Cash: "What kind of dance was it?"

Annibel: "It was just like a rock 'n' roll dance."

Cash: "Was it a school dance?"

Annibel: "No, at the community center in Garberville."

Cash: "And that was the last time you saw her?"

Annibel: "The last time I saw her was with some guy named Steve Hardy."

Cash: "Well, the reason they want to talk with you—I'm sure you're aware she was also strangled."

Annibel: "Yes."

Cash: "Any idea why they want to talk to you about her?"

Annibel: "No more than . . . I don't know why. I guess because I strangled somebody, so they just want to."

Cash: "See what you might know?"

Annibel: "Uh-huh. I wish I could help you there. I can't."

Cash: "And you say LaDeRoute—what was your relationship with her at the time?"

Annibel: "She lived with me."

Cash: "Were you boyfriend/girlfriend at all?"

Annibel: "Yeah."

Cash: "What were the circumstances of her disappearance?"

Annibel: "I don't really know. She got up one morning. She was going to college. The last time I saw her, she packed up some shit. I was gonna go by the storage unit she had in Eureka that was leaking. And she had a sheet and some garbage bags. And she was gonna go to school. That was the last time I saw her."

Cash: "They never did find her?"

Annibel: "I don't know. I moved to Denver for a year after that. And came back."

Cash: "The evidence that was left and the blood, the blood on the bed or . . . do you know if any blood was left in the room?"

Annibel: "I had no idea."

Cash: "While you were at the substation, I stayed at the house and talked to Beth to make sure the kids got off to school and everything. And try and make sure that we did it as low-key as possible."

Annibel: "And I appreciate that. My wife is a wonderful person."

Cash: "We tried to make it as low-key as possible, but I did talk to Beth about that prior case going on up in Humboldt County. She said that she was aware of it."

Annibel: "Yeah, I talked to my wife about it."

Cash: "And she said that the blood the police got . . . like I said, you probably know more about this case. The blood inside the bed was supposed to be her from her [Andrea's] period."

Annibel: "I don't know. I never did see any blood on the bed. The only person . . I bought the bed from a guy named Bruce Johnson. And he had knee surgery. And he told me that he bled on it. It was his bed. I never saw any blood. So I don't know. I have no idea."

Cash: "Any idea of her whereabouts now?"

Annibel: "No."

Cash: "Going back to Sherry, were you dating Sherry?"

Annibel: "At the time, Vicki Willis." [He may have been referring to a Vicki from his high-school days. It is unclear whether he gave a wrong last name by accident or on purpose.]

Cash: "Did you ever date Sherry's sister?"

Annibel: "Yeah, she used to be my girlfriend."

Cash: "What's her name?"

Annibel: "Pam. She's actually my twin brother's wife."

Cash: "Oh, yeah. I saw the pictures at your house. I thought, 'That guy looks familiar.' And Beth said you had a twin brother. How would you feel if Mike [Humboldt County Detective Mike Losey] wanted to discuss this alone with you a little bit more. Try and get some things cleared up. Because Mike's willing to come down here and talk to you."

Annibel: "Yeah, I'll talk to him. But I don't know how I can help him."

Cash: "Unless you'd rather talk to us about it. Because there's more to it than what's going on. I honestly think . . . well they went to Denver to get you."

Annibel: "Yeah. Although, they didn't have to do that. I would have come back."

Kiely: "Right."

Cash: "Well, they would have done like Kurt told you. We don't kick down doors. People screw up. People do things wrong in life."

Annibel: "I ain't got a problem in talking with him [Mike], but it just looks like I'm gonna be accused of every unsolved murder that's ever happened."

Cash: "No, that's not it at all."

Annibel: "But that's what it looks like."

Cash: "No one is accusing you. We're asking you about it."

Annibel: "I made a mistake the other night. I made a big mistake. I just fucked up mine and my wife's whole life and everything. And I'm very aware of that. But I'm not running around killing people every time I turn around."

Cash: "We don't think you're a serial killer. That's not what we think here. But we have some information about that

Fort Bragg girl . . . well, she died ten years ago. You guys are the same age. We figured, hey, you guys might have known . . ."

Annibel: "I never hung out though with anybody. My wife's all I ever needed. You know in all honesty, I don't go to bars or anything. My wife usually doesn't go to bars. If he wants to talk to me though, he can talk to me."

Cash: "You been working logs all your life?"

Annibel: "Yeah."

Cash: "They treat you pretty good out at Harwood?"

Annibel: "They don't pay you as much as LP, but they're a lot nicer."

Cash: "Where'd you go to school?"

Annibel: "South Fork in Miranda."

Cash: "Well, I'm not saying I'm the most perfect person in the world. But you know, you'd feel better about yourself getting this off your chest."

Annibel: "I knew you guys were coming to get me."

Cash [About Beth]: "I sat down and talked a lot to her. She's wondered, you know, how to explain it to your daughters. I think you're heading in the right direction."

Annibel: "I want to do the right thing."

Cash: "I know you do. Otherwise you wouldn't be here. It takes a lot of effort and arrest warrants; they just don't issue them for nothing. Fifteen years ago. [Actually it was eighteen years since Andrea.] You might want to talk to them again. But talking to us, you're doing pretty good on our case. That's why I asked the guys to get out. But Sherry . . ."

Annibel: "I'm well aware . . ."

Cash: "And I think you can get a lot of closure about what happened that night."

Annibel: "So I'm gonna be blamed for everybody that got strangled?"

Cash: "Absolutely not. Absolutely not. We're not saying you did it. But if there's somebody out there responsible for that. You did not know about [Georgina], but you lived in Fort Bragg fourteen years. Someone might have confided in you."

Annibel: "I remember reading about it in the paper, and that's the only thing I know about it."

Cash: "Okay. We're not blaming you for anybody else. Or Andrea. But Sherry, she's dead. I mean, sometimes as you say, shit happens."

Annibel: "Okay, the last time I saw Sherry, she was dancing with Steve Hardy."

Cash: "You didn't see her anytime after the dance?"

Annibel: "No, sir. I don't believe I did. Sherry, I mean, she was staying with her friend at Alderpoint. And there's a lot of rough people out there. I understand the Weather Service was out there at one time. [He probably meant the Weathermen, a supposedly well-armed left-wing group of radicals.] "They're hard-core. A lot of automatic gunfire. Last year I worked out at Alderpoint. They dug up seven bodies out on [inaudible] ranch."

Cash: "Whose ranch is that?"

Annibel: "I'm not sure. It was just lots of rumors. That's what I heard working the mill. They dug up seven bodies. People would suspect that they were there to steal pot. That was one reason I moved to Fort Bragg. I just kind of wanted to get away from it all. I knew that I was gonna start a family, and I didn't want them out in the boonies. I figured that's not a good place to raise a family anymore. One time I had a guy pull a shotgun on me. While I was riding my horse. And I'd been riding on the same trail all my life. I come around the corner on my horse, and a guy jumps out in the middle of the road and says, 'You're not going any farther!'"

Cash: "That'll scare the shit out of me."

Annibel: "It scared the shit out of me!"

Then John segued into an event that supposedly happened in Fort Bragg.

Annibel: "You know what really blows me away is something I [inaudible], and the police never did anything about it. You remember a guy [name deleted] who was set on fire by his wife in Fort Bragg?"

Cash: "Black guy?"

Annibel: "Yeah. His daughter was staying at my house that night. She [the wife] came up to my house about ten minutes before the alarm went off and said something terrible had happened. Well, she got her daughter, and I went back to bed. And about five minutes later, the fire alarm went off. And Beth and I went walking down pushing the stroller. Walking around and saw their house burnt down. We knew what had happened. She definitely set the house on fire. And they just let her go."

Perhaps John was hoping for the same leniency, by telling this story of trying to help the police.

Cash: "Well, it's not over. We know how you were a witness in that case. I have the Fort Bragg police report."

Annibel: "Yeah, it's just kind of odd she said there's been a horrible accident before the alarm even went off."

Cash: "Exactly."

Annibel: "He was disfigured pretty bad. His face, it was ninety-percent burnt. So he was in intensive care for a long time. My wife saw him on TV about a year later. Getting a Thanksgiving dinner from some charity thing."

Cash: "Well, we're on the phone right now with Mike, and see how soon he can get down here and talk to you. So here's the plan. Mike's on his way down. He'll be here in a couple of hours. You can go back and sit in jail, or you can hang tight here."

Annibel: "Actually . . . jail. I want to get my cigarettes."

There was a pause while cigarettes were procured and Andy Cash got John some more coffee. All of the detectives were sure that John was about to give up more information about the murders of Sherry Lynn Smith, the disappearance of Andrea LaDeRoute, and possibly about the murder of Georgina Pacheco.

Mike Losey came down from Humboldt County to talk to John about Andrea LaDeRoute, and Detective Juan Freeman came to talk to him about Sherry Lynn Smith. They asked him to give them more information about his connections to those two and if he had killed them. They tried reasoning with him, cajoling him; they asked him to search his conscience, brought up about the victims' families. Nothing worked. John remained steadfast that he had neither killed Andrea or Sherry. Of course, he had said the same thing about Debbie Sloan only hours before.

CHAPTER 8

The Ticking Clock

The original newspaper reports of the arrest of John Annibel for the murder of Deborah Sloan were fairly short. In the *Santa Rosa Press Democrat*, Police and Courts column, there was a small item: FORT BRAGG MAN ARRESTED IN DEATH. It said in part, "Mendocino County authorities on Friday arrested a forty-one-year-old Fort Bragg man in connection with the death of a Laytonville woman whose nude body was found earlier this week along Branscomb Road. Debra [*sic*] Sloan was strangled before her body was dumped about fifteen feet from the edge of the road, said Captain Broin of the Mendocino County Sheriff's Office."

The Fort Bragg newspaper had a similar small article. COAST MAN ARRESTED IN MURDER. It reported, "John Annibel and Sloan knew each other, but not for long, according to sheriff's spokesman Kevin Broin. 'It wasn't a stranger situation,' Broin said. He praised detectives and deputies working on the case for how quickly they were able to solve the homicide. 'I'm really proud of that crew. They worked late into the night to get that case solved.'"

The name John Annibel perked up interest in the Humboldt

County newspapers as well. The *Humboldt Beacon* out of Fortuna reported in a headline: ARRESTED MAN MIGHT BE LINKED TO TWO LOCAL DEATHS. It went on to say, "A man arrested on December 4 in Mendocino County on a murder charge may be tied to two open homicide cases in Humboldt County." The article spoke of John's reporting that his girlfriend was missing to Fortuna police in March 1980. It stated, "Annibel said he had last seen Andrea LaDeRoute about 6:45 AM, March 17 as she waited to catch a bus to her classes at College of the Redwoods." Of course this was John's story that he had been telling the detectives.

Sergeant Steve Rogers of the Fortuna Police Department, who was now the main detective on the LaDeRoute case, told reporters, "One circumstance that seemed suspicious at the time was although Annibel reported LaDeRoute's disappearance to the police, he never tried to contact her family. Her sister lived in Eureka and had seen LaDeRoute just the week before."

The article spoke of John suddenly leaving the area for Colorado without informing his employer, Pacific Lumber, or keeping the date he'd set to meet with detectives on March 31. The article also stated that John was never tried for lack of evidence in the 1980 disappearance of Andrea LaDeRoute. Now with a similar murder of Debbie Sloan in Mendocino County, Sergeant Rogers of the Fortuna Police Department said that they were taking a second look at the LaDeRoute case. And the Humboldt County Sheriff's Office said that it was looking once again into the 1976 murder of Sherry Lynn Smith.

The *Eureka Times-Standard* picked up this refrain. In an article titled: POLICE REOPEN MURDER CASE, it spoke of the cases concerning Sherry Lynn Smith and Andrea LaDeRoute and their similarities to the Sloan case. Humboldt County Sheriff's Chief Deputy Gary Philp said that John Annibel had always been a suspect in Smith's death. Sergeant Rogers told the reporter that blood collected from the cottage John and Andrea shared on Ninth Street in Fortuna was still in evidence.

The newspaper article also touched on the fact that back in 1976 there were rumors of a serial killer on the loose in Humboldt

County. The article stated, "At least four women, including Smith, had been found raped and strangled. The other victims included an nineteen-year-old Humboldt State University student [Janet Bowman], found dead near Blue Lake in October 1975. And a twenty-one-year-old Colorado State University student's [Karen Fisher] body was found in January 1976 near Trinidad Head." It also mentioned in passing the body of Vickie Schneider on Clam Beach near Samoa.

The focus on John Annibel kept widening in the area's newspapers. On December 12, the *Santa Rosa Press Democrat*, reported, "A Mendocino County mill worker suspected of strangling a Latytonville woman and then dumping her nude body alongside a road, might be linked to two Humboldt County killings dating back twenty-one years, authorities said on Friday."

Art Harwood, president and owner of the Harwood Lumber Mill, told reporters, "It's really bizarre. He's a good worker. None of us would have ever suspected he might be involved in something like this. We were happy to have him as an employee. The whole thing is baffling."

What was interesting in the *Santa Rosa Press Democrat* article was a statement that read, "It turns out Annibel was initially a suspect, although no charges were filed against him in two unsolved Humboldt County cases, according to authorities."

This was of course in direct contradiction to the facts. John Annibel had been charged in the disappearance of Andrea LaDeRoute in April 1980. The charge was homicide [187], and his bail had been set at $100,000.

Humboldt County Sheriff's Detective Juan Freeman did say that Sherry Lynn Smith's case had been reopened and John was once again considered the prime suspect.

The *Ukiah Daily Journal*'s headline for December 12, 1998, was COAST MAN SUSPECTED IN MULTIPLE MURDERS. It chronicled all the familiar details, but once again it reported something inconsistent with the facts. According to the *Ukiah Daily Journal* Fortuna Police Sergeant Steve Rogers said, "Police got an arrest warrant and brought him [John] back to Fortuna [in 1980], but charges were never filed primarily because the body of the victim has never been found." Of course charges were filed, but John was never brought to trial.

The Andrea LaDeRoute case was a Fortuna PD case. Why Sergeant Steve Rogers said that charges had never been filed against John Annibel was baffling. The reporters not knowing any differently, did not pursue the discrepancy.

The *Ukiah Daily Journal* December 13 headline was: MURDER INVESTIGATION WIDENS TO INCLUDE COAST. The article reported that Mendocino County Sheriff's spokesman Captain Broin said, "We are looking at particular similarities to cases where people have died of asphyxiation. All we're doing is covering our bases."

One of the bases they were covering was a new look at whether John Annibel had strangled Georgina Pacheco to death in September 1988. John had been a Fort Bragg resident for four years by that point, even though his name had not come up as a suspect at the time. Now Georgina's murder started looking awfully similar in certain aspects to the murders of Sherry Lynn Smith and Debbie Sloan.

Broin did add, "Pacheco originally was seen in the company of an unidentified man three days before her body was found. This would have put her and the unidentified man together on September 7—almost a week past the family's last contact with her on September 1. Maybe she had been hiding from them because she thought she was pregnant. Or there may have been other factors involved. Why Broin gave the story about the unidentified man such credence is unknown."

At John Annibel's arraignment for the murder of Debbie Sloan, he faced the following charges:

Count 1: "Said defendant, John Arthur Annibel, did on or about the twenty-ninth day of November 1998, commit the crime of murder, a felony violation of Section 187/189 of the California Penal Code, in that the said defendant did willfully, unlawfully with deliberation and premeditation, and with malice aforethought, murder Debra [*sic*] Sloan, a human being."

The charges were signed by District Attorney Elizabeth Norman for Deputy District Attorney Mark Kalina. Kalina had worked many years in the Mendocino County District Attorney's Office and had a good reputation. Kalina had received his education at the Golden Gate University School of Law in San Francisco, and at the University of California, Berkeley. He'd been a deputy public defender for a short time in Marin County, and then a public defender in Mendocino County from 1990 to 1995. In April 1997, he came over to the district attorney's office, where he became a deputy district attorney.

Mark Kalina knew his law and was a good choice to head up the prosecution against John Annibel. If things had tended to slide on the case against Annibel in Humboldt County in 1980, that was not going to be the same under Kalina's watch in Ukiah.

Kalina compiled a list of witnesses and law-enforcement officers to testify against John Annibel. On the witness list were detectives Andy Cash, Kurt Smallcomb, Christy Stefani, Frank Rakes, and Tim Kiely. Other officials were pathologist Jason Trent and Humboldt County Investigator Mike Losey. Civilian witnesses included Beth Annibel, Alan Sloan, Catherine Watts, Gordon Watts, Pauline Sanderson, Cindy Sanderson, and Lisa Lawler [Andrea LaDeRoute's sister. She had married a man named Sandy Lawler].

John Annibel's attorney was Public Defender Linda Thompson, and she immediately began working on the precept that John had not been given a Miranda warning when he spoke with detectives on December 4, 1998. She reiterated, "Defendant asserts that he was subjected to interrogation with the legal meaning of the term prior to being read the Miranda warnings. It is the defendant's contention that all of the statements elicited from him on the fourth were involuntary and taken in violation of Miranda."

John also contended that things he had said on December 7 in the second interview were also in violation of the Miranda warning. These contentions by John were noted in the *Ukiah Daily Journal*. A headline stated: ANNIBEL'S ATTORNEY RAISES MIRANDA CHALLENGE. It followed up with an article that stated in part, "On Friday, the second day of Annibel's preliminary hearing on murder charges in Mendocino County Superior Court, public defender Linda Thompson said most of the statements Annibel made to sheriff's detectives after his December fourth arrest were illegally made."

The issuance of Miranda warnings are now a part of the fabric of justice in the United States. No suspect may be arrested without the warnings being given by a law-enforcement officer. But just what occurred to Jose Miranda to make such warnings a part of the system? Linda Thompson included some of the original statements made by police and Jose Miranda.

Detective: "It's a bad thing that happened tonight, right?"

Miranda: "Yes, but I shouldn't like to continue talking about that."

Detective: "We pretty much know what happened. I need to fill in just a couple of areas. Did she attack you in anyway? Did she hurt you in any way?"

Miranda: "I don't remember. I should not like to talk about this."

Detective: "Okay. We found a knife in the bushes. There was blood on the knife. It was your knife. We will be able to tell whose blood it is. If it was yours from if you cut yourself, or if it was from somebody else. We know there's blood on your clothes. And we will know if that's from you or somebody else. We know there's blood on your shoes, and we will be able to tell if that blood is yours or from somebody else. There was blood in your pants pocket from when you put your hand in your pants. We will be able to tell if that blood was yours or somebody else's, because we took your blood sample. We'll be able to take trace evidence from your hands and match it to the other evidence."

Miranda: "No, I don't want to talk more about this. I feel badly. I should not talk more about anything."

One officer tried to make Miranda open up by citing their common beliefs in the Roman Catholic church.

Detective: "Now you have all the feelings of tonight here in your chest, okay? No one knows what you are thinking. You only know what you're feeling. We are also here to feel what you are feeling. Do you understand? You're a Catholic, no?"

Miranda: "Yes, I am Catholic."

Detective: "Okay, and have you done catechism through the classes?"

Miranda: "Uh-huh."

Detective: "What have they taught you in the classes?"

Miranda: "Well, the love of God. The respect of God. And the way we can live by Him. To respect Him, we follow what he says."

Detective: "Okay, I also love God. I know that one of the basic things of the church is repentance. Isn't that right?"

Miranda: "Yes."

Detective: "I also know that one of the basic steps of repentance is that we admit that we erred. We can't continue forward without saying that there was a problem. And now we are trying to help in this respect. Do you understand me?"

Miranda: "Yes."

Detective: "Okay, I know that it is important that you talk to us about this problem. Because if you don't talk to anyone, you are going to fall."

Miranda: "But it is . . . no, I shouldn't talk of that."

Detective: "Do you want to talk about this later?"

Miranda: "Perhaps."

Detective: "Well, when you say 'perhaps,' what does 'perhaps' mean?"

Miranda: "Later. Tomorrow."

Detective: "But you don't want to talk now. Why?"

Miranda: "I should like to relax. Think about the error I committed. More things."

Detective: "About?"

Miranda: "About my life. About what I am going to do. About what is going to happen to me. Right now, I don't have the slightest idea what is going to happen to me."

Detective: "Well, you're eighteen years old. You are still young, okay? You have never done anything bad in your life. The girl didn't do anything to you?"

Miranda: "I don't know. I don't remember."

Detective: "You remember, but you don't want to say now?"

Miranda: "Maybe that's it."

Jose Miranda on numerous occasions told the officers he didn't want to talk anymore. In years to come, his right to invoke silence would become the basis of a Miranda warning. In fact, many law-enforcement officers now carry the Miranda warning on a printed card. The warning states, "You have the right to remain silent. Anything you say can and will be used against you in a court of law. You have the right to an attorney. If you cannot afford an attorney, one will be appointed to represent you if you wish." This has been the law of the land since the landmark Supreme Court decision in 1966.

In the first round over the admissibility of his interview, John Annibel and his lawyer won. Judge Ron Brown decided that John had not been properly Mirandized, but he still left the issue up for further debate. At least for the time being, no mention of John confessing to the murder would be heard.

At the preliminary hearing on February 25, 1999, the *Ukiah Daily Journal* wrote: "Accused murderer John Annibel was depicted in court as a misogynist who was angry with his wife and wanted to get even with her on November twenty-eighth, the day he met up with Debra [*sic*] Sloan."

Detective Christy Stefani said on the stand that John frequently referred to women as whores. Catherine Watts said that John had come by her house and asked where he could find a woman and a motel where he could stay for a couple of nights since he had separated from his wife. Watts was fairly nervous and reluctant on the stand. She had been much more candid with Detective Stefani in December.

Watts did say that John was acting very strangely that day and threatened to kill her dog. Then Watts said, "When I gave him a dirty look, he told me, "I'll kill you too if you ever look at me like that again!""

Watts eventually admitted that she told John that he would most likely find a woman his age at the Crossroads Bar in Laytonville.

A cashier at the Red Fox Casino testified about seeing John and Debbie at the casino sometime around 7 PM. She said they were both gone when her shift was over at midnight.

The owner of the Cottage Motel said that when they cleaned the room in which John Annibel had stayed, they found feces on the bedspread. Fecal matter had also been found on the body of Debbie Sloan. It probably got there when she was being strangled to death.

Pathologist Dr. Jason Trent said that Sloan had suffered blunt-force trauma to the back of her head prior to be being strangled to death. And Beth Annibel, while on the stand, said that John had cleaned his car interior twice after returning home in November.

The defense seemed to have won a huge victory when John's contentions that his rights had been violated during the police interviews was upheld by the judge. But this was a temporary victory, and Judge Brown reviewed the evidence between February 1999 and June of that year. When he came back about the legality of the interviews, a great deal was at stake.

Mark Kalina was ready for the battle over admissibility of John's statements and his understanding of his rights about Miranda. Kalina put various detectives who had interviewed Annibel in the past on the stand. Two of these detectives were Leo Bessette and James Ivey, who had spoken with John about the murder of Sherry Lynn Smith in 1976.

Bessette was asked about the Miranda warnings he had given John in 1976 while being questioned about Sherry Lynn Smith.

Kalina: "Did you advise Mr. Annibel of his Miranda rights on May fourth of '76?"

Bessette: "Yes, I did."

Kalina: "Now do you know if you did that or Detective Ivey did that?"

Bessette: "I did that."

Kalina: "Do you know why you did that?"

Bessette: "Just a habit of mine, I guess."

Kalina: "When you're talking to what people?"

Bessette: "When I'm taking a statement from someone that I feel needs to be advised of rights, I advise them. I had a little card in my wallet and I read it off that."

Kalina: "Did he indicate to you on May the fourth of '76 that he knew about what his rights were?"

Bessette: "Yes, he did."

Kalina: "And did he waive his rights?"

Bessette: "Yes, he did."

Mark Kalina also had Investigator Mike Losey on the stand talk about Miranda warnings when John had been arrested in Denver in 1980.

Kalina: "And your recollection concerning any advisement of Miranda rights occurred at what time relative to his arrest?"

Losey: "Immediately following his arrest and transport to the Denver Police Department."

It is hard to know if John was being very clever with the officers in his interviews of December 4 and 7. Only he knows if he tried to lead them into a trap by answering questions before being Mirandized. Ultimately, however, he did not know the law as well as he thought. There are other cases in the law book that deal with admissability of evidence, and one of the laws in California is *People v. Silva*. The judge in John's case ruled that, "It becomes clear after reading the [Miranda] interrogation that the case at bar is totally different from the case cited by counsel. In the case at bar [John's case], the defendant freely discusses a variety of matters with the police. The times he is reluctant to speak are when the officers ask about the specific circumstances of the killing. This case is very similar to *People v. Silva*, wherein a murder suspect waived his rights and submitted to an interview. His answers became evasive every time a question focused on the murder. When the police officer persisted in asking about whether the suspect was driving at a crucial point in the chain of events, the suspect said, 'I don't know. I really don't want to talk about that.' The court held that in context the statement was not an invocation of the right to remain silent, but merely indicated unwillingness to discuss a certain subject, not a desire to terminate the interview."

So the judge in John Annibel's case allowed the admissions of guilt he had made during his interviews, especially the one on December 7. It was a huge ruling for the prosecution; otherwise, all the evidence of the interviews with Smallcomb and Kiely would have been thrown out, and the only evidence getting in would have been circumstantial.

If the defense lost a huge battle on the admissibility of John's statements at his police interviews, they gained an equally important one soon thereafter. Judge Brown ruled that none of the statements or suppositions about the Humboldt County homicides would be heard by jurors. That meant that any mention of the deaths of Sherry Lynn Smith, Andrea LaDeRoute and Georgina Pacheco in Mendocino County were off-limits to the prosecutor.

By the fall of 1999, there was a new lead prosecutor on the Annibel/Sloan case named Rick Martin. Martin had led an extremely colorful life in the judicial system. It had started out prosaically enough when he graduated from the San Fernando Valley College of Law. He then became a deputy district attorney for Lake County, California in 1982. Between 1985 and 1988 he had a private practice that specialized in civil litigation. Then he went back to the Lake County DA's office from 1988 until 1996.

It was in 1996 that his legal career took on a whole new and exotic twist. Martin became Attorney General for the Micronesian state of Kosrae in the Federated States of Micronesia. Kosrae is located in the South Pacific, north of New Guinea and south of Saipan. Fringed by a beautiful reef, it is a prime destination for scuba divers from around the world. The island is inhabited by Micronesians who sailed there in the immemorial past from other islands in the Pacific. The king and his royal court originally inhabited the citadel of Lehu, surrounded by walls of volcanic basalt.

In 1824 the first Europeans arrived, followed in 1852 by New England missionaries. The native people took to Christianity, and as the official website notes, "Now Kosrae is one of the most devout and conservative of Micronesian islands." What they mean by conservative is the people's use of the old ways. Many islanders still prepare food, build houses, farm, fish, and build tools, as their ancestors have done for hundreds of years.

Into this island paradise Richard Martin arrived in November 1996. He became responsible for providing legal advice and counsel to the governor and state agencies. He was the chief law-enforcement officer in Kosrae, responsible for prosecuting criminal and civil matters on behalf of the state, national, and international contracts. He also enforced and allocated revenues and managed operation of the island's police force.

It was a three year stint of tropical breezes and palm-fringed beaches. Even the main resort of Kosrae Village was a scene right out of the movie *South Pacific*, with its cottages made of local wood and thatched roofs of coconut-fiber bindings. Martin enjoyed the legal domain there until January 1999, when he returned to the mainland and became Chief Deputy District

Attorney of Mendocino County. He returned just in time for the murder case of Deborah Sloan to land on his desk.

The jury trial for the murder of Deborah Sloan got under-way on September 7, 1999 at 9:30 AM. As the minutes ticked away, key items and issues came into play in the courtroom. Public Defender Linda Thompson requested further jury instructions and was denied by Judge Ron Brown. Thompson then noted that the victim's mother and sister were in the gallery and she objected to their being there while she presented her opening arguments, since they would be called as prosecution witnesses later. This was also denied.

Juror number eight told the court that she'd heard something about the case, but that it would not affect her ability to be fair and impartial. Judge Brown said that he would question her at length during a recess.

DDA Richard Martin finally began his opening statements. He told the jurors, "John Annibel savagely strangled forty-two-year-old [Deborah] Sloan to death last November in a Laytonville motel, wrapped her body in a blanket, then threw it over a steep embankment on Branscomb Road." Later he added, "It takes six to eight minutes of solid hard strangling to kill someone. If you stop for any reason, you have to start all over again. So it could take longer."

Martin told the jurors it didn't take long for the investigators to link Sloan's body with John Annibel. Within a week he had been arrested for the murder. Martin said that during his first interview, John denied knowing Sloan. Later John changed his story and admitted that they had partied together and stayed in the same motel room on a Saturday night.

Martin stated that John invented a story that he had awakened to find Debbie Sloan dead in his bed. John said he thought she had died of a heart attack. He did admit to dumping her body down a ravine, and even showed the detectives the area on the Pacific Coast where he threw her clothes over a cliff.

It was during the second interview, Martin told the jurors, that John admitted to strangling Debbie Sloan to death. Martin said that John had even demonstrated on Tim Kiely how he had done it. Martin told the jurors that John then began to invent a story about Sloan trying to blackmail him for having sex. Martin declared that the crime was intentional, not spur of the moment, and should be considered first-degree murder.

Deputy Public Defender Linda Thompson began her opening remarks by saying that she didn't deny that John had killed Debbie Sloan, but that he had become overwhelmed by extreme emotion because Debbie had tried to extort $500 from him after having sex. Thompson portrayed John as a hard worker who loved his wife and children. She contended, it was Beth Annibel who had betrayed her husband's trust by cheating on him over the years. It was the discovery of his wife's latest infidelity, Thompson said, that pushed John over the edge. [This was in direct contrast to Pam Smith Annibel's contention that the argument on Thanksgiving had been over pies and not infidelity.]

Thompson told the jurors, "As his wife's transgressions multiplied, John became bitter, and the split had been preceded by a major fight." Looking for solace, she said, John had gone to Laytonville and met Debbie Sloan at the Crossroad's Bar. While at the Crossroads and Boomer's, several witnesses attested to the fact that Debbie was "in very good spirits."

Thompson contended that John passed out on the motel bed after having sex with Debbie. Thompson also said that John had consumed twenty alcoholic drinks that day. "He awoke suddenly just before 3 AM," Thompson said, "with Sloan beside him, demanding $500. If John didn't give her the money, Sloan threatened to tell Beth Annibel about her husband's infidelity. John became enraged by the threat, grabbed Sloan by the throat, and began choking her.

"He did choke her," Thompson declared. "He may, or may not, have slammed her head on the motel-room heater. When he did start to think, John's wife's face flashed before him, and he let her go. It was too late. Sloan was dead."

Thompson claimed that John wanted to tell the police, but he didn't know how to explain what had happened. Instead, he wrapped Sloan's body in a blanket and took it out to his car, placing it in the backseat. He drove onto Branscomb Road, reached a spot five miles east of Westport, and stopped. He dragged Sloan's body from the backseat by her feet and pushed the body over the embankment. The corpse slid fifteen to twenty feet down into the ravine, according to Thompson.

Thompson said that some of the statements John told the detectives during the second interview on December 7, 1998 were out of fear and frustration. One particular damaging statement she alluded to was, "Yeah, I wanted to kill her." Thompson said, "John admits to killing her, but he did not plan or premeditate the killing. Therefore, John Annibel isn't guilty of either first-degree or second-degree murder, but of manslaughter."

While the others jurors were on a break, juror number eight remained in the courtroom. She confided to Judge Brown that a coworker's sister may have been a victim. (It's not certain in documentation if she said "a victim" or "the victim"—meaning Debbie Sloan.) Judge Brown listened to what she had to say and denied the excusing of juror number eight.

When the trial resumed, road-worker Linda Mitchell was the witness, and a map of John's route from Laytonville to Branscomb Road and the body dump site was displayed. During the next half hour, there was a quick succession of witnesses— Gage Ferguson and Carl Mechling described the place where Debbie Sloan's body had been discovered.

Next in line was Debbie Sloan's mother, Pauline Sanderson. She spoke about Debbie in general and then specifically about a ring that was found that belonged to Debbie. A photograph of the decedent was admitted despite an objection from Thompson.

Cindy Lane, Debbie's sister, was questioned about Debbie's blue jeans, tennis shoes, and jacket, all found where John had discarded them. Then Catherine Watts told the jurors about John's comments before the events had occurred, and how he called women, especially his wife, "whores."

Detective Christy Stefani took the stand at 3:25 PM and discussed the investigation up to the time of John's arrest, and his first interview on December 4. She spoke of his hostility to her for bringing up domestic violence against Beth.

The trial resumed the next day with Alan Sloan, Debbie's

ex-husband, on the stand. He spoke of seeing Debbie and John on November 28, and had a video-rental receipt to prove he had been at the location in question.

The next batch of witnesses were from the Crossroads Bar, Boomer's, Red Fox Casino, and Cottage Motel. Rachel Korpa, who helped manage the motel, identified a motel receipt signed by John Annibel and described the interior of the room in which John had stayed.

In the afternoon, Dr. Jason Trent began a long discussion of Debbie Sloan's wounds and cause of death. He identified photos of Debbie's face and arms. Linda Thompson opposed the showing of the photos, but was overruled. Dr. Trent explained about the wounds on the victim's scalp and neck. He even drew a diagram of a hyoid bone within the neck, as well as pointing out photos of wounds to Debbie Sloan's hyoid bone and neck. There was a close-up photo of Debbie's left eyelid and other regions of her face as well.

MCSO Officer Darrell Forrester was asked about photos and evidence pertaining to Sloan's knees, hands, and pubic-hair brushings. The photo of the pubic hair was opposed by Linda Thompson, but she was denied. Detective Andy Cash was questioned about a vaginal swab taken from the victim, and Inspector Frank Rakes spoke about photos containing brown boots, two blankets, and the interior of John's room at the Cottage Motel.

Deputy David Edwards was shown a photo of a nylon sleeping bag, and identified it as one he had taken from the Annibels' storage locker in Fort Bragg.

The next day, Evidence Technician Debbie Foster described her work on the case, and Barbara Allard spoke of seeing a male putting a blanket into his trunk late at night at the Cottage Motel. She said whatever was inside seemed to be heavy.

California Department of Justice Senior Criminalist Kay Belschner discussed photos of the victim's pubic hair that had been analyzed. She also spoke of fibers from the blanket being found on Debbie Sloan's clothing.

Outside the presence of the jury, the videotape of John's December 7 confession was discussed. It was agreed by all parties that the tape would be played before the jury, but all references to any of the other crimes would be deleted. There would be no mention made of Sherry Lynn Smith, Andrea LaDeRoute, or Georgina Pacheco.

Detective Kurt Smallcomb, who was now a lieutenant with the MCSO, testified about the investigation on Branscomb Road, the discovery of Sloan's clothing near Westport and about John's interaction when the clothing was found. Then the edited version of the videotape was shown to the jury. After the videotape was shown, and a few more remarks, the prosecution rested. The headline for the *Ukiah Daily Journal* was: "ANNIBEL TRIAL ON FAST TRACK."

On September 13, 1999, Deputy Public Defender Linda Thompson, outside the presence of the jury, asked the judge for an acquittal of John Annibel based upon PC 1118.1. She was denied.

Linda Thompson's witness list was short, and so was the time they spent on the stand.

10:37 AM—Timothy Zaer, 10:55—MCSO County Public Defender Investigator Carl Bartlett, 11:01 AM—a recess. Gordon Watts took the stand at 1:30 PM, and the defense rested at 1:35 PM.

On September 14, it was time for the closing arguments in the John Annibel/Debbie Sloan murder case. Richard Martin's closing remarks were dramatic in the extreme. He told the jurors, "Annibel was eye-to-eye with Debbie Sloan, looking in her face as he strangled her. When you're that close, you know darn well you're killing someone. Annibel's eyes are the eyes of a killer, and that's what Debbie Sloan was looking into as she died. Forensic pathologist Dr. Jason Trent testified it took Sloan six to eight minutes to die. That is a very long period of time."

To demonstrate the point, Martin produced a clock and set it to ring at six minutes. The hands began ticking off the minutes and there was absolute silence in the courtroom. At two minutes, Martin said that Debbie Sloan's face turned red. At three minutes, he said her face turned blue. At around five-and-a-half minutes, Martin declared, "She is unconscious." When the clock rang at six minutes, it was a startling sound in the otherwise silent courtroom. Martin announced to the jurors, "She was dead."

Defense lawyer Thompson's closing argument was muted by comparison. She told the jurors that John Annibel's killing of Debbie Sloan was a crime of passion, and not premeditated murder. "He strangled Sloan acting under emotion, after she threatened to tell his wife they had sex unless he paid her $500. When he began to think about what he was doing, he stopped. But Sloan was dead.

"This is not a case of first-degree murder. This is not a case of second-degree murder. It's clearly a case of manslaughter."

In the end, the jury of five men and seven women deliberated for less than a day. When they came back to the courtroom, they found John Annibel guilty of first-degree murder. He now faced a prison sentence of twenty-five years to life.

As a footnote to the verdict, the *Santa Rosa Press Democrat* added, "Annibel remains the only suspect in two unsolved Humboldt County murders, according to authorities. In 1976, he is suspected of strangling Sherry Lynn Smith, whose body was found on property near where the Annibel family then lived. Humboldt authorities said Annibel had earlier argued with the victim. In 1980, Annibel was identified as a suspect in the death of his girlfriend, Andrea LaDeRoute, who disappeared from their Fortuna home and has not been seen since."

John may have been on his way to prison for one murder, but another case was about to come out of his past to haunt him.

CHAPTER 9

The Wilderness

For Lisa LaDeRoute Lawler, there was no closure as there had been in the Sloan case—hers was a hell of a different sort. There was no body to bury, no finality—her sister Andrea was just a missing person, vaporized, a ghost. Lisa was tormented by the fact that Andrea could still be alive, perhaps an amnesiac, but in her heart, Lisa knew that Andrea was dead, and she believed that John Annibel had killed her.

Lisa said later, "My goal became finding her remains, so that she could have a proper memorial service. In my spare time between my job and everyday life, I searched in the woods, on trails, along rivers and creeks, and under bridges. I searched every where for signs of her. I always came up empty, but I kept searching anyway. I knew she would have done the same for me."

In part, to give herself something to do, to keep herself from going insane, Lisa began to compile a portfolio on everything relating to Andrea, John Annibel, and other un-solved murders of young women in the area. She especially focused in on young women who had been strangled to death and their bodies left out in the woods or isolated areas. These crimes particularly concerned those of Sherry Lynn Smith, Karen Fisher, and Janet Bowman in Humboldt County.

Lisa would later gather Humboldt County crime statistical reports. One in particular was a compilation of crime statistics having to do with the years 1977, 1978, 1979, and 1980. Under the heading "Seven Major Offense Arrests, Adult," for homicide in Humboldt County the chart listed: 1977—2, 1978—3, 1979—1, 1980—0.

"Zero!" she said. "That didn't make any sense for 1980! These statistics were for arrests, not convictions. So what about John's arrest for murder in 1980? He was arrested on a 187 charge—murder. So why wasn't this listed? This was the chart that the DA's office turned in to the California Department of Justice."

Even more galling to her was a report called "Evidence Collection Report for 1980," and subtitled "Major Cases Worked by Evidence Technicians in 1980." It listed an "Armed Robbery and Assault case for 03/15/80—Fingerprint ID of suspects aided District Attorney in obtaining plea without jury trial. Three arrested and convicted." The next case listed was, "Armed Robbery and Shootout—05/06/80. Extensive crime-scene work and photos. Both suspects found guilty."

Lisa said, "There was nothing listed about all the tech work done on Andrea's case starting in late April and early May 1980. I was assured that hundreds of hours of tech work had been performed. So why wasn't that listed in the official report?"

In frustration about the lack of progress in Andrea's case, Lisa wrote Humboldt County DA Bernard DePaoli a formal letter on May 6, 1981. It read:

> Dear sir.
> I am inquiring about the LaDeRoute case that took place in March 1980, regarding a missing person and possible homicide. I would like to express my dissatisfaction with your department. Although I feel that I have been as cooperative as possible, I also feel that my rights, being the only supporting relative receiving

important information, have been neglected. I have been in a constant state of limbo regarding the case, if a case even exists.

I would appreciate any information concerning the case of my sister, in regards to why all charges have been dropped on Mr. Annibel. I also want to know what is being done, or what can be done. I will expect to hear from you within ten days.

Cordially yours,
Lisa LaDeRoute

On May 18, 1981, there was a reply to Lisa's letter from Assistant District Attorney Rick Moench. He wrote, "I'm sorry you feel dissatisfaction with the way the case has gone. I have seen you occasionally at the store or around town and wished you had spoken to me sooner about your concern." He went on to write that he wanted to stay in touch with her because relatives and friends of victims often provided new information about a case, especially rumors that they had heard. Moench said that Andrea's case was stalled for lack of new information. He also said that investigator Floyd Stokes would return certain items of Andrea's to her.

Eventually this did happen. Lisa received the following items that had been stored by Andrea in the Rainbow Mini Storage locker.

• One table model sewing machine, covered with a tapestry. (Her great grandmother had been a seamstress for forty years and the tapestry was of good quality.)
• Four plastic heavy-duty garbage bags, containing clothes.
• One wooden dresser, with four drawers containing sundry items and clothing.
• One cardboard box containing a Sunbeam hairdryer.
• One large stuffed bear.
• One plastic garment bag with photos.
• One radio.

• One small brown suitcase containing miscellaneous items.
• One bowling-ball bag with ball inside.
• One pair of boots, leather-type, knee-length.
• One brown leather purse.
• Books and record albums.
• Miscellaneous dishes.
• One antique phone.
• One blue canvas book bag.

That was it. That was the sum of items left to Lisa from her entire sister's life. A few items Lisa did not receive were two address books and a photo album. These were kept as evidence.

What really burned Lisa to no end was that many of these items were stored in the care of her aunt. One day Lisa discovered that her aunt was having a garage sale. When she hurried over there, many of Andrea's items had already been sold. Lisa was furious. "These items were not only the last physical items I had of Andrea; they might have been evidence as well. I thought my aunt's excuse for selling them was pretty lame. She said she thought they were things that would upset me, and it was best to sell them."

Almost a year later, the case was still going nowhere, and Lisa could see no indications that anyone in authority was doing anything about it. She hired a private investigator from the Redwood Investigative Services to check into what was being tried and what had been accomplished.

The private investigator on the two-year anniversary of Andrea's disappearance sent Lisa a letter about what he had discovered. He told her that he'd talked with DA Investigator Floyd Stokes and learned that approximately two thousand man-hours had been expended in investigating Andrea's disappearance and possible murder. He said an infrared search had been conducted in the Humboldt Bay area. Lisa wondered why, if two thousand man-hours had been conducted, it had not shown up on the 1980 DA's report to the state. "All that work and effort should have been recorded," she said later.

Repeated attempts by Lisa to look at evidence or files collected on Andrea's case were denied by the Fortuna Police Department and District Attorney's Office. In frustration, she turned to old newspaper articles on microfilm at the county library for anything that concerned Andrea, John Annibel, or cases of local young women who had been murdered in the last few years. She started with articles that dealt with Sherry Lynn Smith and John's possible involvement in her murder. Lisa also found articles about the strangulation of Janet Bowman in 1975, which included the report by the anonymous letter. She also found articles on Karen Fisher in 1976 and Vickie Schneider in 1976. These three cases had certain characteristics consistent with the murder of Sherry Lynn Smith. All of the women had been strangled and their bodies left in isolated areas. They all were either young women or girls. One of the articles even mentioned the other three murders along with Sherry Lynn Smith, suggesting they were connected.

Lisa said later, "After John's release the detectives instructed me to never find myself alone and to let someone know where I would be at all times. They said that John was a clinical psychopath and if I 'hung out to dry, I could get plugged.'

"A few years later, two friends who were at Andrea's apartment the night I confronted John were murdered. Terry McCloskey was missing for nearly two years before they located her skull with two bullet holes in it. She had been buried in a shallow grave.

"David Cross was stabbed to death while he was sleeping. Attached to the knife that they found in his chest was a twenty-dollar bill. No one was ever arrested for the murders of Terry McCloskey and David Cross.

"A few years later, Ethel Reed, the one who had yelled at John, 'We know you did it John! We know you killed her!'— she was killed in an automobile accident on the highway. She was thirty-one years old. Around this time someone tried running me off the road on Highway 101 between Eureka and

Fortuna. I believe they were trying to kill me. I didn't get a good look at them because they zoomed by too fast."

For years, Lisa kept searching for clues about Andrea, especially when the anniversary of her disappearance rolled around. Very few new clues filtered in, and the official investigation seemed completely stalled. By now, a different detective for the Fortuna PD was supposedly in charge of Andrea's case, but Lisa could find no forward movement in that regard.

Then in 1992, a very strange story surfaced via Andrea's old boyfriend Billy Ryan. Billy was supposedly the last one to have seen Andrea alive back in March 1980 when he spied her and John coming out of a tavern in Fortuna. (This story differed somewhat from another one where Billy would later claim to have actually been in the bar with Andrea and John.)

Lisa said, "Billy had a fifteen-year-old female cousin who said an acquaintance had recently confessed to her aunt about killing Andrea. Billy's family, however, did not go to the police with this information. The information was passed through three people before I got the news. When I heard the story I confronted the source and told them I was going to have to inform the police. I asked Billy's mom if she would talk to the police about what she'd heard. She agreed.

"According to Billy's cousin, when she finally got the confessor to explain himself, the confessor stated that he and another guy were making love to Andrea, and because she was so wasted and fighting back, they tried to rough her up. One guy began beating her until she was knocked out. They didn't realize they had killed her at first, but when they did, they tried to dispose of her body by removing all her clothes and cutting off all of her hair. This was to prepare her body for a wood chipper that they placed her in.

"The confessor said that the hardest part of all was when they let go of her feet when she was in the chipper. He also said that he couldn't get the bloodstains off his hands for over a week.

"Billy's cousin asked why he was confessing and the confessor said that he still loved Andrea. This cousin was too young to have known whatever happened to Billy's ex-girlfriend, so she asked her Aunt Jo if she ever knew anybody by the name of Andrea. Billy's mom told her yes. They didn't go forward from there, though, about telling the authorities, because they didn't want to get involved.

"At this point, because of the lack of cooperation throughout the years from authorities involved in my sister's case, I notified an officer that I had spoken to during the disappearance of Terry McCloskey, before she was found. He had been helpful. His name was Dave Douglas.

"I explained briefly the situation about my sister and the new information I had received. I told him I didn't know who to make my report to because none of the agencies involved could even locate my sister's file. Officer Dave Douglas told me situations like mine were not handled in his department [Eureka PD], but he would offer to find out who I should talk to and get back to me. Within a few minutes of my talking to him, he phoned me back with the number of the Fortuna Police chief.

"After Dave contacted the Fortuna Police chief and related my concerns to him, the chief agreed to contact me about my sister's case. He even said how strange it was to be hearing from me. That he had been having dinner with Detective Losey, who worked for a different agency. I think it was the sheriff's office, and the chief said that on the previous Sunday evening, over dinner, they had been reviewing Andrea's case file, and that was why no one in the office was able to locate her file. I thought this was a pretty strange coincidence, since no one had been looking at the file for quite a while.

"I told the chief that I needed to report new information from Billy Ryan's mom, but I asked if Mike Losey could be present to fill in the investigator who would be working on Andrea's case. The chief said he would contact Mike Losey and they would even meet me at my home if I was comfortable with that. I agreed.

"The chief gave me the name of an investigator, and I can't remember the spelling of his last name. It started with an 'M'. He would be taking my statement. The chief said he would have M call me and schedule a time for me to meet with him and Losey. When M called, he wanted to meet me at my workplace. This was not appropriate for me. Then he suggested I meet him at the station in Eureka. I asked if Mike Losey would be available. He said he hadn't been able to connect with Losey yet, but would let him know what time to meet us at the station.

"The appointment was scheduled around Mike Losey's shift as a deputy sheriff, so that he could be present to fill M in about the case history. Losey was going to be doing this on his own time because he said the case was always one that really bothered him, but when I got to the station, M informed me that he left a message for Losey when and where to meet, but Losey wouldn't be able to make it. It became clear to me that this was just one more instance of the same situation that had occurred so many times in the past with everyone else.

"At the Eureka Police station, M took my statement and then told me he had reviewed my sister's case, but after a few questions I was sure he hadn't reviewed very much. So I asked him about the original suspect, John Annibel's involvement. M told me that the former suspect's involvement was a long shot, and that he would try to set up a surveillance of the confessor who had talked to Billy Ryan's cousin.

"None of this made any sense to me. To say that all the prior evidence which led to the original suspect's arrest was a long shot, in my opinion clearly showed M's total lack of knowledge about this case. I tried to ignore my feelings and asked M about the blood that was found in the apartment that my sister had shared with John Annibel. M's lack of response to my question indicated to me he was unaware that blood had been found, and he wasn't even interested that blood had been found there."

Instead of zeroing in on a viable suspect, Andrea's case seemed to be slipping off into Neverland. This surreal set of circumstances became even more so for Lisa not long after her talk with M. She recalled later, "I had just arrived at my boyfriend's place when the phone rang. My boyfriend answered the phone and handed it to me. It sounded as if someone had their phone next to a television, but the movie kept changing voices in the middle of sentences, as if the voices had been spliced in to an audiotape. After nearly ten minutes I realized that all of the lines from the different characters were replaying the situations that had developed during my sister's entire initial investigation.

"These were situations that only someone intimately involved with the case would know. Things like the garbage bags that I spoke about during my hypnosis with the detectives present. The whole scenario of my sister's case was played back to me from a VCR with movies that had been spliced together. When the part came up about the garbage bags, the caller slammed the receiver down."

This wasn't the only odd occurrence that happened to Lisa around that time. She noted, "I came into contact with Billy Ryan once more. He was playing a bunch of mind games. It was a cat-and-mouse type of thing. He came by with some cotton gloves as [if] to prove he could be around me and not leave any fingerprints.

"I asked him how the police had originally located him to get his first statement about John and Andrea, and did he really see John and Andrea together coming out of a tavern on March 16, 1980. Billy ignored the first question and answered the second. He said that Andrea had been driving John's Camaro and she and John had been coming out of the Town Club.

"This alarmed me, because I had never known Andrea to drive John's car. I didn't even think she had a driver's permit, much less a driver's license. Billy's behavior became very erratic.

"Then Billy said, 'I want to show you some paperwork.' He went and got a paper from his car. It was a bill of sale for the car supposedly from M. Billy said that he'd gotten the car from M and that he did work for him.

"The next day, I spoke to M and discussed my concerns about Billy's behavior and his statements. I was told that Billy was a known "speeder" [meth user] and didn't make much sense a lot of the time. M denied that Billy had ever used his vehicle.

"Still, I felt threatened and I took my concerns to the Fortuna chief of police and explained the registration that Billy had showed me concerning the car he was driving. The registration showed that the car had previously been registered to M. The chief responded, 'That's bullshit!'

"He may have said it was bullshit, but the registration proved that it was true. So I asked the police chief how he knew that Billy was not involved in Andrea's disappearance. He answered that he didn't, and then added if Billy's behavior continued and I felt threatened, I should make a report to the sheriff's department.

"A week or so later, Billy kept driving by my place. I was by myself when he showed up in the middle of the night. He said he needed to use my phone. I asked him, 'What keeps bringing you around?'

"He wouldn't say.

"I was fishing for answers, so I said, 'Are you having dreams about Andrea? Are you here to protect me?'

"'No,' he responded. And then in a very strange voice he said, 'She knows I would never hurt you.'

"I was startled and said, 'No, you mean the person who did this would never hurt me, don't you?'

"He didn't say anything. He just stared at me.

"I freaked out and told my boyfriend, Sandy, to come over and get rid of him. Billy did leave my place, but we found out the next morning that he had slept all night in the yard. Billy started to come into my place, and Sandy said, 'Lisa, get out of the house!'

"I ran out, and Sandy told me later that he showed an antique black powder-type pistol to Billy, and told him, 'I thought I told you to leave her alone! I'm telling you now, don't ever come here again. Let me make it very clear for you.' And Sandy showed the pistol to Billy.

"Billy took off and never came back. He had really freaked me out. I wasn't sure if he wanted to kill me or not.

"A few weeks later my apartment was robbed of more than $1,000 and the black powder pistol. It felt like a warning to me, though I don't know if Billy did that or someone else. I had lost my keys around the time that Billy showed up. I was scared because I felt like Billy knew something about Anghs.

"Throughout the years, my family and I have persisted in trying to express our concerns to the Humboldt County District Attorney's office by phone, in person, and by certified mail, yet most of our calls and letters went unanswered.

"On February 8, 1995, I sent a certified letter to DA Terry Farmer with a return receipt that requested that my concerns be addressed or at least acknowledged. I never received a response from the DA's office except for the signature of the receipt. In fact, during Terry Farmer's long term of office, he never gave me the time of day.

"And although the former DA Bernard DePaoli in 1980 was quoted as saying charges would be refiled, but not immediately, no charges ever were refiled. Incidentally, Mr. DePaoli had been convicted of several crimes involving fraud and embezzlement after he was no longer the DA but a practicing lawyer in Humboldt County."

Lisa had seen just a few short items in the local newspaper about former DA Bernard DePaoli who was now a practicing attorney in Eureka. The items were very small and wedged into the "Area and State News" column. One of the articles from March 26, 1989 stated, "DePaoli is accused of bribing Alan Dale Bradley, a convicted felon who was subpoenaed to testify in the murder-for-hire trial of Philip Kellotat. DePaoli is Kellotat's attorney."

The article went on to say that DePaoli was suspected of being the middleman in a bribe to make Bradley change his testimony against Kellotat. The trial was taking place in Shasta County.

There was another small article buried in the newspaper on October 29, 1989, and a third on July 22, 1990, once again in the middle of the paper. The news eventually faded away and Lisa never knew what happened to DePaoli.

She said later, "This story should have been front-page news. DePaoli was the district attorney of Humboldt County from 1978 to 1982. He still lived in the county and practiced there as a defense attorney. These were serious charges. So why were the articles so small and hidden in the middle of the paper, where it was easy to miss them? I didn't get it."

At least one good thing happened to Lisa in the early 1990s, and that was when she met Sandy Lawler. She recalled later, "We started dating in 1992 and one of the first things I found attractive about him were his beautiful blue eyes, his strong smile, and engulfing laugh. His laugh reminded me so much of Andrea, that I thought of her every time he laughed. When we first got together, I actually nicknamed him Sandy Claus, because he was so jolly. Besides, he has a cute little nose and round, full cheeks, just like the pictures of Santa Claus Andrea and I saw as kids.

"When I first saw Sandy, he was walking in the middle of the road with a little child on his shoulders and a girl with him. I didn't really have a feeling one way or another about him, but when I passed him, I remember looking back in the rearview mirror of my car at him.

"I was working two jobs at the time, six days a week. I had no idea until later, when his family told me, that Sandy would watch me drive past his window every day. Then one day I was mowing Max's lawn on a hot summer day, and I was wearing a new summer outfit, a kind of bathing suit, tank-top kind of thing. I saw this guy drive by on a motorcycle, and all of a sudden I heard a loud noise. I turned and looked and the guy was trying to pick the motorcycle off the ground. It was Sandy. I was afraid he might have really hurt himself, but I guess all he really hurt was his ego.

"Finally he asked me out on our first date by the opening line, "Aren't you my neighbor?" From that moment on my life had just begun.

"One evening we were going to a benefit dinner on a yacht that sailed out on Humboldt Bay. It was to raise money for a little girl who needed a liver transplant. Sandy and I had been talking about getting married, but nothing was definite. When we were getting on the boat, I told Sandy it would be neat someday to charter a boat and have the wedding ceremony on it. I asked Sandy to ask the captain how much it would cost and we could make reservations some time.

"Well, I was in for a big surprise. He got down on his knee

right then and there and proposed to me. He said, 'Do you want to get married?'

"I said, 'You mean here? Tonight?'

"He said yes.

"Well, in front of eighty strangers we had the most romantic wedding day I could have ever hoped for. There was a full bar on the boat and a great band, and they took one of the white linen tablecloths from a table, and used it as a wedding veil, since this was all so sudden. We even borrowed some rings and a garter belt. The captain married us. It was a beautiful wedding, and there just happened to be a couple of people we knew from high school. Other people took pictures of us and videotaped the whole wedding. They mailed us photos of the wedding later."

Sandy was good to Lisa. He became the rock in her life that had been sorely missed since Andrea disappeared. Together they searched trails, riverbanks, creek beds, and forested hills for any signs of where Andrea's remains might be. Despite searching everywhere in the region, Lisa and Sandy always came up empty.

Through 1996 and 1997, hope that the "disappearance" of her sister would ever be solved dwindled for Lisa. In her heart she knew that Andrea was dead, and she believed that John Annibel had murdered her. Whenever Lisa asked the Fortuna Police Department or Humboldt County District Attorney's Office where the case stood, she got the same refrain—there was no new information and nothing more was being done on the case.

Finally, in March 1998, Lisa spoke with Sergeant Steve Rogers, who now had Andrea's case. She related later, "He said he sent blood samples to a friend at the Redding, California DOJ lab in 1998. There was not very much blood to send, he said, and there had been no activity on Andrea's Social Security Number since 1980."

Lisa brought up a Humboldt County case involving the disappearance of seventeen-year-old Karen Mitchell at a mall in Eureka, and Sergeant Rogers agreed that there were some similarities. According to Lisa, Sergeant Rogers told her, "I'm looking at the case [Andrea's case] again. I wasn't allowed onto the property on Fruitland Ridge [the property where John Annibel's parents lived]." Other than that, he didn't go into detail about what else he had been doing.

Lisa wondered if Rogers was looking into the case, why he couldn't obtain a search warrant to look on the Annibel property.

Sergeant Rogers told Lisa that he had spoken with Rick Malcomb, the man who had gone with John to Colorado in March 1980. Then Rogers related that Rick Malcomb's brother, Randy, had been at the residence that John and Andrea shared. This had been when investigators arrived in April 1980. Lisa wondered why this fact had not been previously related to her.

Rogers related that he had sent fifty pages of documents related to the crime to the crime lab in Redding, and that the DOJ still had the original blood samples. Lisa told him she wanted to have her own blood compared to blood that had been found on the wall and bed in the place that John and Andrea had shared.

Sergeant Rogers spoke to Lisa about a crime tech named Joe Rynearson. Rogers said that back in 1980, Rynearson was just getting started in his field, and that he had processed the crime scene in Fortuna. Then Rogers said, "He [Rynearson] is interested in this case. He thinks it's interesting."

Lisa told Rogers, "If it was a crime of passion, it would be one thing. If there is a possibility the person had a previous involvement, and some kind of psychotic attachment to this type of behavior, then he will continue doing these kinds of crimes. If someone had done something before Andrea, this might not have happened. If this is true, we won't know until we pursue the evidence. How many more have happened since then?

"It's been nineteen years. It's not so much a matter of letting it die. It's more that somebody's got to stop it. If it really was her blood, and there must be other evidence to substantiate it—I mean, there is no body, so it needs other evidence to support it being a homicide, or it never would have been classified that way."

Rogers: "Well, that's one of the problems. There was insufficient evidence to prove there was a death."

Lisa: "Except for his previous involvement [in the Sherry Lynn Smith murder].

Rogers: "Yeah."

Lisa: "How many more have there been? I can't live with that. With the idea of the involvement of more. Every year I have a hard time with it. Every time I pick up the paper and see Karen Mitchell's face. I don't know if it is related. But how do you know if it's not?"

Rogers: "You don't. It's a mystery."

In frustration, Lisa phoned the DOJ lab in Redding to ask about Andrea's blood samples. The person she talked to said that if this was a homicide case, then the blood samples would have been returned to the originating agency, in this case, the Fortuna Police Department. The person did admit, however, that a small portion of blood samples would have been frozen and kept at the DOJ.

Lisa told the person, "At this point, it is critical to whether they will pursue the case or not. I don't know if he's mislead-ing me. If there's no way of pursuing the case, then he should say so."

Lisa related later, "This is the way the whole investigation has gone for the last nineteen years. And we're talking about a possible serial killer. They classified it as a homicide within a month of her disappearance, but they never found the body even though they found other information to classify it as a homicide. They found blood at the crime scene. They were able to determine it was her blood type. Blood samples were taken. If they don't pursue this, I think there will be other Sherry Smiths and other Karen Mitchells."

Then November 1998 arrived, and one small article in a newspaper changed everything. The article declared, "Coast man arrested in murder. Fort Bragg resident John Annibel, forty-one, was arrested Friday on suspicion of murdering

Deborah Sloan, forty-two, of Laytonville, and dumping her nude body off Branscomb Road."

Lisa said later, "It was like a rock fell on me. I knew that all my attempts to have the Humboldt County DA's office do something over the years had failed, and now another person was dead because of John. I felt just awful. It was like I'd been screaming and screaming and no one heard me. Like one of those awful dreams where you scream but make no sound. Now somebody else had to suffer because those who should have done something, did nothing."

Lisa searched for every news article she could find, not only in the Eureka newspaper, but other ones as well. One article in particular gave her new hope. The headline read: POLICE REOPEN MURDER CASE. It went on to say, "Annibel is being questioned about the 1976 rape and strangulation of South Fork High School student Sherry Lynn Smith and the 1980 disappearance of his live-in girlfriend, twenty-year-old Andrea LaDeRoute of Fortuna."

The article stated that Humboldt County Sheriff's Chief Deputy Gary Philp said that Annibel had always been a suspect in Smith's death. Sergeant Rogers of the Fortuna PD said that blood had been found in the apartment that Annibel and LaDeRoute shared, and that the blood was still in evidence. He stated that DNA testing, which was not available in 1980, was now being conducted.

Once again the notion that perhaps John Annibel had been a serial rapist/murderer back in the 1970s reared its head in the local newspapers. But Deputy Philip told a reporter that he doubted whether Sherry Lynn Smith was killed by the same person who had possibly murdered Julie Bowman and Vickie Schneider.

These stories of multiple murders would not die, however. The headline of the December 11, 1998 *Ukiah Daily Journal* was, "COAST MAN SUSPECTED OF MULTIPLE MURDERS." It went on to tell about Sherry Lynn Smith and Andrea LaDeRoute. Speaking of LaDeRoute, Sergeant Rogers told a reporter, "The evidence right now is being reexamined in the Department of

Justice crime lab. I don't know what's going to become of this, but I'm hopeful the case can be brought to a close."

Lisa LaDeRoute Lawler was even interviewed by the newspapers. In an article titled: WOMAN HAUNTED BY 1980 CASE for the *Eureka Times-Standard*, Lisa told the reporter that she was still haunted by the disappearance of her sister, Andrea. Lisa told of at least two occasions when John had abused Andrea. "I came home one night and she was standing at the top of the stairs completely naked and crying hysterically. She was crying that he'd tried to suffocate her."

Lisa also told the story of John attacking Andrea at the Annibel property on Fruitland Ridge, when he went berserk and claimed she had killed his cats. Lisa said that if John's father hadn't pulled John off of Andrea, he might have killed her then and there.

At least the trial and conviction of John Annibel for the murder of Deborah Sloan was of some comfort for Lisa, but it still did not bring Andrea back, or even indicate where her remains might be found. To Lisa, Andrea was just as lost as ever.

In October 1999, an article appeared in the *Eureka Times-Standard* entitled: "LONGTIME SUSPECT COULD BE CHARGED. " It stated, "Justice may have finally caught up with a former southern Humboldt County man suspected of two long-ago slayings, a sheriff's investigator said last week."

Juan Freeman told the reporter, "It's a tragic thing that sometimes the way these guys get caught is that they kill one person too many. Thank goodness Mr. Annibel got caught. I think he was a viable suspect in my case [the Sherry Lynn Smith case]."

Sergeant Rogers was also interviewed on the Andrea LaDeRoute case. He told the reporter it might be a couple of more months for DNA test results to be returned from the California DOJ lab. Then he added, "We haven't given up. We'll never give up."

A couple of months went by, and then a couple more. Months turned into years. There had been a flurry of activity once more, until it too died out. Lisa LaDeRoute Lawler realized that hope was once again fading away.

* * *

A very strange thing happened to Lisa Lawler at the very end of 2001. It had all the bizarre aspects of Billy Ryan's off-the-wall behavior of years before. Lisa and her husband, Sandy, managed some apartments in the area. One of the apartment complex's most unruly tenants was a man named Roger Hudnall. He became so belligerent, in fact, that Lisa had threatened to evict him. According to Lisa, Hudnall was stalking a female tenant in the complex.

In July 2001, Hudnall pretended to be an FBI agent and told Lisa he was working undercover. He phoned Lisa and told her that she would be arrested if she tried to evict him from the apartment complex. Instead, Hudnall was arrested for posing as an FBI agent and a restraining order was imposed to keep him away from Lisa and the apartment complex.

In retaliation, Hudnall sent a letter on November 24, 2001, to the FBI offices in San Francisco, that became marked "return to sender." The return address was that of Lisa Lawler. When Lisa opened the returned letter, a white powder spilled out into her hands. This was in the era of the anthrax scare right after 9/11 in which a few people died. Lisa phoned the Eureka Police Department, who got her in touch with local FBI agents. This was a terrorist threat.

According to an affidavit from the FBI, the letter, which had a return address to Lisa Lawler, stated, "I am sending you some anthrax in the mail. Like I have done before in D.C. and kill some postal workers. If you let me out I will leave the U.S. I will kill my night manager, Sue Lynn Johnson, and Mr. Hudnall. Planning to kill Mr. Bush on Dec. 7, 2001 in D.C."

On December 10, Eureka police met with Hudnall at his residence in Eureka. During the meeting, Hudnall confessed to sending the letter and its contents, saying, "I just wanted to scare the bitch! It's only talcum powder."

On December 14, FBI agents, U.S. Marshals, and officers of the Humboldt County Drug Task Force swept down on Hudnall and arrested him. He was held without bail and the charges included a maximum penalty of $250,000 and possible five years in prison for mailing a threatening communication, and $250,000 and possible three years in prison for impersonating a federal officer.

According to the *Eureka Times-Standard*, "A federal grand jury has issued an indictment against Roger Hudnall, the man accused of sending a letter to his former landlord in Eureka that contained threats and a suspicious white powder. Hudnall, forty-five, was arrested on December 14 at 7:20 AM by FBI agents, U.S. Marshals, and officers from Humboldt County Drug Task Force."

As time went on, Lisa wondered if Roger Hudnall was just a pawn to make her stop pushing for justice in her sister's case. She wondered if Hudnall, like Billy Ryan, had been used by someone with more intelligence and power to try and keep her quiet about her sister Andrea, and just let things stay as they were. For some reason John Annibel seemed to be off-limits in Humboldt County. Lisa said later, "I couldn't understand it. He wasn't some rich person's son. He was just a punk. Why did he keep getting a 'get-out-of-jail card' for free?"

Then in August 2002, a miracle happened. While reforesting trees up on Redwood House Road near Carlotta, where John Annibel had once worked and gone hunting with his dad, workers for the Pacific Lumber Company stumbled upon a human skull. It contained only a fragment of skull bone, but luckily that turned out to be an upper jaw with teeth. The teeth could be a valuable asset in identifying the skull.

As soon as a small article appeared in the newspaper, Lisa told her husband, "It's Andrea!" She had an overwhelming sensation that some of her sister's remains had been finally found. Lisa had ignored other discoveries of skeletal remains found in the forest over the years, but this time she was sure. The feeling was so strong it was nearly overpowering.

Lisa was right. On Friday, August 30, 2002, twenty-two years after Andrea LaDeRoute went missing, the *Times-Standard* declared: SKULL IDENTIFIED AS FORTUNA WOMAN MISSING SINCE 1980.

The article stated that the County Coroner's Office positively identified the skull as belonging to Andrea LaDeRoute. The article recapped the story of John Annibel and Andrea, and added one more thing at the bottom of the page—"More details are expected to be available after a press conference at the Fortuna Police Department today."

Lisa was shocked, when she read the article. Not one person in authority had told her that a press conference had been scheduled for that very day. If she had not read the morning's newspaper, she would never have known.

There was a press conference indeed. Sitting at a long table were Coroner Frank Jager, Fortuna Police Chief Kent Bradshaw, and Sergeant Steve Rogers. A room full of print reporters and television news reporters filled the room. Sergeant Rogers told them, "It's been a career goal of mine to see this case solved." Then he told about the 1980 arrest of John Annibel and the fact that he had been released for lack of Andrea's body.

Jager told reporters that materials other than the skull and jawbone were found, but he would not release details of what those were. He added that an expert forensic anthropologist from the San Francisco Bay area would be assisting him in further examinations.

Lisa, however, was not a part of the conference at all. She said later, "I couldn't understand why they didn't even tell me about it. I went and got there late with my husband and Aunt Carmen. When we walked in, it looked like Chief Bradshaw's face turned white. Like he didn't want us there at all. One of the reporters finally asked me about Andrea. His name was Dave Silverbrand. He was very concerned.

"So after the press conference was over, Silverbrand met me in the parking lot and asked if I would say anything. And I told him I wasn't supposed to talk to the press. And he said that wasn't the dictum he had received from the police. They had told him he could ask any questions he wanted of the victims' family members. I didn't know what to think. Why were there such mixed messages?

"So I did have a conference with Dave. And some things got on TV and for awhile there was some interest. But then Dave had a heart attack, and that was the end of that."

Once again, the flurry of activity faded off into almost

nothing. Then in May 2003, an article appeared in the *Eureka Times-Standard* stating: "SUSPECT NAMED IN 1980 HOMICIDE," with the follow up lead, "Live-in boyfriend named as alleged culprit in killing of Andrea LaDeRoute." The article stated that the Fortuna PD had named John Annibel as the suspect in the 1980 killing of Andrea LaDeRoute, and they filed a report with the Humboldt County District Attorney's Office regarding the homicide. The article said that advances in DNA testing linked blood found at the apartment that Annibel and LaDeRoute shared to Andrea.

One thing with the DA's office did concern Lisa that year of 2003—it was a surprise announcement by DA Paul Gallegos that he was picking Mendocino County white-collar-crime prosecutor Tim Stoen as his number-two man in the Humboldt County DA's office. Lisa knew that Stoen came with a lot of baggage, and she surmised that any progress on Andrea's case would have to go through him. She worried that everything might become bogged down on Andrea's case because of Tim Stoen's history.

During the 1970s, Tim Stoen had been chief counsel for Jim Jones and the People's Temple. In fact, Stoen had signed an affidavit at one point that would haunt him ever afterwards. It concerned the paternity of a son named John Victor Stoen, born to Grace Stoen, but just who the father was became a matter of contention later on. In the affidavit Tim Stoen wrote, "I, Timothy Oliver Stoen, hereby acknowledge that in April 1971, I entreated my beloved pastor, James W. Jones, to sire a child by my wife, Grace Lucy [Grech] Stoen, who had previously, at my insistence, reluctantly but graciously consented thereto."

His letter went on to say that John Victor Stoen was born on January 25, 1972, and that he felt honored to raise the child. He hoped the child would grow up to be a devoted Christian like his natural father, Jim Jones.

"I declare under penalty of perjury that the forgoing is true and correct."

Years later, after having a falling out with Jim Jones, Tim Stoen would claim that he had been coerced into signing the affidavit—that in fact he was the natural father of John Victor Stoen. By this time, however, John and over 900 other people were living in Jonestown, Guyana, and Tim Stoen was not welcome there.

By 1978, Jim Jones's world had become a mix of megalomania and paranoia, fueled by the abuse of prescription drugs. A small notation was written in the U.S. State Department Embassy log book in Georgetown, Guyana in October 1978—"Mr. Tim Stoen informs the department that in view of the failure of the judicial process in Guyana, he is prepared to retrieve his son by force if necessary."

Around the same time a small article appeared in the *Ukiah Daily Journal* under the headline: "TROUBLE BREWING IN GUYANA." The article stated, "One father has even threatened to hire mercenaries to raid Jonestown and liberate his son by force. Trouble that could lead to an international incident may lie ahead."

It led to more than just an international incident. There is good reason to believe that Tim Stoen's threat to take his son back by force, and California Congressman Leo Ryan's visit to check upon the conditions at Jonestown and take out people who wanted to leave, pushed Jim Jones over the edge.

On November 18, 1978, as Congressman Ryan and fifteen Jonestown defectors and their family members were ready to board a plane at Port Kaituma, Guyana, a flatbed truck with nine armed gunmen raced onto the airstrip with pistols, rifles, and shotguns. Ryan and several others were gunned down in cold blood, while others fled into the jungle. One gunman finished off Congressman Ryan with a shotgun blast to the head.

At the same time in Jonestown, Jim Jones exorted all his followers to commit suicide by drinking cyanide-laced Kool-Aid out of large vats. Those who were reluctant to do so were forced by armed guards to drink the deadly mixture. Amidst cries and wailing, Jones gave a rambling speech. In part he told his flock, "Lay down your life with dignity. Don't lay down with tears and agony. Be kind to the children and be kind to seniors, and take the potion, and step over quietly. This world is not your home." When it was over, 913 lives had been snuffed out, including that of John Victor Stoen.

New Humboldt County Assistant District Attorney Tim Stoen might have lived down this episode in his life, and proceeded quietly about his work in the county, but it was not to be. Both he and Paul Gallegos brought a lawsuit against the Pacific Lumber Company for violating several logging standards and codes. A political firestorm ensued and Lisa Lawler became caught up right in its vortex.

Opponents of Tim Stoen, and his boss Paul Gallegos, initiated a recall election in the latter part of 2003. The PALCO suit was the underlying theme, but the news in the forefront was that Paul Gallegos, and by extension Tim Stoen, were soft on crime. One of the most flagrant instances as far as Gallegos's opponents were concerned was the Pedro Martinez-Hernandez case. Thirty-nine-year-old Martinez-Hernandez, according to police reports, had sexually abused an underage girl more than 2,500 times over the years. Instead of bringing forth multiple counts against Martinez-Hernandez, the DA's office only brought forth one count. Hernandez was eventually convicted and sentenced to sixteen years in prison.

Many people in the county were outraged. HCSO Deputy Sheriff Troy Gurney, under the banner of "Safety Yes! Recall Gallegos" told a reporter, "There's no excuse for Gallegos allowing a predator to plead to one count."

The recall campaign got nasty. Someone broke into Pacific Lumber offices and stole some information. Someone also broke into Paul Gallegos's home and turned the heat up to an intense degree. A former prosecutor at the Humboldt County DA's office, Gloria Albin Sheets, said that Gallegos's campaign manager was illegally leaking inside information to the press. She also said that Gallegos and his supporters were using the Pacific Lumber suit to mask a "lack of concern about crime and incompetence."

And on top of everything else, opponents of Gallegos were bringing up Tim Stoen's past. Many of the details of Jim Jones and Guyana once again made their way into the newspapers.

Lisa Lawler probably would have never become involved

if not for a group of surviving family members of victims holding a press conference at an anti-Gallegos rally. They spoke about their loved ones who had been murdered, and how they thought Gallegos wasn't tough enough on criminals.

To counter this, Lisa, with her friend Marie at her side, held a news conference of her own. She spoke to the *Eureka Reporter* and stated, "The purpose of this press conference is to express our opinion that Paul Gallegos is not being soft on crime. During Terry Farmer's time as DA I had trouble getting in touch with people at the district attorney's office. Despite calls and certified letters, he never contacted me. No response, not a phone call, nothing.

"After Andrea's remains were found, I contacted Paul [Gallegos] and I and other family members met with him. This is open communication. I don't know Paul. I have no feeling about him one way or the other except that he has been open with me. If it were your sister or your loved one, you would want Paul."

Lisa had indeed experienced more positive contact with the DA's office and Paul Gallegos than under the former DA Terry Farmer thus far. All of that changed, as far as Lisa was concerned, after Paul Gallegos won the recall election. She said later, "I felt betrayed and exploited. All the contacts with Paul and his office suddenly stopped. He and others wouldn't return phone calls or letters. I felt like a door had been slammed in my face. Everything I had endured with DePaoli and Farmer was happening once again. It was like a nightmare."

CHAPTER 10

Investigator Harris

Initially the investigator didn't want this case. The brief description he'd read on the matter made it seem hopeless. Whatever link there was between the young woman named Sherry Lynn Smith who was murdered in 1976, and the other young woman named Andrea who disappeared in 1980, seemed tenuous at best. He'd seen his share of cold cases that seemed so promising in the beginning wander off into oblivion, every lead reaching a dead end. Even though he was an investigator by what he did, he was not affiliated with any government agency. His was more the private kind of investigation, and he'd seen plenty in his time. Some of it he didn't particulary want to remember. This whole thing on Sherry and Andrea seemed like a lost cause.

But then the investigator had always been intrigued by seemingly lost causes. He'd taken on the pseudonym of Harris only half-jokingly, in honor of his hero of lost causes, Shorty Harris of Death Valley fame. Shorty was a prospector who had lived in the late-nineteenth and early-twentieth centuries. Shorty had wandered the Death Valley region for decades, missing one gold or silver strike after another. In the words of one writer, "He chased the moon, and the moon was gold." Shorty was indeed a rainbow chaser whose domain was a vast and lonely landscape.

Shorty may have been a rainbow chaser, but he had one great quality—persistence. He spent twenty-five years in his quest for El Dorado, and then one day in the summer of 1904, Shorty and his partner, Ed Cross, stumbled upon a low ridge of promising-looking rock on the eastern side of Death Valley. What they discovered was the fabulously rich Bullfrog Lode, so named because the first piece of gold-bearing rock was about the size of a bullfrog and had a green tinge to it. In the next few years, Shorty, the perennial loser, would also discover the rich lode at Skidoo on the western side of Death Valley, and even have a town named after him, Harrisburg. Twenty-five years of wandering in the wilderness had finally paid off. Shorty always had trouble hanging on to his fortunes, but it didn't seem to matter to him. For Shorty, the journey, not the destination, was the important thing. If he found gold at the end of the rainbow, all the better. If not, he had blue skies above and more freedom than any man could ever want.

Harris the investigator admired Shorty's tenacity—his willingness to keep on in what seemed a hopeless search. Harris admitted that the self-styled sobriquet suited him well for the Sherry Smith/Andrea LaDeRoute cases. These were cases that had gone nowhere for years, circling around and around, only to come out where they had begun.

What turned Harris from a skeptic, and lukewarm follower of the case, to a more interested party, was a short article in a redwood county newspaper with a headline of LOST WOMAN FOUND. The article was only two paragraphs in length, but it would change Harris's life in very profound ways. In part the article stated, "The skull was positively identified as LaDeRoute on Thursday. Technical advances allowed the department to reexamine blood found in LaDeRoute and Annibel's apartment which turned out to be LaDeRoute's."

The article went on to say that Coroner Frank Jager confirmed that other evidence besides Andrea's skull and jawbone had been found at the scene, though he was not specific. He told reporters, "There were other items found that will help us in our investigation. Jager also said that an expert forensic anthropologist from San Francisco was going to be brought in on the case.

After reading the article, Harris was sure that Andrea LaDeRoute's case would now be solved by the Humboldt County authorities, and he would be a mere observer of the whole situation from afar. He knew that back in the summer of 1980 District Attorney Bernard DePaoli had told reporters that charges against John Annibel for the homicide of Andrea LaDeRoute would be refiled as soon as her remains were found. On top of the newly discovered remains, Harris knew that the county authorities retained other evidence, such as blood from the bedding and walls of the cabin that John and Andrea had shared, and some other evidence that had not been mentioned in the newspapers. Harris had his sources and they seemed to be reliable. Harris now considered it only a matter of time before the case moved forward to trial. The 1998 murder of Debbie Sloan would be the template for the LaDeRoute murder case, and might even lead back to the Sherry Lynn Smith case as well.

Harris waited patiently enough—he was deep into another case in a different California county during 2002 and 2003. He waited and waited, but nothing happened. What was wrong with the DA's office up there, he wondered. Why wouldn't they act? There seemed to be enough evidence. It was really not his business, but the inconclusiveness of it irked him. What about the victim's family? He'd heard that Andrea had a sister named Lisa. What did she think about all of this? And what about Andrea, herself? Didn't she deserve justice?

Harris had some time off in September 2003, so he took a trip north on Highway 101 to do a little more research on the Andrea LaDeRoute and Sherry Lynn Smith cases. It was just to be a scouting mission, nothing more. He had a lot of reservations about doing it, however, and part of the reason was the redwood region itself. He and his family had a past there, and not all of it was good.

Harris admitted that the Redwood Empire was beautiful;

ethereal and photogenic. It was also redolent of personal failure. He had moved there at one point for its very beauty and serenity. He had bought a house surrounded by towering redwoods, where gray squirrels leapt among the branches above his patio. Lush ferns and other plants surrounded the house, and the deck looked out over a beautiful landscape. But the dream had all come crashing down. He chalked it up to *cherchez la femme*, the wrong woman at the wrong time, the wrong place, and to self-admitted flaws in his own character.

The redwoods had even an ever deeper history than that for Harris. His father had returned from World War II to carve a small redwood-lumber company out of the forest where he could raise a family. The property his dad owned seemed like paradise—a land of tall redwood trees, small gurgling brooks, and fern-enshrouded nooks. The property included hundreds of acres that spanned steep, wooded ridges and narrow, shadowed ravines, teeming with wildlife and vegetation. From the highest hill on the property, you could get a glimpse of the Pacific Ocean to the west, just a thin strip of blue like the blue of a jay's wing. To a young boy it was a magical kingdom.

But Harris's dad couldn't compete with the big lumber companies and he was working himself to death with his small crew of lumbermen and limited transportation capabilities. In grudging defeat, the Old Man had given up the property and the life he loved, to take on a more stable job in the San Francisco Bay Area. It was a job he hated, but stuck out for almost forty years. There was that streak of tenacity once again showing itself in the family. Harris and his dad would go back to the redwood region once in a while, just to look, but neither one of them ever wanted to live there again.

Harris wondered if his own experience in the redwoods had made him a desert lover. Like Shorty Harris, the investigator Harris found Death Valley intoxicating. It's vast and lonely reaches, its barren mountains and deep canyons. It was a place where you could see for a hundred miles, and things couldn't creep up on you there the way they could in the redwoods.

He agreed with a passage from the novel he'd read called *On Spider Creek* by Robert Roper, which captured the mystery and fantasy and heart of darkness of the redwood region—a region that could spawn tales of Bigfoot and other mythical creatures. One old timer in *On Spider Creek* told of creatures that infested the dark woods to such a degree that they seemed to be lurking behind every tree—"coyotes, grizzlies, black bears, honey bears; mountain lions with big tusks hanging over their lower lip and regular mountain lions, and wildcats, mule deer, dick deer, red deer, and rat deer. . . . All kinds of weird creatures with double heads and magic poisons in their beaks and feathers and fur mixed amongst their scales so that you couldn't hardly tell a bird from snake except from which ones could fly."

Harris knew the old-timer's tale was not literally true, but it was metaphorically true. For all its cathedral-like beauty, the redwood forests were also a realm of rot and decay and death. There were quiet streams and fern grottos of infinite beauty, along with rotting logs crawled over by huge, slimy banana slugs. Shafts of sunlight beams dappled down through flowering dogwood branches and heavily guarded marijuana patches alike. It was a place where children could play happily in the cool waters of the Eel River on a warm summer's day, and musty duff could hide the fractured skull of Andrea LaDeRoute. It was a place of ethereal splendor and sudden death. Harris both loved and hated it. It had cast a spell over him once, but spells are not always felicitous.

Yet in 2003, Harris found himself making his way back through the familiar locales of Cloverdale, Hopland, and the Russian River valley to Ukiah. He was on the same route that Sherry Lynn Smith had taken on her bus ride twenty-seven years before in 1976. Harris stopped off in Ukiah because he wanted to read the official files on the Debbie Sloan case and see what aspects they might have in common with Sherry Lynn Smith and Andrea LaDeRoute. He did find tantalizing bits of information relating to all the cases. One was a four-page synopsis on the Smith murder, and the other was a three-page synopsis of the LaDeRoute disappearance. These scant pages gave a few names of people who knew the victims and certain circumstances about the cases as well.

What really caught Harris's eye was a small addendum to these pages. Written by some lawyer in the Sloan case, the addendum read, "It is the People's position that the uncharged acts [upon Smith and LaDeRoute] are relevant and admissible pursuant to 1101(b) Evidence Code to show intent, motive, common schemes or plans, and absence of mistake."

It went on to say that both acts involved female Caucasian women with brunette hair, and both were in the same age range as John Annibel. It also stated that there was blunt force trauma to the head of Sherry Lynn Smith, and circumstantial evidence of blunt force trauma to the head of Andrea LaDeRoute. The document noted that John knew Sherry Lynn Smith, and Andrea was his live-in girlfriend. Both victims had been strangled to death, and their bodies had been discovered in isolated areas.

Reading more of the case files, including court transcripts on the Sloan murder and its similarities to the Smith and LaDeRoute cases, it did seem that there was a link between the murders of Sherry Lynn Smith, Andrea LaDeRoute, and Debbie Sloan. So many of the circumstances were a very close match. Harris discovered one more thing at the Ukiah judicial center. It was only a small item that would send him off in a totally unexpected direction. He read a newspaper article that was only a few paragraphs long, but which posited a question: Had John Annibel been responsible for the strangulation of a twenty-year-old Fort Bragg woman named Georgina Pacheco in 1988? He had never before heard of this link.

After further research, Harris decided that the MO on the Pacheco case was just too similar to the other cases to pass up. After all, he knew that John Annibel had been a resident of Fort Bragg in 1988, the year Georgina was murdered. Harris decided to take a detour to Fort Bragg before heading up to Humbodlt County. If there was any more information on Georgina Pacheco, it would be found there.

In his research at Fort Bragg, Harris did find more tantalizing bits of information about Georgina Pacheco. There were some files on record that in many ways made her death sound similar to the murder of Sherry Lynn Smith, and Harris

also learned of many possible suspects, including John Annibel. Georgina's sister, Laudalina, or as everyone called her,
"Laud," managed a pizza parlor on Main Street in Fort Bragg,
and he decided to pay her a visit.

Their first meeting was a strange one, to say the least. Not
wanting to beat around the bush, and knowing there was no
easy way to introduce himself, Harris said that he was investigating about the death of her sister. Laud misunderstood him
and thought he was talking about either Zee or Julie, not
Georgina. She suddenly had a panicked look on her face,
wondering if she had just lost another sister, until Harris managed to get everything straightened out and clarify that the sister
he was talking about was Georgina.

Laud took Harris into her small office and for the next
couple of hours they discussed every angle about what they
knew concerning Georgina's murder. Harris had some new
things to tell Laud, and she had a lot of information that was
new to him. At the end of their meeting, Laud asked Harris if
he would like to go see the spot where Georgina's body was
found. He said that he would.

The trip to the site was shorter than he expected. It was just
south of town, down Highway 1, and then inland a short way
into the woods. He had expected the body dump site to be a
greater distance from Fort Bragg. Nonetheless, the route
twisted and turned, and the pavement finally ended. Harris had
completely lost his sense of direction, and he knew that it must
have been a local person who had chosen this spot as the
dump site. A person just passing through wouldn't even know
this road was there, much less be able to find their way around
late at night.

As they got out of Laud's vehicle and stared at the bushy tree-
lined spot where Georgina's body had been found, Harris noticed tears streaking down Laud's face. It was as if the events
had happened the day before, and not fifteen years in the past.
He also realized that the spot looked a lot like both the Sloan
body-dump site on Branscomb Road and the Sherry Lynn
Smith dump site up on Eel Rock Road. He wasn't saying that
John Annibel had murdered Georgina Pacheco, but it was a pos-

sibility. All three of these women had some of their clothes pulled off and were probably raped and strangled to death. After they were dead, their bodies had been dumped in a spot other than where they were killed, hidden under some brush, and all on isolated roads that only a local would know. He wasn't the only one who thought this way. Harris learned that both Detectives Smallcomb and Kiely entertained similar theories.

Harris picked up a few more bits of information as he obtained court documents and police reports relating to the murders of Debbie Sloan, Sherry Lynn Smith, and Georgina Pacheco. On the Pacheco murder, both Harris and Julie (Georgina's sister) agreed that Robin Johnson knew a lot more than she had been saying back in 1988. In fact, Julie thought Robin knew the killer and had sent detectives off on a wild-goose chase away from him on purpose. It made Harris think about Christine Anderson back on the Sherry Lynn Smith case. Fourteen-year-old Anderson had also indicated she knew who the killer was, and had even bolted from a pickup truck when officers tried picking her up as a runaway. It made Harris wonder why the Anderson lead had faded away to nothing, since it had initially seemed so promising.

Georgina's sister, Julie, told Harris one more intriguing fact about Georgina. She and Georgina had been great pals, and in the last week before her death, Julie found out that a girl named Melissa had written Georgina a letter. One sentence in the letter stated: "Don't do that again!"

"Don't do what again?" Julie asked Georgina.

Georgina didn't answer her, and a week later she had disappeared.

Harris also learned that the investigation had never really stopped on the Georgina Pacheco case. The Mendocino County Sheriff's Office was good about cold cases, and every once in a while they reviewed the old documents and tried to develop new leads. Harris discovered that leads were still coming in by 1999, though they tended to make the case even more complex, rather than less so. On top of all the other suspects in the case, John Annibel, Josef Gavette, and Victor Gray still weren't out of the running.

In February 1999, Josef Gavette had thrown everybody a

curveball. A psychiatrist named Dr. Anker had been treating Gavette's wife up in Medford, Oregon. She passed on information to him that she wondered if her husband had murdered Georgina Pacheco down in Fort Bragg, California eleven years earlier. Dr. Akern passed this information on to Detective Kurt Smallcomb.

The information that was shared concerned Joe Gavette saying that in the summer of 1988 he had sex with Georgina and she liked it rough. In his own words, "This sex was nasty. We hurt each other. I even choked her with my hands."

Smallcomb talked directly to Josef Gavette, who said he had been out at a party on Boice Lane in 1988. When he went outside he met Georgina Pacheco near a trailer and talked to her there. Then, according to Gavette, he and a guy named Shawn Thomas and Georgina took a walk out into the woods near the "Y." Gavette said that Georgina wanted sex, so they did it outside while Shawn watched. Then Gavette claimed that Georgina wanted to experiment with a cord around her neck to heighten her sexual pleasure. He said he didn't want to do it, but she talked him into it.

All of this, according to Gavette was not on the night that she died. Gavette said that he saw her three days later and she told him she was pregnant with Victor Gray's baby. Then according to Gavette, Georgina told him that she was going to tell Gray that the child was Gavette's.

Much of his story didn't make much sense, and Smallcomb learned that Gavette had a history of mental illness. Gavette may have thought he committed these acts and imagined most of the details. Georgina's sisters said she was a real coward when it came to pain. They couldn't imagine her asking to be hurt during sex or any other time. Laud said, "Georgina was a big chicken when it came to pain."

When Shawn Thomas was asked about Gavette's story, he said that none of it had happened.

It was around 1998 or 1999 that the Sheriff's Office really started looking into the John Annibel angle of the Pacheco case. A dead girl, raped, strangled to death, and left in the forest certainly fit his MO. The office requested that DNA evidence from

John be sent to the North Coast Criminalistics Lab. Tim Kiely requested a sample of blood consistent with B or O types for a new PCR test.

Harris knew that the Pacheco case was a difficult one. Unlike the Sherry Smith and Andrea LaDeRoute cases there were too many suspects, rather than one truly viable one as in the Smith and LaDeRoute murders. All law-enforcement personnel in the Smith and LaDeRoute cases pointed their theories toward only one suspect—John Annibel. Harris decided to take another trip to Fort Bragg and enlist the help of Laud and Julie in tracking down any new leads on Georgina.

Up to this point, Julie had not been involved in any evidence collection. The death of her big sister had hit her hard, and she was particularly angry at Robin Johnson. Very correctly she had determined that Johnson had thrown the investigators offtrack in the crucial early days with her phony sketch of the "suspect."

Amazingly, Julie had never been to the spot where Georgina's body had been found. That day, she, Laud and Harris went out there. When he asked her how she felt about being there, she said it was okay. In fact, it was kind of a relief, she said.

The rest of the day was spent tracking down old leads and going to places that had been important back in September 1988—Noyo Harbor, the site of the old Sprouse Reitz, areas where Georgina hung out, places where John Annibel had lived. In fact, Harris learned that at one point, John and Beth lived only a block away from Georgina. It would have been very likely that he had seen her at some point, especially in a city as small as Fort Bragg. As Laud pointed out, "Everybody knows everybody else here. It's not that big a town."

There were still ties to John in Fort Bragg, since that was the place he had been living for fourteen years before being arrested. Laud, Julie and Harris went over to a house where a guy and his wife lived who both knew the Annibels. She had baby-sat the Annibel kids at one time, and the guy had worked with John at Louisiana Pacific. The guy said that John did have a drug habit, and maybe even dealt. They both said what a nice person Beth was but that John did not always treat her well.

Even after sixteen years, there were an amazing amount of people who remembered Georgina and the events of 1988. To Julie and Laud, it seemed like the events of that September were only yesterday. The trio picked up odd bits of information that led from one person to another. What became clear to all of them was that various people were lying about events, and they caught several of them in their lies. Laud and Julie were very clever about surreptitiously eliciting information.

Thinking that there might be a connection between the Pacheco and LaDeRoute murders, Harris decided to contact Andrea's sister Lisa, who still lived in Eureka, to see if she would consider meeting with Laud and Zee. He knew it was risky business. There might not be any connection at all, and he had no idea how Lisa would react to his suggestion. She might be incensed that he was poking around at old wounds, but he also had experience from past cases where victims' family members who didn't know each other at all were able to get comfort from each other. One thing he knew for sure, they shared something that no one outside their fraternity or sorority of pain would ever know to its full extent. It was the same situation Zee had endured years ago when the woman trying to comfort her had said, "I know how you feel," and Zee felt like screaming, "No, you don't!" Harris realized that unless you were someone in their shoes, you'd never know the full extent of their loss and pain.

When Harris did contact Lisa LaDeRoute Lawler on the phone, she seemed vary wary. He could tell she wanted to know what his angle was—why he was calling her out of the blue. She'd been burned before, and she didn't want it to happen again. He understood her wariness. He also thought this might be a good opportunity for her to share things with others who had been in her same position. Laud and Zee were all for the meeting.

Finally after much hesitation, Lisa said that she would agree to a rendezvous, and Harris set it up for a site about halfway between all the different women. The place he chose was not by accident—it was Boomer's Bar and Grill in Laytonville. He wanted them to see the place where Debbie Sloan had been on the last evening of her life. If they were lucky, they just might be able to contact Debbie's ex-husband, Alan Sloan, and he could join them. It would not be only a place where they could talk about their losses, but also share names of people John Annibel might have known. If any of those names were the same, it would be significant. Eureka, Laytonville, Fort Bragg, and Ukiah were not close to each other, and if certain names kept popping up, they might be important leads. Harris wished that Pam Smith Annibel could be there as well, but that was an impossibility. He wasn't even sure if she was still married to James or living in Colorado. She was a mystery herself.

On May 22 Harris met Zee and Laud at a café in Willits and rode up with them to Laytonville. They went into Boomer's and sat down at a long table, waiting for Lisa and her husband to arrive. It was a long ride down to Laytonville from Eureka and road construction was holding them up. Several couples walked through the door, but Harris, Laud, and Zee ignored them. Then a slender woman with dark hair, and a burly man walked in past the bar. Harris, Laud, and Zee somehow knew it was the Lawlers, even before the couple walked up to their table. They were correct.

Everybody at the table shook hands, and to get things rolling, Harris showed everyone police photos of several aspects of the Sloan case. He thought this might break the ice. The one thing every person involved might have in common was John Annibel. Lisa certainly did, and Laud and Zee might have a connection as well. If nothing else, they had once lived only a block away from him without knowing it, and he was at the top of the list next to two others as a suspect on Georgina Pacheco's murder, as far as MCSO was concerned.

Lisa said later, "I felt this strange uneasiness. They were real friendly and nice and everything and this feeling had nothing to do with them. It was really my own insecurities about what to say and how to react around them. Which I thought was odd, since of all people, I should really have been able to identify with their feelings. But for some unknown reason our first meeting had an intensity about it, although I wasn't really uncomfortable. I was just aware of it. Afterward I could honestly say that I understood how others who have suffered this can feel."

As for Laud and Zee, they were taken aback about the absolute lack of support that Humboldt County authorities had given Lisa. For years Laud had remained good friends with Detective Miller and still went to see him occasionally at his office. Zee became friends with Kurt Smallcomb, and they even played on the same softball team together. Both Laud and Zee knew that these and other detectives had done everything they could to solve Georgina's murder, and still periodically took out the files and read them afresh. It was a case these guys were truly interested in solving.

"We couldn't believe it," said Zee. "How could they treat Lisa so terribly? She's the one who lost a sister, and they almost treated her like a criminal. It made me mad when I thought about it."

Before everyone left for their respective homes, they all went to the Red Fox Casino and met Debbie Sloan's ex-husband, Alan. He talked with them for a long time and shared stories about Debbie. He also knew John firsthand, and said John was a guy who would back down from a fight with a man but who acted like a tough guy around women. Alan thought that John was very capable of killing Andrea and Georgina.

Harris had one more thing to do before going home. He took a drive up to Eureka and stopped at Sunset Cemetery, the place where Sherry was buried. Her grave was in a large grassy area that sloped downhill toward Humboldt Bay. Harris took a small high-school photo of her out of his wallet and gazed at it. Sherry's fifteen-year-old face beamed back at him with the confidence and joy of youth. That she now lay in a grave below his feet seemed almost inconceivable. She should have had a long life with its happiness, heartaches, triumphs, and mistakes like everyone else.

Harris stuck the photo back into his pocket and quietly said, "I promise you, Sherry, I will do everything I can to bring you justice."

CHAPTER 11

E-Mail Alley

After the meeting of the sisters in Laytonville, Harris mainly worked with Lisa Lawler in Humboldt County. It was not that Georgina Pacheco's case wasn't as important as Andrea's, it was just that he really didn't know if John had murdered Georgina. The links were more tenuous and there were just too many other viable suspects, and he had no contact with Pam Smith Annibel. As far as Andrea went, however, he concluded there was just one suspect—John Annibel, and he based this assumption on the findings by the Humboldt County Sheriff's Office and Fortuna Police Department reports.

Since Harris and Lisa lived hundreds of miles apart, their main means of communication was by e-mail, with occasional phone conversations or snail mail. One thing was for sure—Harris and Lisa were off and running right from the start. Each began researching different areas as to what had really happened in 1976 to Sherry and in 1980 to Andrea. Neither one doubted that both cases were linked, and the connection in their minds was John Annibel. Humboldt County law-enforcement documents backed them up on this.

Lisa e-mailed Harris with an interesting bit of information

on April 27, 2004. She said, "I received information from Mike Losey between 2000 and 2001 when I was really pushing for DNA testing [the blood in the apartment that John and Andrea shared]. Mike stated that an item had been found in the apartment near the bedroom area that my sister shared with Annibel. At first he was reluctant to tell me what the item was. He did say that the item had what appeared to be blood on it, and as a result it was submitted for testing, but came back inconclusive at the time. After a few more persistent conversations, I point-blank asked Mike what the item was and he said it was a hacksaw."

That was certainly an interesting item to Harris. Why would a hacksaw possibly have blood on it other than it having been used to saw through Andrea's bones? Harris had just been involved with another case where the killers had used knives and saws to dismember a body. Had Annibel murdered Andrea in the apartment, dismembered her in the bathtub, and then sneaked her body parts out in garbage bags during the night? It certainly was a possibility as far as Harris was concerned. Especially when Lisa spoke of John having multiple garbage bags at the apartment in Fortuna that he and Andrea shared. He had made it a point to place the garbage bags out of Lisa's sight at the time. Harris already knew about Debbie Sloan being transported out from the murder scene in a blanket and sleeping bag. John could have put Andrea's body parts in garbage bags for transportation. Or, if her body was still in one piece, in a blanket that was covered with dirt and twigs and spoken of in police reports. Either way, John's site of disposal for Debbie's body had proven to be the woods. No one would think twice if he was putting garbage bags into his car. People were always hauling every kind of item imaginable around in garbage bags.

Another thing Lisa mentioned was curious. She wrote, "I have three videotapes from years ago. The 1998 interview was the most damning one because the reporters supported my belief that Annibel should never have been released, or at least tried again for Andrea. The interview even included a statement from Floyd Stokes, who was one of the original detectives in Andrea's case. He felt there was always enough physical and circumstantial evidence to take Annibel to trial. He came right out in the television interview and said it. And he'd been a big investigator on the case in 1980."

Lisa added, "While doing some research at the local library in 1990, I accidentally stumbled upon the Annual Humboldt County DA's report to the state. Despite two-thousand-plus man hours of investigation, there was no homicide "arrests" listed for 1980 in Humboldt County, despite the fact that John Annibel was arrested in Colorado and brought back to stand trial in Humboldt County." This was the first time Harris had heard this information.

To get Harris up to speed, Lisa sent him a portfolio of news articles, letters, comments and reports she had gathered about Andrea over the years. It also contained items that concerned Sherry Lynn Smith and Debbie Sloan as well as Janet Lee Bowman, Karen Fisher, and Vickie Schneider.

On May 24, 2004, she sent Harris another e-mail entitled "News Flash!!!" concerning the fact that she had just learned that John Annibel had been transferred from prison to the Jamestown work camp in the Sierra foothills. Lisa was incensed when she learned that Pauline Sanderson, Debbie Sloan's mom, had not been informed of this move. She also wondered why a murderer like John was being placed in a work camp at a Level II facility after having been transferred from a Level III facility.

Jamestown was a California prison in the Sierra foothills near Sonora. Most of the facility held low-risk prisoners who were being taught firefighting skills. Then they were sent out to fight wildfires during the summer months. There was a Class III facility for inmates who needed more security. Lisa hoped that John was in there. She said, "If he was on a fire line, he could just walk off if the thought popped into his head."

The next day Lisa wrote, "I spoke to the authorities there and they confirmed that he was, in fact, at Jamestown. I spoke to Pauline about this. None of us were informed, so how the heck could we show up at the next parole hearing or give input when they hadn't provided us with the correct info? Unbelievable!"

On June 8, Harris asked Lisa for any address she knew of in Fort Bragg where John and Beth had lived. He wanted to go there and talk to people who may have known John, and he wanted to check on the Georgina Pacheco angle again to see if it had any validity. One of the reasons Harris wanted to go there was because there was a lot more information in Mendocino County on Annibel than there was in Humboldt County, even about Humboldt County cases. It had become apparent that if he wanted to get facts on the murders of Sherry Lynn Smith and Andrea LaDeRoute, documented information was available to him at Mendocino County and not Humboldt. The only items he had so far from Humboldt County were old newspaper clippings and some interviews with people. Where were all the documents? If the Humboldt County investigators had done two-thousand-plus hours of work on Andrea's case alone, there should be a paper trail a mile long, and all Harris had so far were three measly pages of court documents concerning John from Humboldt. He knew from past experience that there should be a lot more documents available to the public than that. So what had happened to it?

Frustrated by the lack of cooperation from the Humboldt County DA's office in particular, Harris e-mailed Lisa a message on June 18. "All information on Annibel seems to go in and never come out as far as the Humboldt County DA's office goes. It's like there's a black hole up there as far as Annibel is concerned. All of this would be fine if the DA's office was moving ahead on the case, but I see no movement at all. What is wrong with them? All we're trying to do is help them."

Lisa had her own frustrations with the authorities and media in Humboldt County. It was if no one cared about her sister or justice. She wrote, "I know that firsthand. After they found Andrea's remains, we were not told that a press conference had even been scheduled. I had to read about it in the newspaper. I was told by Sergeant Rogers not to make any statements. So when my aunt, my husband, and I showed up in Fortuna to listen, we did not ask any questions. We felt like outsiders and when the media approached us, we told them, 'Sorry, we can't make any comments.'

"Dave Silverbrand from KIEM news said, 'When you're

ready to talk, please call me.' We responded that we would like to, but we've been instructed not to make any statements.'

"Dave looked puzzled and said, 'That's strange, because we were told we could interview the family.'

"Just before we were approached by Dave, there were about ten media members there, and at the end of the conference I watched Sergeant Rogers approach a media member and whisper in his ear. I just knew we were in trouble. I wasn't the only family member who felt that we were not supposed to be there.

"So when Dave Silverbrand caught us in the parking lot, as we were leaving with my portfolio, which I had hoped to share with someone, in hand, we explained the situation to him and again he seemed very puzzled. He said that the authorities had given him an open door to interview the victim's family.

"Not too long after that, something in the newspaper regarding the case inspired me to seek out Dave's home phone number and I contacted him for an interview. The thing that inspired me to do it was the newspaper kept saying that no charges had been filed against John. That really upset me because they were printing wrong information. I called Dave that Sunday afternoon, leaving a message on his home phone. He immediately responded and scheduled an exclusive with me the next day, which is the same day it aired."

[There was a segment about Andrea and Lisa that aired on KIEM in which Lisa showed photos of Andrea and related a synopsis of the case.]

"After the interview, Dave told me he would be investigating the case and would keep me informed. When I contacted him a few weeks later, he said that the district attorney's office has several thousand cases a year to determine whether they go to trial or not, and that there was only one person assigned to make that determination. He was pretty much giving me the brush-off. I didn't understand these inconsistencies. Dave was really eager initially, because I know he's been in the area ever since Sherry was a victim.

"Unfortunately, Dave had a heart attack and nothing else was done after that. And so there was the same old pattern of enthusiasm and then nothing. So to say I have trust issues with the media is an understatement. What I don't understand is, why was the media so supportive until after the interview with me? It's almost as though the case never existed and it all occurred in my head. I know I'm stretching here, but I can't understand why the media would go from enthusiasm to avoidance. Throughout the years I have gone through three DAs, I've written the grand jury at least two times, and I even hand carried the last portfolio to the grand jury's in-box at the court house. Now I'm mad as hell and I believe I have just cause!"

In mid-June, Lisa spent her lunch hours trying to get information on John's arrest in Denver, Colorado, by the local police department. It was all a waste of time and energy. There seemed to be another "black hole" in Denver about Annibel as far as documents were concerned.

Unexpectedly, Lisa informed Harris that she had a phone call from Paul Smith, Sherry Lynn Smith's dad. Paul was up from his home in Las Vegas, Nevada, and visiting in Eureka. He told her that he would bring his own portfolio by so that she could see the notes he'd taken over the years about Sherry's murder case.

By July, Lisa and Harris had become friends. In many ways they were very different in personality, background, lifestyle, and age. But they admired the tenacity, truthfulness, and drive that each showed in pursuing justice for Andrea and Sherry. Lisa shared with him, "I am always struggling with my job, as is my husband. We're always screening the job opportunities in our area. Even with a degree, starting wages are $8 to $8.50 per hour here, and without benefits. So in scanning, job searching, faxing, and e-mailing, my life feels completely out of sorts."

It didn't leave a lot of time for her to work on Andrea's case. Lisa told Harris one more thing—if not for the fact of trying to get justice for Andrea, she and her husband would have left Humboldt County long ago, seeking better job opportunities elsewhere. But Lisa knew that Andrea would never have abandoned her, so she could never abandon Andrea. She had to stay no matter what.

Harris was also feeling "out of sorts." In other counties, in other cases, he'd always had cooperation from the local authorities. It wasn't like he was asking for the Crown jewels or restricted information. All he wanted was information that should have been open to the public and would actually help their case if he developed new information. He knew that sometimes people talked to him who wouldn't talk to a uniformed officer, or even a plainclothes cop. It happened all the time. So where was this information up in Humboldt County? What the hell was going on up there?

Eventually Lisa and Sandy met Paul Smith and he handed over to them a portfolio he had been compiling on all the cases involving John Annibel. It contained a lot of information Lisa hadn't seen before, most of it concerning Sherry. Paul just handed the entire thing over to her. He was running out of steam on tracking the cases, and he was also ill. He'd run into the same roadblocks with the Humboldt County authorities that Lisa had. He was disgusted with them and said, "I could have helped them. Instead they shut me out."

Paul's most damning statement was when Detective Juan Freeman spoke with him right after John had been arrested for the murder of Debbie Sloan. Paul wasn't as angry at Freeman as he was for whomever was higher in the chain of command at HCSO. Paul related, "Freeman was all excited and told me that they were going to solve Sherry's murder now. And then the very next day he said that they didn't have the evidence. So what happened to it? It was a complete flip-flop from one day to the next."

Lisa informed Harris, "I noticed a strange car at my workplace. Strange because this guy was just sitting in his car and didn't look like the usual drug-type lookout. He pulled up right next to my office window. I was alone in my office that day, so I called the neighbor from the business next door. When my business neighbor showed up, he went right up to the window of the car and asked the guy what was going on, and told him he was parked on private property. The guy in the car said he was doing surveillance on the motel across the street. The business neighbor came inside and told me what the guy had said. At that point the guy in the car drove away. When he did, I realized he would have had a hard time viewing Motel 6 across the street. I also realized his side view mirror was pointed right at my office window. I wondered if I was being spied on."

By this point, Harris wasn't brushing off anything that Lisa said. He told Lisa, "There's a lot of murky stuff going on up there. Be careful!"

Lisa also related one odd fact to Harris that he didn't know. She said that unlike most people, Andrea considered her lucky number to be thirteen. "It was just always lucky for us. It's kind of strange, I know, but that's just the way it's always been."

Harris went up to Humboldt County in mid-July and began to talk to Lisa about going to visit the site where Andrea's remains had been discovered on Redwood House Road northeast of Carlotta. He knew that a visit by Julie to the place where Georgina had been found seemed to have been helpful to her. Lisa was very torn about going there. She had never been to the location. She wanted to, and yet she was also afraid. Who knew what kinds of images and feelings would be dredged up? What if it was a horrible place of rotting tree trunks and murky, shadowed ravines? The thought of that being Andrea's last resting place was almost too much to bear.

There was one other thing that made Lisa hesitate. In the past she and Sandy had been riding on his motorcycle out in that same vicinity. It was early morning and shadows lay across the roadway. As Lisa rode on the back of the motorcycle, she was suddenly stunned as a mountain lion broke out of the woods and dashed right by their motorcycle. It happened so fast that Sandy didn't even see it, since his vision was concentrated farther down the road.

The encounter with the mountain lion terrified Lisa. She had nightmares of it attacking her and pulling her off the motorcycle. To go back into that same wooded area on Redwood House Road seemed to be tempting fate.

Harris realized that Lisa was very frightened about the mountain-lion incident. He also wondered if this incident tied in with deeper psychological trauma for Lisa that concerned the area where Andrea had been found. He wasn't sure if those demons would be dispelled by Lisa visiting the spot or not, but he decided to give her all the support she might need.

Lisa was still terrified that a mountain lion would sneak up on her and attack her there, even though Harris said that he and Sandy would be with her, and no mountain lion would attack with so many people around in broad daylight. Still she was afraid, so to give her more assurance Harris asked his cousin and his cousin's son, who lived in the region, to come along. Lisa also invited one of her women friends to join them. There would be six people in all going there—more than enough to scare off any mountain lions, especially in the middle of the day.

In two separate vehicles, they journeyed up Highway 36 to Carlotta and then turned off onto dirt and gravel Redwood House Road. It climbed steeply up through redwood trees and pines, near Yager Creek on the edge of the embattled Headwaters region. Just down the hill were several old-growth redwood groves that had never been touched by the hand of man. Pristine and ethereal, they were a temperate-zone rainforest, decked with immense foliage and lush, green fern grottos.

As the mile markers passed by, Lisa became more and more agitated and nervous, almost overwhelmed by powerful emotions. This was the road on which Andrea's body had been transported to its final resting place. Suddenly, without warning, Harris shouted at his cousin, who was driving a van, "Look at that!"

It was the number thirteen painted on a tree by timber workers. The number thirteen had always been Lisa and Andrea's lucky number.

At first Lisa was so preoccupied that she didn't even see the number, until Harris pointed it out. Then a broad smile crossed her face. The painted number seemed to erase whatever misgivings and fears that had been troubling her.

Along with the others, Lisa walked to an area by a tall, old redwood tree that had been mentioned in a report as being near the spot where Andrea's remains had been found. She placed a small vase of roses that she had taken from her yard on the forest floor. Then everyone had a moment of silence for Andrea.

Later Lisa said, "The spot was beautiful. I had been worried that it would be ugly and overgrown. But the area was quiet and peaceful and lovely. It made me feel better about where she had been found."

A very curious thing happened one day in the summer of 2004, when Harris and Lisa went to the clerk's office at the Humboldt County Superior Court to ask for more records on John Annibel. While they waited for the clerk to return with the file folder, Lisa looked at someone walking in the door and turned absolutely pale. The person who had just walked in was Roger Hudnall, the same person who had pulled the anthrax hoax on her in 2001. She had no idea he was out of prison and back on the streets of Eureka. Was he stalking her? Did he intend to harm her right there in the courtroom lobby of the clerks office? Lisa was absolutely petrified.

When Lisa whispered to Harris who the person was, Harris's first thoughts were, "Somebody in this courthouse let Hudnall know Lisa was here." He said later, "We had already indicated to one person in charge that we would be going to the clerk's office. Whoever it was within the court, they sent Hudnall in to scare her away. Why they would do this, I didn't know, but I didn't believe in coincidences of this magnitude. One of the people she feared the most, just happening to show up at the same time we indicated that we would be there. I mean, come on! If you believe that, I've got some great Florida swampland to sell you."

Harris decided to take the offensive rather than sit back and be frightened. He said later, "If they thought they could pull this kind of crap on me and Lisa, then I was gonna do them one better. So I walked up to Hudnall, stuck out my hand, and with a big smile on my face I said to him, 'Long time no see, Roger. How are you doing?'

"Because we had never seen each other before in reality, he looked at me with surprise and confusion. I knew he didn't know me. And now he didn't know what to do. Because I had a black briefcase in my hand and was well dressed, he might have thought I was a lawyer or a police detective or even with the FBI. I didn't tell him I belonged to any agency. I just let his imagination run wild.

"'Do I know you?' he finally said.

"I laughed and said, 'Oh, sure, I used to see you all the time around here a few years ago. So what have you been up to?'

"He didn't answer, but looked even more confused and concerned. He soon left without ever stating why he was there.

"I thought this was a pretty good message to whoever sent him there in the first place that we were on to their tricks. It would show them we were on to their little mind games and they weren't going to scare us off."

A few days later, incensed by the lack of movement by the DA's office, and especially by DA Paul Gallegos, whom she had supported so strongly during his recall election, Lisa e-mailed Gallegos about the lack of progress, but got no response. Soon thereafter she faxed DDA Worth Dikeman, who was supposed to be handling the case. In part the fax read, "I e-mailed DA Paul Gallegos requesting that he explain whether he would be filing charges against the suspect responsible for my sister's homicide, or at least explain to me in writing why he was unable to. I also requested that I receive a copy of her death certificate as my family has never received an official one.

"My sister, Andrea LaDeRoute, is a homicide victim as a direct result of domestic violence. Her case file supports that there is evidence of this. I have repeatedly tried to get authorities to pursue her case, and I am repeatedly told that they are working on her case, that it is an active case, that it's a complicated case, and after twenty-four years, even though they recovered her remains in August 2002, they still don't know if they will ever file charges against the suspect. I have not been given any timelines in which to check back with them or when they will make a final decision.

"The DA's office has denied my family access to her case file and records. As a result of prosecutors not pursuing evidence in a 1976 case with the same primary suspect as Sherry Lynn Smith's murder, Andrea became another unfortunate homicide victim in 1980. There have been other homicides in which authorities in both Humboldt County and Mendocino County suspected John Annibel. It wasn't until 1999 that Annibel was actually convicted of the murder of Deborah Sloan in Mendocino County.

"The authorities in Mendocino County have reviewed the information that I have involving my sister's case, and have stated based on information I alone have—which of course does not include everything that the Humboldt County District Attorney's office has—that if the case had occurred in their county they would have already taken it to trial on Annibel.

"One of the original investigators from the Humboldt County District Attorney's office stated publicly in 1998 that he and others always felt that there was enough information to take the case to court, and that they never understood why prosecutors hadn't done so.

"Yesterday would have been Andrea's forty-fifth birthday. She died at the age of twenty. I would appreciate any assurance or help you can give me in this matter. I don't understand why my sister's case is not being pursued as other cases have."

Like many other requests from Lisa to the DA's office, she received no reply.

For whatever reason, Sandy and Lisa Lawler were invited to a picnic of DA Paul Gallegos supporters at a park along the Van Duzen River in the summer of 2004. It did not escape Lisa's attention that Andrea's remains had been discovered only a few miles away up Redwood House Road. Lisa later told Harris, "The whole thing was a complete joke! Not only did no one approach me or Sandy, even though we were in front near the food table for more than four hours, Paul didn't even arrive until 4 PM. I told my girlfriend, Marie, that we needed to approach Paul, because by that time we wanted to leave. Marie went up and thanked Paul for his invitation and gave him kudos. I stood there waiting to be snubbed while five or six of his supporters stood around. He stuck out his hand and said, 'Paul Gallegos,' as if I didn't know who he was. I responded, 'I know!'

"It had been pretty strange sitting there for four hours with people looking at me like they knew me. I didn't notice these same people staring hard anywhere else. The afternoon was a complete waste of time. But it was only 2.5 miles from there to Redwood House Road, so we took the opportunity to drive up the hill again. Our friends seemed really pleased to experience the site with us.

"I felt just as at peace as I did before. It is such a beautiful place. I just wanted to find one item that belonged to Anghs from there. I just wish to God that the Humboldt County DA's office would give me as much information as Mendocino County DA's office gave to Georgina's sisters. Somehow I can't help but feel if I knew more I might be able to help them with Andrea's case. I know I am just an everyday citizen and probably pretty naïve. But even still, I just don't understand why they insist on closing me out of my sister's case. Do they really believe that I could jeopardize her case any further than they have? No criminal charges filed in twenty-four years! Why don't they see me as a good resource to help support their investigations?"

Why indeed? Harris wondered the same thing. It was true that civilians could sometimes muddy the waters in a case, but after twenty-four years, what did Humboldt County have to lose? Mendocino County was using Laud and Zee in anyway they could to help solve Georgina's murder, and that was after sixteen years. So what was the problem with using Lisa in a similar manner up in Humboldt? No one knew Andrea's habits, friends, and the places she liked to go better than Lisa. Lisa could be a real asset to them.

And yet in late August, eighteen-year-old Tiffany Porter told a reporter for the *Eureka Times-Standard* that she had been riding on a motorbike only yards from her house when she nearly hit a mountain lion crouched in the tall grass. She claimed that the big cat chased her, she screamed, gunned the high-powered bike toward her house, and ran inside. When the cat got to the pavement, it ran off.

All of this was suspiciously like the incident that had happened to Lisa in the 1990s.

Harris was very dubious about this latest reported episode in the newspaper. It was just too convenient that a mountain-lion story like this should show up in the newspaper, right after Lisa had spoken at the DA's picnic where a mountain-lion incident had happened to her. Harris told Lisa, "A girl on a motorbike gets chased by a mountain lion? Give me a break!"

Even statements by two California Department of Fish and Game wardens, who went to investigate Porter's claim, seemed to back Harris up. They said they couldn't find any sign of the mountain lion and they called the encounter "unsubstantiated."

Harris said to Lisa, "I think this newspaper story is just another incident like Roger Hudnall coming into the court clerk's office when we were there. Someone does not want you to go up to the spot where Andrea's remains were found. What's the easiest way to keep you away? By bringing up a story about a mountain lion chasing a young woman on a motorbike."

Lisa and Sandy went to the Pacific Lumber Company offices in Scotia to try and talk to the foresters who had discovered Andrea's remains. They were not allowed to talk to these individuals, and at all levels they met a wall of silence just as profound as that which they encountered at the DA's office.

A whole new factor came into the mix in August 2004, and the factor was that Pam Smith Annibel responded to a letter that Harris had sent her, hoping that she might be helpful. Pam e-mailed him back, saying, "We would be happy to provide you with information on our sister Sherry. My sister, Paulette, and I are going to get together this weekend and discuss the details of Sherry's life and hopes and dreams. There is a lot we can share with the world. Her teachers were correct when they said that she was a friend to everyone and charming and outgoing. More than us. She did trust everything someone said or did."

Then Pam added about herself and Paulette, "We have become the most protective parents that I know. I didn't know until I read your letter that Sherry was beaten in the head just like Debbie and Andrea. No one is willing to help us or tell us any information. That seems so wrong. Families need to have their questions answered. Whenever I start feeling sorry for myself, and our loss,

I think of others and their losses as well. Debra's [*sic*] children lost their mother. Their pain right now is probably greater than ours. It took my twenty-five years to come to terms with my loss. My baby sister, Paulette, though, has still not come to terms with this. Sherry was our best friend."

On August 22, 2004, Lisa told Harris, "I'm ecstatic that we have Pam's support! As I write this, I am experiencing deep, deep chills which are making it hard to write."

Lisa had other things to say as well. She had just contacted Rick Moench, the DA Investigator who had flown to Colorado in 1980 to bring John back for trial in Humboldt County. Now Moench was a judge in Kern County, almost 400 miles away from Eureka. According to Lisa, Moench had told her, "There was a lot of physical evidence that was not pursued then."

Harris wanted to know, "What evidence?" It was a judge saying this, not just some malcontent. The evidence must have been profound if Moench could remember this twenty-four years later. So why didn't they pursue it?

The very next day, Lisa sent Harris an e-mail, blowing off steam and venting. "Sorry that things have gotten a bit out of control from sending e-mails and my job being so demanding. It really pisses me off that my boss expects me to do what was done by two people before. And all of this in the midst of trying to preserve some momentum on my sister's case. And I mean that sincerely. I believe that you and I are closer to resolving her case than the Humboldt County DA's office ever was! I still don't understand their resistance. I'm in this for the long run, and I will continue regardless of what personal obstacles they use to block my path.

"Now as to Rick Moench, I had left messages for him on his answering machine. A lot of messages went back and forth and then at approximately 10 AM I got a call by someone I didn't recognize, but the area code was the same as Mr. Moench's. Unfortunately I was up to my neck in my boss's whims, so I couldn't excuse myself to even take a call. At lunch I called the number back and explained that I would try to call again during my lunch hour and my 10 AM and 3 PM breaks. This went on for three days.

"Finally, on the third day, I was forced to go get supplies. On my way back to the office, my cell phone rang at approximately 3:19 PM. I knew it was Mr. Moench. We identified each other and I said, 'I'm sorry we keep missing each other. I know I was supposed to talk to you during the 3 PM break this afternoon. However, my break today is picking up office supplies.'

"I wasn't prepared for my questions and I'd left my portfolio at home. I picked up a dull pencil sitting in the passenger seat of my car and a small notebook. He was so comforting in expressing his concerns. I didn't know if he was a good guy or not, and I don't have much faith in anyone who worked at the Humboldt County DA's office, but he was going out of his workweek after twentysomething years to make contact with me. This was a good sign.

"He said, 'Lisa, how are you?'

"I said, 'Well, I could be better. I really appreciate you taking the time to call me back.'

"He said, 'I always felt something would come of this.'

"I said, 'I'm not sure where to begin, or how much information you can give me. As you know, Andrea was reported missing and the same suspect was ultimately convicted for yet another homicide in 1998.'

"'Yes, I heard that,' he said.

"'Well, a lot of us have been talking, and we're trying to put the pieces of the puzzle together, and we were just hoping that you could share what you know. I understand that it's been many years, and I'm not sure what you can remember and what you can share, but we'd be appreciative of any help you can offer.'

"Mr. Moench said, 'I can remember it today as though I was standing in the apartment looking at the paneling on the wall. They'd found blood on the wall, but we were unable to type it without something called umisol [perhaps he meant luminol].'

"Mr. Moench said back then in 1980, authorities believed this process was hazardous to the individuals taking the samples because they thought it was carcinogenic. He said he remembered that no one performed the tests because of this fear.

"I told Mr. Moench about Debra's [*sic*] case, and he affirmed he was aware of that case. But when I told him that part of

Andrea's remains were found in 2002, he was taken aback and surprised. I had to tell him at least twice what remains were found and where they were located.

"Immediately afterward, he said he remembered the paneling and that he knew that 'they' had a lot of physical evidence. Without saying as much, he indicated that they had just been waiting for a body.

"He went so far as to say, 'At the time, I called in a favor and had the Navy do a search in which Andrea's purse was located between the bay and channel.'

"Mr. Moench wanted to talk more, but I felt pressure that I needed to get back to my job. So I told him, 'I loved talking to you, so if there's anything that you can think of, please call me.'

"He said, 'Anything I can do, that's what I went to school for. I'll let my subconscious awaken, and if anything transpires, I'll call. Please call me anytime. I want to help in anyway I can.'"

That very same day, Pam contacted Harris. "Whoever found Sherry's body—I'd heard that it was a horseback rider [it was actually a motorcycle rider]. I was in Fortuna at a dance on a Friday. I heard that John left with my sister at around midnight, and I learned that in fact, he was irritated at her for taking so long to say good-bye to her friends. I was at the Annibel's home when I saw John pull up at 3:15 AM on May 1st. He left again at about 6 AM in the morning for a few hours. Then he came back and told me that he wasn't supposed to say anything, but Sherry wanted to hang out at Alderpoint before going home. That was a lie, of course, because she had called my sister Paulette and my mom, and let them know that she was coming home after the dance. And he thought he could get away with this lie, because Sherry's body had not yet been found. He probably hoped it would never be found, and it might not have, if that guy hadn't stumbled upon it when he did.

"Sherry knew John through me, and would have thoroughly trusted him to take her home. But John always had a morbid mind. He was always saying creepy, off-the-wall remarks. I remember when the OJ trial was going on, John thought how great it was that OJ got away with murder. My husband can vouch for what a mental case John is.

"I didn't know that John took a polygraph test. His mom kept that a secret from us. I still have my issues with that. John does have a more rare blood type than most. My husband has the same blood type. They are fraternal twins, not identical twins. One good and one bad, as the saying goes.

"I'd always been told that Sherry had a lot of skin and blood under her fingernails. They say that they saved that, but who knows? I never heard anything about them finding her suitcases. The first I heard about that was from you."

Harris wondered where Pam had heard about the blood and skin under Sherry's fingernails. Paul Smith had said the same thing, and Pam and her dad weren't close after he had divorced her mom. Paul had moved away and remarried and didn't stay in contact with his daughters. Had samples of skin tissue been collected? Were they still around? Why hadn't they been analyzed? Certainly with DNA testing, not available in 1976, these samples could now be significant.

By August 26, Harris was having serious doubts about the Humboldt County DA's office. He told Lisa, "I can no longer believe the DA's office in Humboldt County is on your side. They don't want you to know the truth about what happened, and they don't want me to know the truth as well. Why this is, I don't know. We have to be our own detectives now. They are not going to do anything about it. It's just as you said once: 'Andrea's body could be lying on the sidewalk and they would walk right past it. It is shameful!'

"I don't believe for one second that Roger Hudnall just happened to be at the court clerk's office the day we were there. He was sent by someone to scare you. But who and why? That's the big question. Why would any of these guys want to protect John Annibel? It's not like he's some rich guy's son, or politician's son. A lot of this doesn't add up—and yet, incidents like the Hudnall one keep happening."

A few days later, Pam Annibel was able to give Harris some more information he hadn't heard before. "Rick Malcomb's mom and John's mom were the best of friends. They did everything together. I just this weekend asked Rick about his trip to Colorado with John, and he said that he and John had been drinking in a bar in Fortuna all day long. It was a spur-of-the-moment decision to pack the car and head east since Rick was unemployed at the time. He saw it as a great opportunity to find work. John must have seen it as an escape for himself.

"Rick also knows how weird John is. They both arrived unannounced at our house in the evening. It was within days that John was arrested at my home. It was a bunch of uniformed detectives who came busting in with their guns drawn. They took him and his car and it wasn't until then that I realized he was a cold-blooded killer. When he was arrested for Debra's [*sic*] murder, the first thing I said was, 'Thank God he finally got caught.' Too many had to die.

"Fred Lane, by the way, was a stepcousin to the Annibels. I do recall him saying to me that Sherry decided to ride with John, but she was supposed to be going home to Miranda, not up the hill. That must have been something John told her to get her to go with him, because I was there."

By mid-September 2004, the e-mails were constantly flowing back and forth between Harris and Lisa Lawler. Lisa e-mailed him, "I wanted to take this time to express as best I can how grateful I am to you. I know that you can see firsthand how the loss of my sister has changed my life. Losing her has been the most tragic and painful thing I have ever had to endure. Unfortunately, the pain is only magnified each day, each year, each birthday, each memory that I recall of her. I fight myself to keep from thinking about how her life was lost. Just taken away from her before she even began to live. It's difficult when I am faced with the reality that she died a horrific death, all alone and left to rot.

"All these years, twenty-four in fact, I have tried to make some sense of her precious life being taken, and I have tried to work to make sure whoever did this horrible act would not be able to do it again. I have written to everyone I could possibly think of. Each time the return phone calls were left with, 'Well, we don't have much to go on.' I even wrote the grand jury twice to investigate my sister's death. Again, no response.

"My father actually drove down from Portland just before he died so he could talk to the Fortuna police officer, M. He waited for over an hour before someone told him that M would not be returning that day, but would call him. My father had an answering machine, as did I. No one ever contacted my father. My father died a few years later. No one ever contacted him from the Fortuna Police Department.

"Throughout the years these situations have occurred repeatedly. No response to letters, phone calls, certified mail. It wasn't until I started going to the media in 1998 that my phone calls began to be returned. The more I learn about my sister's case, and the perpetrator, the more difficult it is to comprehend. I realize now more than ever that the authorities who had the opportunity to stop this individual from murdering again, have literally worked to prevent this suspect from being charged. They even suggested at one point that the DA would offer this suspect complete amnesty if the suspect would just let us know where Andrea was."

Lisa said, "As best I can recall, Mike Losey called me at my work and said, 'I'm really glad John's going to be locked up. He got just what he deserved for Christmas—twenty-five years to life. At least he won't be able to do this to anyone else again.'

"Then Mike added, 'We've been thinking about trying to find closure for you and your family. So we want to run something past you. What if we could get him to tell us where Andrea is, so that you could finally put her to rest? I don't know, but I think the Native Americans (such as Lisa), have strong feelings about this. In exchange for amnesty?'

"I replied, 'Amnesty? What do you mean?'

"Mike said, 'We would agree not to file charges on him, if he gives us a full disclosure.'

"I answered, 'I would have to think about that, I can't answer for the whole family,' knowing that would include Sandy and my aunt. 'I'll have to talk to them and let you know.'

"Later, after I spoke to Sandy, he helped me see that's not what I really wanted. It would be a slap in the face to Andrea. John wouldn't have to serve any more time for killing her.

"For the longest time it was hard for me to even believe that the system could fail so pitifully. And even those closest to me thought it must be me, not the authorities, who were wrong. That

I was just blowing the whole thing out of proportion. So for years I struggled with this painful reality alone, except for my understanding husband who has supported me the best he knows how.

"When Debra's [*sic*] body was found, and John Annibel was convicted, I had all but given up on ever trying to expose the truth of what really had happened to Andrea. I had continually run into a brick wall each time I tried to persuade the DA's office or the Fortuna Police Department to do something. Then on 8-9-02, Andrea was found, and I can't tell you what kind of experience that was for me. I'm still trying to absorb the reality. My husband and I had been looking for her throughout the Eel River area for years. Under bridges, on wooded trails. When she was found it was so wonderful to realize she was finally home, and yet so painful to know the reality I had guessed at all along.

"Unfortunately, after she was found, the current DA Paul Gallegos informed me he doesn't know when or if he will ever file charges against the suspect. I can't even get her remains back for a proper memorial service! He says they want to keep what remains were recovered just in case they go to court. I can't even get a little of her back for a service!"

Around this time, Pam Annibel gave Harris a more detailed account of what had occurred at John's arrest in Denver in 1980. "The day John was arrested was a Saturday and they were in plain clothes and drove a plain brown car. They took his car, the brown Camaro.

"They asked me, James and Rick Malcomb to all come down for questioning, which we did. They talked to us all individually. They really didn't ask me much other than the time John and Rick arrived, and John's demeanor at the time. I told them that he showed up unexpectedly the week before and they had arrived rather late at night, like around 9 PM. It was dark outside and snow was on the ground. James and I were watching TV and looked out the window and said, 'What the heck are they doing here?'

"John said that Andrea was missing and he didn't know where she was, but that she was going to leave him. He said that he had dropped her off at a bus stop and that she was taking classes at Humboldt [Pam may have meant College of the Redwoods].

"She was on her way to school, and that was the last time he saw her. He said he had no idea what could have happened to her. That is what I told the detectives. John did not seem shook up about it. He said he just wanted to get out of Humboldt County.

"I guess they detained him for a couple of days before sending him back to Humboldt. I have no idea how the process went. They took his car back to Humboldt, too. Mike Cortopassi was living here at the time, and it was he who talked to Lisa and told her that John had showed up in Denver. I truly regret not realizing that John was a killer at the time.

"It was after he was released from Humboldt [about May 1980] that he came back here. It was then that I began to realize he might be a killer. He lived in our home for about six months before I kicked him out of our home, with the blessing of my husband. I think James thought the same thoughts I did, but we didn't deal with the fact that his own brother could be a killer.

"Of course, James knows now and is willing to tell me and the family how sorry he is, even though he is not responsible for John's actions. Even though we have been married for twenty-eight years, James feels great shame for what his brother has done. James is nothing like John. He is sweet and caring, and a good husband and father. He's said that John can never get out of prison. They should never think that he is just some harmless old man. John is a born killer and will kill again if given the chance. John is probably already plotting his next victims."

Harris and Pam and Lisa were starting to become a team. If no one else would investigate these old crimes, then they would. Harris contacted Lisa about what Pam had just told him and Lisa said, "That was good information you got from Pam. Good work!

"I don't know how John learned that Anghs was thinking

about leaving him. She and I discussed keeping it a secret, at least until she got moved out. That's why she got the storage room she had just rented to have a different billing address other than where she and John lived. She didn't want him to know. She only had the storage unit a few weeks. I still have the envelope her bill was addressed to. How he learned about her storage unit and her planning to leave him really has me puzzled, because I believe that if Anghs even suspected he knew, she would have left him immediately and stayed with me.

"One thing I think everyone has overlooked is Anghs at College of the Redwoods. The week that she disappeared, it was the first week of finals, and Anghs's courses were DHR, which was hands-on lab work. During finals week her schedule was completely different. She was only scheduled to attend two or three finals for the entire week. Anghs did not have to leave for class at 6:30 AM on March seventeenth as John reported because she didn't have a class or final that day. I know, because I still have the class schedule. So when John said he took her to the bus stop, or that she went to the bus stop by herself, I know that he is lying. He obviously wasn't aware when he lied that she didn't have a class that day.

"I also recall that John normally left for work before Andrea left to catch the bus. She would actually walk about eight blocks to catch the bus. In fact, John had told me and Max that, 'I left for work that day, and when I came home, she was gone. And there was no note. Anytime she wouldn't be home, she always left a note.' Later on he admitted that he didn't go to work that day because he'd been caught on it.

"Unfortunately for him, the police must have learned that he didn't show up for work that day, as he had reported he did. So then his alibi became that he and Anghs had a fight, and he was too upset to show up for work that day. Which was why the police started looking at her disappearance as a domestic dispute. The Fortuna police chief even told me two weeks after she disappeared that was why they were treating it differently than a missing person's case. She was an adult in their eyes and not a missing child.

"Even though John told the police he didn't go to work that

day, he never notified his employer of four years that he wasn't going to show up. Even more than this, Andrea's watch was found in the apartment after she was missing. She wouldn't have gone to classes without her watch. Her wallet was found two weeks after she disappeared, which suggests she never left the apartment. She had just received a check for $340 from financial aid, and she would not have left without her wallet.

"So, what was the argument about the night before? Was the argument about her leaving him? When did he learn about her planning to leave him? What did he know of her plans? And if he took her to the bus stop, why was he in possession of her wallet? Most of all, if he was so upset about her being missing, then why did he do nothing to help find her? No contact to family, no phone calls, no assistance with posters. And leaving the state immediately after I told him I thought we needed to work together if we were going to find her—and Ethel had just accused him of killing Andrea. Well, it's obvious. Once Ethel accused him of that, and Mike Losey was coming back to check on him, John got scared and ran."

On September 28, Pam Annibel had some very interesting new revelations she shared with Harris that he hadn't known about. Pam said, "The Annibel family moved to Fruitland Ridge when John and James were twelve years old. James and John started doing different things. James was hanging out more with the older kids. The oldest brothers, Ted and James, hung out together, and they started excluding John from everything they did. John would always tell on his brothers, so they made him an outcast.

"Some other friends of James and Ted would really belittle John all the time. One friend was a girl named Sherry Nordgren— John really hated her. One night John was really drunk. He hit Sherry over the head with an ax handle. She told the guys that John had wanted her to walk up with him to the horse corral. That's when he swung the ax at her and hit her in the head, and she was bleeding. She told the boys that John had tried to kill her. This was when he was about thirteen or fourteen years old. He was a very angry person when he was drunk."

It was obvious to Harris that if John was getting drunk at

the age of thirteen or fourteen, there had been very little
parental supervision of him in his teenage years. It was under-
standable in some respects. Both of his parents worked to make
ends meet, and they were away from the homestead for long
hours at a time. But the fact that John had his own cabin with
little or no restraint likely had disastrous consequences later
on. With very little self-control, John was a ticking time bomb
ready to explode.

Harris told Lisa in response to her growing sense of hope-
lessness that Andrea's case seemed to go on and on with no
end it sight, "Please, don't feel hopeless. I feel more confident
all the time that we're going to solve this. People are talking
who haven't before, and we're learning more details all the time.
We're on the offensive, not them. We've got some good people
on our side, and all the power is flowing toward us, not them."

By "them," Harris meant John Annibel and some of the authorities in Humboldt County, past and present. In his mind they
were all part of the same problem. Why anyone would want to
protect him, though, was a mystery.

CHAPTER 12

The Labyrinth

Lisa and Harris kept wondering what the big dark secret in Humboldt County concerning John Annibel was, and how he continued to avoid trial there. Lisa told Harris, "After I e-mailed you last night, I couldn't put the puzzle pieces together. I wondered why Annibel would target females that were closely connected to him. Sherry Lynn Smith was last seen by several people leaving the dance with John. Andrea, according to him, was last seen while he drove her to the bus stop. Debbie was seen with John on the night before he had killed her, too.

"You would think he would be afraid of getting caught—or maybe that's it. He had no fear of being caught even with all the circumstantial evidence because charges against him kept being dismissed, at least in Humboldt County. How could any murderer be that confident that he would get away with it?

"So, I guess this case is really twofold. On one hand a murderer who has committed several murders, though only charged with one, and a DA's office who allowed him to commit them by not pursuing charges with the evidence they had."

Information hopped back and forth between Lisa, Harris,

and Pam like a bird on a telephone wire in the fall of 2004. Pam informed the other two of something they had never before heard. "I wanted to tell you today," she said, "about another possible crime that has come to our attention. James and I were talking to Rick Malcomb this weekend about things that happened years ago, and Rick mentioned that his first wife, Linda, had told him about a strange encounter that she had with John back in 1978. Rick and Linda were separated at the time, and Rick was working with his brother up in Oregon. Linda was living in Loleta at the time.

"One night, John came knocking on Linda's door about 3 AM. He asked her if he could crash on her couch because he said he was too drunk to drive home. She said sure and she went back to bed. When she got up early the next morning, John was already gone. It was only a matter of days later when the police found a body of a girl not far from Linda's home. At that time, nobody put two and two together."

This was news to both Harris and Lisa. Who was the murdered girl? Why hadn't this come up before? Harris was intrigued by this information. John had deposited Debbie Sloan's body in the ravine around 3 AM, he had returned home from the Garberville dance about 3 AM, and Harris surmised he had probably killed Andrea around 3 AM, after the bars had closed. Three AM seemed to be within John's comfort zone for murder. Try as they might, however, Lisa and Harris could find no information about a murdered girl near Loleta in 1978, though they noted in a report that there were three homicides in Humboldt County in 1978. So who was the murdered girl that everyone was talking about?

Lisa had an interesting conversation with Pam on October 24, 2004. It concerned John and his abandonment of Andrea in Colorado in 1979. Pam said that a guy named Gary Lorenzo remembered that incident. Now it was a matter of finding the right Gary Lorenzo. Lisa and Pam talked for more than three hours on the phone, sharing information.

Then Pam remembered a name from the distant past, and shared it with Harris. The name was Steve Harding. Steve had cared for Sherry very much back in 1976 and she remembered a conversation they had. "Just before James and I moved out to Colorado, Steve asked me how I was doing. It was in regards to Sherry. My reply was, 'As good as can be expected.' Then I told him, 'I look at every guy and wonder if he could be the one.'"

Pam added, "My guess, back at that dance, John must have told Sherry that he would take her to come and visit me before he took her home. I know the detectives in Humboldt will never get their act together regarding Sherry.

"I remember one time, John came out to see us on a three-day visit after the spring of 1976. He said he was doing some investigating of his own to help my family find out who killed Sherry. He made a big deal out of the fact that he was going on dates with a lot of different girls that were Sherry's friends. Who they were, I don't know. I remember that he did say a couple of names, but for the life of me I can't remember them now. The fact that he said he was trying to find the killer was a lie. I think he was just checking up on the girls to see what they knew."

In late November 2004, Harris sent Pam and James John's full confession in regards to Debbie Sloan's murder to Kurt Smallcomb and Tim Kiely. Pam was stunned by all the information in there and all of John's lies. She told Harris, "The part where John said I was his girlfriend was really something! I was never John's girlfriend! I was friends with both him and James back then, when we were in the eighth grade. Sometimes I talked to John more and sometimes I talked to James more. John really always had a crush on Vicki.

"Then there was the thing with Beth. John many times created arguments with Beth when they were married so that he could leave. He would be gone for days and then come back as though nothing had happened. In his confession, he made a comment about getting something out of his duffel bag. Well, that tells me that he planned on an argument that day [Thanksgiving 1998]. He was packed up and ready to go. He also had a sleeping bag with him. These are not things that someone who loves his wife so much would casually keep in their car.

"John planned on leaving that day and looking for any gal that he could. I think he craved to kill women. It gave him a real rush or power trip. James kept commenting about John's confession about how evil he really was. John tried to portray the caring husband and that he's not a thief. I could read between the lines that in reality he doesn't care that much for his own kids.

"One thing I do know: Debra [*sic*] was with the wrong person at the wrong time. John killed her because he had the need to do it. I mean, why would you kill for your wife if you didn't honor your marriage enough to be true and faithful? In fact, Beth had been seeing someone the year before—she was with John for security. She was so young when he met her. She needed someone to take care of her. They did not have a blissful marriage. I'll sign off for now. It starts to raise my blood pressure when thinking about all of this."

Lisa also received a transcript of John's confession from Harris. She said, "I couldn't put it down. I took my time digesting everything about John's state of mind." And then she wrote "Thank You!" Forty times.

If Lisa was thanking Harris, this was not the case in her fax to Worth Dikeman, the Deputy DA who supposedly had her sister's case at the Humboldt DA's office. She wrote:

Please accept this as my formal written request in trying to obtain information regarding my sister Andrea LaDeRoute's case, which occurred 3/17/80. When I spoke with you last July, you informed me that you had been reviewing the case, so therefore I am presenting this request to you as the prosecutor assigned to Andrea's case.

I have repeatedly requested information, verbally and in writing, regarding the status of my sister's case for the past twenty-four years. However, I have still not received any written information, such as the final disposition on the arrest and arraignment of John A. Annibel, who was extradited in April 1980. I recall making a sworn statement in front of Judge Buffington, and approximately twelve others who were there, in which my statements were recorded. I am asking at this time that I receive a copy of that court document, as well as the final disposition from the April 1980 arrest and discharge and any transcripts from the questioning [See Public Record docket #G36893]. I also wish to have other public documents provided for me.

I would also like copies of the transcripts generated while I was under hypnosis, as was requested and performed at the District Attorney's Office. At the time I was told I would receive copies of the transcripts. To date, I have yet to see them.

Additionally, I would like to be informed in writing why I am not entitled to specific information such as reviewing the coroner's file for Andrea. Since the recovery of my sister's remains, I realize that her case has been reevaluated, and as such, I am requesting a written disposition of her case. Please respond to my request in writing by December 6, 2004. I understand that you are busy, but according to penal codes, all felony cases of serious crimes have precedence over all other criminal and civil cases.

I am requesting the information as the sole representative for my sister, Andrea, the homicide victim, pursuant to the following California Penal Codes and statutes:

"Pursuant to Penal Code 1118.10(d): As used in this section, "final disposition" means an ultimate termination of the case at the trial level including, but not limited to, dismissal, acquittal, or imposition of sentence by the court, or a decision by the prosecuting attorney for whatever reason not to file the case."

"Pursuant to CA Penal Code 1315.1: When a disposition described in section 1315.1 is one of dismissal of the charge, the disposition report shall state one of the following reasons as appropriate: (a) Dismissal in furtherance of justice, pursuant to Section 1385 of the Penal Code."

Lisa listed several other statutes of the California Penal Code and then wrote:

I appreciate everyone's efforts in working on my sister's case, and I understand that it has become a very complex case. However, I hope you can appreciate that I have been very patient waiting for information, including whether or not charges will ever be filed.

Respectfully,
Lisa Lawler

Like her other faxes, letters, and phone calls to the DA's office, this one went unanswered as well.

Lisa told Harris, "I expect them not to respond, as usual. I've already downloaded the writ of mandate and I'm prepared to file it as soon as the ten days expire. Because of my past jobs, I've filed, without an attorney, three small claims, fifteen unlawful detainers and writs of possession, three bankruptcy cases, one restraining order, and three labor disputes. I was twenty when I filed my first case."

That same day Harris heard from Pam. She said, "James and I both agree that John was lying throughout his confession about Debbie. He was going on about how he really cared about his daughters. It was unbelievable! I truly believe he liked the sound of her [Debbie] dying after he choked her. My personal profile of him is that he killed so many times because he got a rush from watching his victims die. John is a born killer."

As December rolled around, Harris pondered the fact that it had been forty years since the great floods on the Eel River that had torn the region apart in 1964, and sent the Annibel family and others like them scurrying to higher ground. The *Eureka Times-Standard* pondered this event as well in a series of articles describing the destruction and chaos of that time. Dairy farmer Oma Rowley recalled looking down Main Street in Ferndale. She told a reporter, "I remember seeing nothing but water." Her aunt and uncle had owned the Alton store. After the flood, many of the items from the store were found miles away. "I remember cleaning that store after the flood, and the mud was so deep, it pulled your boots off."

Even on Christmas Day 2004, Lisa contacted Harris. After opening presents she told him that "every day is Christmas Day for Sandy and me." Then she admitted that Andrea was foremost on her mind. She said, "I'm going to finish the complaint.

With God's help I'll be able to fax a draft of it tomorrow. My initial thought is to file on issue of personal injury. Items will be mostly for emotional distress because of failure to respond to my numerous requests asking for the disposition of her case and return of her personal property, such as her photo album and her address books. This is just the tip of the iceberg of what I plan to state in my personal-injury claim.

"In addition, I will include a petition for disclosure, citing the laws that I've already stated in my letter to Worth Dikeman. I will also include a notice of inclusion, which requires that my case be decided within the one-year period without any exceptions or exemptions. Once I have filed a complaint of this nature, I am entitled to discovery, just like any other attorney would be. Although, I'm sure my requests will continue to be denied, I'll either sink or swim with this. Here goes!

"I've decided to take another method, meaning I'll file a complaint versus filing a writ. I want to:

1. Get the DA to provide me with info that I'm entitled to, and stop stonewalling me, and for them to be accountable for their actions and lack of actions.

2. Present in court all of the discovery on John Annibel in Sherry's case and Andrea's case, to determine if criminal charges are warranted. With the intention of judicial review someone can agree that there is enough substantial evidence to pursue criminal charges.

3. Let the DA's Office know that after twenty-four years, I'm not playing around anymore.

"I really don't want to take the wrongful-death approach, but since personal injury will be difficult to prove without including wrongful death, I don't have much choice. I feel I should include Andrea as a plaintiff. It is one of those unorthodox moves, but it really is one of those moves you make to ensure that they can't eliminate any information.

"It has never been my intention to sue for monetary gain; however, in order to file a complaint, I have to list a monetary value. When you review the forms, you'll understand. If I choose an unlimited amount, the case would have to be heard by a jury. There are pros and cons to that. Yet—I expect to get complete resistance from the court and county during this process. Once they have rejected my complaint, then I will proceed with the writ of mandate. Since I will be stonewalled by Humboldt County, I can trying filing my writ in the Second District Court in San Francisco."

Harris agreed she needed to try through the courts system. He also gave her a word of warning. "Once your papers start going through the court, I really worry for your safety. Please get all the protection you can from Dave Douglas [now the police chief of Eureka]. I'm really glad you live within the Eureka city limits. If you were on county land, I believe things would be worse. It's obvious that Dave is a good guy."

A few days into 2005, Pam Annibel contacted Harris and said, "If the detectives working on Georgina's case would like to talk to me, that is fine with me. I would love to talk to those guys that grilled John. I would love for anyone to solve any murder, including Sherry's."

By January 11, Lisa was getting more harassment. She told Harris, "I've received several strange calls at work this week. When I finally confronted the person, they hung up on me. I couldn't tell if it was a male or female. My whole life seems to be in the balance right now. It is a good versus-evil-period, and I'm trying to fight the evil."

Soon thereafter, Lisa revealed some startling news to Harris—someone she knew was in contact with Tom Smith, one of John Annibel's old buddies from the 1976–1980 days. Lisa said, "A woman named Julie and my mom were friends. They were so alike in personality. When my mom died, I saw and felt so much of my mom in her. It was almost uncanny. Then we didn't see each other for a long, long time.

"About five months ago, I just happened to see Julie walking down the street. We noticed each other at the same time. Both of our faces lit up, and I pulled her over while she ran toward me and we ran into each other for the biggest hug.

"Last week, Sandy and I started making plans for our Super

Bowl party. Julie's boyfriend, Robert, had agreed to come with her because he is a big football fan. Then a few days ago, Julie called me and asked if she could bring a couple of friends over. They were named Tom and Lynn. Something told me to keep asking questions about Tom and Lynn. Julie said, 'They're named Tom and Lynn Smith.'

"I asked where they were from, and she said from around the Fortuna area. I asked how old they were, and she said that they were probably in their mid-forties. I told her I might know them. It may not be them, but if it is, he and I are going to say, 'Oh, my God!'

"Of course, it was Tom Smith, who had given John a ride home the day he got out of jail in 1980. John was in that very car when he looked over at me at the stoplight and gave me that evil stare.

"We went over to Robert and Julie's house later on, and she told him I might know Tom Smith. It was the serious way he looked at me that made me feel I needed to explain. I asked Robert if Tom had a younger brother, and he said yes. I said I wasn't sure if it was the same Tom, but if it was, I knew him through Mike Cortopassi. Before I could say anything else, Robert smiled and said, 'If you know Cortopassi, then you know Tom.'

"Tom Smith is the guy who Mike Cortopassi once said was a good buddy of John's. Tom's younger brother, according to Linda in Redway, is the guy who went to Colorado with John and Andrea in 1979 when John dropped her off in the middle of nowhere. This was a couple of months before she disappeared.

"All these years when I questioned detectives if they'd ever questioned Tom Smith, I always got, 'I never heard of him before. Did you tell other detectives?' Even more recently, within the last couple of years, Sergeant Rogers said we would never find him.

"Mike Cortopassi and Tom were good friends. In fact, that's how I first met Mike. It was because he and Tom were out cruising together. My girlfriend and I were out on the sidewalk, and they finally stopped to get our names. Mike and I were together to such an extent he wanted me to move to Colorado with him in 1980, and I probably would have done it if Andrea hadn't turned up missing.

"Oh, at the Super Bowl party, I'll pretend to be noninterested. If it's really him, he'll know who I am because of all the pictures of me when I was younger in our house, and of Anghs, too. I'm hoping he'll want to talk. All I know is, if this is *the* Tom Smith, then this is no coincidence. I don't know how anyone could have put Julie and me together after nine years. This all has to be for some purpose, and I don't see how I can pass up this opportunity. I know it could be dangerous, but I'd rather know when they're coming than have them sneak up on me in the yard so to speak."

The "they" in Lisa's conversation wasn't directed just at Tom Smith and Julie as far as she was concerned, but rather at the whole district attorney's office in Humboldt County, as well as some of the Fortuna Police Department.

Harris told her, "I think your meeting with Tom on Super Bowl Sunday is very important. I believe this is an opportunity that can't be passed up. But be careful. I don't know where all of this is going, and too many funny things have happened already to you."

February 5, 2005 dawned in Eureka, and in between a rush of preparations, Lisa e-mailed Harris. "Even though I'm trying to keep the situation in perspective, I am also trying to plan how to react if I do know him. If he acts like he doesn't know me, I'm going to follow his lead, and just observe. Maybe some time later he might see something that triggers his memory.

"I just wish I knew for sure. The suspense is hanging in the back of my thoughts, and intensifies with each minute. Deep breaths and staying busy—that's what I've go to do."

At 4:42 PM, she e-mailed Harris again. "I am very nervous, but I'm staying busy trying to plan the biggest party of the year for Sandy. He loves football so much. He says it's like Thanksgiving and Christmas all in one day. Wish you were here."

The suspense was getting to Harris as well. He couldn't concentrate on the Super Bowl game. Neither one of the teams playing was "his team." All of it seemed somehow disjointed and uninteresting. What the hell was going on up there in Eureka in Lisa's house? Was Tom Smith a "good guy" or a "bad guy"? Was he even *the* Tom Smith? Harris stewed and waited for a message from Lisa.

At 4:45 PM it came with a two word title—"It's him!"

Lisa wrote, "It's him, so far so good. He acknowledged me, and he seems to want to be close enough to me to talk. I've only been around him a few minutes. I'll keep you posted throughout the game."

She did just that, with bits and pieces of information flowing over their computer screens.

"It's definitely him," Lisa wrote later. "He saw all the pictures. I found out from him where Mike Cortopassi lives now. He's just forty-five minutes down Highway 36, which is really close to where Anghs was found. I found out that Mike's grandmother just passed away a month ago, and he inherited the property. Gotta go."

Later, "Mitch [one of the guests] has connected with Tom on a common interest—looking for old Indian arrowheads and coins. Tom said he knew an area in the middle of nowhere where they could go. So they exchanged addresses, and lo and behold, Tom and his girlfriend live only two blocks away from me! Gotta go now. Someone's coming."

The next day Lisa wrote, "I'm still trying to digest everything. I was so exhausted, I almost didn't make it to work today. How weird. That was really him! He's lived around the corner from me for years. Unbelievable! I don't know what to make of all this. Why him? Why now?

"Oh, one more thing," Lisa said. "I read in the paper the other day that Roger Hudnall was arrested for auto theft. I haven't seen his name in the public records since then. So I don't know if he was charged or sentenced. But if he is, he would have also been charged for violating his parole. I thought this might send him back to the pokey for a while. All of this is very strange. Sometimes I feel like I'm in the middle of a murder mystery. Except all of this is real life."

It was around this time, that Harris noticed an interesting article in the *Eureka Times-Standard*. The article concerned Deputy DA Tim Stoen apologizing to Les Kinsolving, who had been a reporter for the *San Francisco Examiner* back in 1972. Kinsolving was one of the first reporters to question some of the tactics of Jim Jones and the People's Temple. Kinsolving wrote about Temple guards packing .357 Magnums. In response several People's Temple members harassed Kinsolving and picketed the *Examiner* offices. Tim Stoen, as attorney for Jim Jones, filed a libel suit against Kinsolving.

In March 2005, Stoen heard that Kinsolving had recently had a heart attack. Stoen wrote him a letter which later appeared in the *Santa Rosa Press Democrat*. In part Stoen said he was sorry for the way he and others had treated Kinsolving and asked for forgiveness. Stoen said he'd made a terrible mistake by believing in Jim Jones utopian plans. He praised Kinsolving for taking on Jones's "Machiavellian" schemes when others were too fainthearted to do so. At the end of the letter, Stoen said that he prayed that Kinsolving could forgive him. Stoen seemed genuinely concerned that he had been wrong about Jim Jones and the trouble the issue had caused Kinsolving.

Yet at the same time, Stoen, on behalf of the Humboldt DA's office, was pressing charges against Debi August, a Fortuna councilwoman, for what many in the county thought were political reasons. August was a realtor in Fortuna, and the charge was that she had used her office to help a friend who was in construction. To many people in the county, however, the real reason Debi August was being charged was because she had been an outspoken opponent of DA Paul Gallegos in the recall election, and an opponent of Tim Stoen in his stance regarding the Pacific Lumber lawsuit. A lot of August's constituents were Pacific Lumber employees.

Meanwhile, Pam Annibel was giving Harris more details about the location where Sherry's body had been found in 1976. She said, "The spot was about ten minutes from the Annibel home up on Eel Rock Road. When you drive up the main road, it forks at the top. The Annibels' home and Ron Stone's home and Fred Lane's home are on the left fork. Sherry was on the right fork just past the dump, and where they found her was very secluded. You have to know that spot because from the road it looks like bushes and trees are overgrown there. John did know the spot. Like I said, he actually asked me if I wanted to see where they found her. I said yes, not thinking at the time why he knew.

"I think the reason John wanted to tell me about Sherry that morning in May 1976 was to take away suspicion from him. The look on his face, though—I remember it was very chilling, as though he was thinking about what he had done, or even how she looked while he was doing it."

In mid-March 2005, Lisa told Harris, "I've pretty much cut off communications with Julie ever since the Super Bowl game. She's been pretty persistent about calling me at least once or twice every day. I don't know why. She just leaves a lot of messages on my answering machine. I don't know what her connection is to Tom Smith or John and it's getting kind of scary. She wanted me to come by and pick up some envelope that was supposed to be in a box near her front porch. I'm not going to pick up some envelope and not know what's inside it! I feel like I'm being set up."

After the whole mess with Roger Hudnall, Harris agreed that this was the best policy for Lisa to adopt.

Quirky things like this kept surfacing. Harris reread an article from the 1998 *Humboldt Beacon*, and a strange thing caught his eye. In the article was one line—"When police searched his [John Annibel's] cabin in Fortuna with a search warrant, they found blood on the bedclothes and walls." Bedclothes? This was the first time Harris had heard about police finding blood on the bedclothes. Was the reporter wrong about this? Or was he right, and the fact did not appear in later police reports?

Another thing Harris noted was a strange marking in Andrea's letter of February 7, 1980. He told Lisa, "In looking over her letter, she is writing about being at College of the Redwoods and her counselors there. But look on page two in the margin. It hits you like a ton of bricks! There is one word. The word is 'afraid.'"

"What does she mean by that? Afraid of John? Afraid of what? The word 'afraid' does not go with anything else on that page. Of course, in a few more weeks from that time, John will have killed her."

By April 2005, Harris was sending Lisa a lot of information she hadn't heard before, and he broke things down into various sections. All of his information came from law-enforcement papers and documents from Humboldt County that had surfaced in the Mendocino County court system during the Debbie Sloan trial.

1. "Ron Stone was at the Garberville dance in 1976. Three different people put him there. But he was probably with his girlfriend, Paula Wise."

2. "Bruce Johnson, the guy John and Andrea supposedly got the bed from, was a friend of John's since elementary school. Bruce Johnson lived in Stafford, but I don't know if he's still there.

3. "Rick Malcomb was a friend of John's since elementary school. He had a brother named Randy Malcomb. According to one police report, Randy may have cleaned up John's apartment in late March 1980. He probably didn't know he was cleaning up a crime scene. According to a report, Rick Malcomb supposedly had two vehicles around John and Andrea's place in March 1980. I don't know if they ran or not. One was a Jeep Wagoneer. The other was a Volkswagen, and I'm only guessing, maybe a Volkswagen Beetle.

4. "John said some things to people in 1980. Here is what is recalled by those people. 'She [Andrea] was going to the Rainbow storage unit in Eureka. Her sister [Lisa] gave her a lot of stuff, and she kept it in storage. Her aunt Carmen also gave her stuff.'

5. "About the laundry on that day you arrived with Max—John said, 'I just got back from the laundry and was folding clothes when Lisa showed up.' He does not

mention Max being there. Also, you said that you and Max got there first. And that John arrived with the bags of laundry later.

6. "John said he phoned you about Andrea being missing. He said this happened on the eighteenth or nineteenth of April. But I thought you said that he never phoned you.

7. "About Andrea's dress and slip, John said, 'I found a dress for Lisa. Not a slip.' He said he gave you Andrea's dress.

8. "John said that three weeks before Andrea went missing, they had a fight. She left him for the night and supposedly spent the night with you at your apartment. John then said, 'Lisa and Andrea went discoing at the Red Pepper.'

9. "John said that it was this fight that made him move to Fortuna with Andrea so he could be with her more often. When Andrea was at Myers Flat, she had to be driven down to the bus stop, and then she had a long bus trip to College of the Redwoods.

10. "When John was asked why he never checked for Andrea at College of the Redwoods, he said that he didn't know anyone there, and it wouldn't have helped.

11. "Here's what John said about learning that he might be arrested in Colorado. 'Tom Smith called from Humboldt County and told me that there was a warrant out for my arrest and they were coming to get me. So I had my mom call the Fortuna PD. And they said it wasn't true. So then I didn't worry about it.'

12. "John did say he was scheduled to fly back to California on Air West the day after he was arrested in Denver.

13. "Now here's something interesting about what John said when you and Terry McCloskey, Dave Cross, and

Ethel Reed showed up at his place. 'Lisa came by my place about midnight. Her and a bunch of her drunk friends. It really annoyed me. I don't like to see people get drunk and make an ass of themselves.' John did not mention your friend, saying, 'We know you did it, John! We know you killed her!' But you and I know that's what made John leave the area the very next day.

14. "Also, there's the odd thing about his Camaro being wrecked in March 1980. John said it happened on a Sunday night. That's the last time anyone saw Andrea alive. John said that the fender hit a pole in front of his house. Could John and Andrea have been having a fight about this? We always thought he killed her because she was trying to leave him. What if Billy Ryan was right, and Andrea had tried to drive John's car that night and dented the bumper? Maybe he got mad enough to kill her. I don't know, I'm just throwing these things out. Something set John off sometime between March sixteenth and the morning of March seventeenth."

Lisa responded to some of Harris's questions, though not in the order he had presented them. She said, "When Max and I went to the apartment, I didn't expect to see John there because it was in the middle of the workday. And when his car wasn't there, I assumed he wasn't, either. I can remember Max thinking I was stupid for knocking on John's door. Right after we taped the poster of Andrea on the front door, John showed up. He had several large garbage bags that he said were laundry, and he put them in the small storage room right outside the apartment.

"I still believe it was a slip he gave me, and not a dress.

"Now if he and Andrea did have a fight, why would he be doing her laundry? If they didn't have a fight, why would he be taking time off work to do laundry in the middle of the day?

"The fight he's probably referring to occurred a few months before she disappeared, when he left her in Colorado. That's when she came to stay with me because she didn't want to go back to Myers Flat. I don't remember if we went out dancing, but we had gone to the Red Pepper in Arcata a lot. It was a discotheque. As soon as he got back from Colorado, he picked her up from where I was staying at my girlfriend's mom's house. A few weeks later they moved into the cabin in Fortuna.

"Yes, Ethel was really drunk and I asked John when I knocked on the door if we could talk to him. He invited us in, even though he didn't have to. I gave him my phone numbers at home and at work. At the time I thought he might not have my phone numbers, since he hadn't called me before. I had been drinking too, but I wasn't sloppy drunk. Just tipsy enough to get up the courage to confront him.

"I noticed on Anghs's card to Mom dated February 14, 1980, where she said that John bought her a car and that she was going to drive it up to see her. I still don't believe she had a license, but she may have gotten a permit. How and when I don't know. Anghs was really intimidated by cars. I think this was because she had no sense of direction. Even just before she disappeared, she didn't know which direction Arcata was from Eureka.

"I wonder why Mike and Tom were talking long distance about Anghs and I. It seems strange to me that Mike would have called Tom. It seems more likely that Tom would be calling Mike to see what I had told him and then reporting the info back to John. But what was it that had Tom so involved? Was he just friends with James and John? It was Mike who told me that John was flying back to Humboldt County. This info had to come straight from John to someone else who had spoken to Mike, knowing that this date would probably get back to me. Was this an attempt to frighten me?

"Why would John fly back, since he didn't think there was an arrest warrant out for him? It couldn't have been for his job, since he hadn't notified them that he was suddenly taking off for Colorado. I think he really wanted to come back to silence me."

Two days later, Harris had a new list of items for Lisa, once again, with more information that had come directly from law-enforcement reports.

1. "According to Rick Malcomb, he came back to Humboldt County from Denver in 1981 and married Linda. They tried staying in Humboldt but didn't make enough money. So they went back to Colorado to work and live. Rick said that he sold his wife's car to John in May 1981. He also said that John stiffed him for about $250 on that car. I don't know what make it was.

2. "Rick Malcomb told someone, 'John always spent a lot of time on back roads.' Well, we know that Andrea's body was dumped on a back road. So was Sherry's body, Georgina's body, and Debbie's body.

3. "Rick Malcomb got the impression from John that Sherry Smith was murdered somewhere down in the Bay Area. John was obviously trying to throw him off-track, and Rick did not grow up in the Miranda area, so he didn't know it well. He grew up in the Fortuna area.

4. "Rick did meet Andrea a couple of times up at the Annibel place. That must have been in 1979. He said he never did see John and Andrea fight.

5. "Rick was not living over at James and Pam's place in Denver when John was arrested. He was living at some other guy's place. Rick was visiting James Annibel's residence on the day that John was arrested. Rick saw everything go down.

6. "John did have a reservation for an 11 AM flight from Denver back to California on Air West. But of course he was arrested before he could come back.

7. "Here is another lie from John. He told a police detective that he had paid three months' advance rent on the apartment he shared with Andrea on Ninth Street in Fortuna. The landlord said differently. In fact, the landlord said that John was already past due for the April rent. John did not stick around to get a refund. Originally he said he was going to send his dad over to clean up the apartment so he could get his deposit back, but I don't think

his dad ever went to do that. There is a good possibility that Rick Malcomb's brother, Randy, did, according to a police report. This is for sure: when the detectives went into the apartment, they found that the blood on the wall had been wiped. Whether John or Randy did that, I don't know."

To all of this, Lisa said, "Wow! I never saw any blood on anything, but the lighting in the cabin was always pretty gloomy. I know in the bathroom, where I turned on the light and looked, there wasn't any blood that I could see. I also didn't see Andrea's wallet on the toilet. I know that I would have noticed that. I was also looking to see if she had taken her toothbrush, makeup, and nail polish. All of that was still there. I also noticed her wristwatch hanging on a nail on the wall. Just this black wristwatch hanging on the wall. Andrea would have taken all those things if she had left John."

Harris was sending Lisa item after item that he had recently uncovered.

1. "John was trying to tell the cops in 1980 that he thought Andrea had gone back to Billy Ryan. Of course he was lying. Billy never saw her after March 16, 1980.

2. "Another excuse John gave the cops for leaving for Colorado was that he owed money to Pacific Finance. He said he just wanted to skip town. At least that was his story.

3. "John did say that when he went to Denver he took one pillow and some blankets. And one of the blankets did have some dirt and twigs on it. You have to wonder if there was blood on the blanket as well. Remember, he used a blanket to haul Debbie Sloan's body out of the cottage motel. And we know from detective's documents that it was Andrea's blood in the apartment.

4. "Since the cops didn't find much in the way of bedsheets at Ninth Street, they asked John about this. He told them,

'We didn't have a lot. Some of what we did have was like rags.' I doubt if Andrea would have been willing to sleep on rags. She liked nice things and had a sense of style.

5. "John and Rick Malcomb did stop by Bruce Johnson's place before leaving for Colorado. This is according to Rick Malcomb. They told Johnson they were going to Denver.

6. "Here's another bullshit statement from John about the laundry at the cabin. 'I just got back from the laundry with my cousin. He had to do some laundry and I did, too. I just came back and was folding laundry when Lisa showed up.' But of course you said you were already there with Max, sticking up a poster of Andrea, when John showed up with bags full of laundry that he quickly put into a storage shed.

7. "Here's another lie from John. 'I just put her [Andrea's] laundry out in the washroom. I figured she would get it if she came back.' So the cops asked him if Andrea had a key to the washroom, and he admitted that she didn't. So how in hell was she supposed to pick it up if she didn't even have a key? Of course she couldn't pick it up. She was already dead.

8. "John told the cops that Andrea had possessed a driver's license for four or five months by March 1980. He indicated it was a permanent one. I wonder if the detectives ever looked into this.

9. "The cops asked John why the garbage can for the cabin was missing. He said it had just been stolen. The cops were pretty interested in that garbage can. Of course a garbage can is a place where someone would think to throw away bloody rags, etc."

Harris also related the stories John had been telling the cops about Andrea to Lisa. John said that one time in Eureka that

Andrea had been so drunk, he had slapped her and left her on the street. Another time he said she had bitten him while performing oral sex, and he hit her hard. Another strange incident was John's purchase of a new garden hose for the apartment.

Lisa responded, "It was so strange to read what you sent me. Now after reading it, some of it is coming back to me. I know John was always asking Andrea for oral sex. It wouldn't surprise me if Anghs bit him while performing oral sex, especially if she felt forced. Especially if she had been drinking. That's one thing undeniable, Anghs couldn't drink. Not even a few beers. She was so tiny and petite, along with her Native American nationality, her body couldn't tolerate the alcohol.

"Now about the garden hose, let's say he did buy it to clean out the garbage can that he claims was stolen. Where would he have taken it to clean it? Outside the cabin? It would have had to been a place with an outside spigot and that didn't already have a garden hose attached. The house in front might have had a spigot, but probably not John's cabin.

"I am still amazed that out of the three times I was in that cabin in Fortuna, I didn't see any signs of blood. I don't even remember seeing a mirror, as one of the news articles or police reports stated. It said they found streaks of blood on a mirror next to the bed.

"I'm also amazed at just how much detail John provided about incidents back then. It's as though he's not concerned at all about giving certain details, and he only leaves out the critical details, like Ethel telling him repeatedly, 'We know you did it, John! You might as well admit it. We know you killed her!'

"And what about any medical records in Fortuna? According to Billy Ryan's sister Lori, she had to drive Andrea to the hospital in the middle of the night after John had beaten her up one time. I can't remember the details, but I think she had bruised or broken ribs. Anghs never said anything to me about this. I wonder why she kept it from me. Probably she knew I would go nuts on him."

Harris was not only sharing information he gathered to Lisa, he was doing so with Pam as well. He told her, "Here is a little bit more about Sherry's crime scene on Eel Rock Road. A car broke traction in the middle of the road and backed up. It came to a stop and then something heavy was dragged from it to where Sherry's body was found. That something must have been Sherry's body. The tire-tread marks did match the ones on John's 1969 Mustang.

"Now, I'm wondering if John later took you to the right spot where Sherry's body was found by detectives. The place where John said she was discovered—was it along a fence? I'm guessing the fence must have been a barbed-wire fence. This fence is mentioned in a police report. Also, if you can recollect, were there any power poles up there? Anything like that bringing electricity into the area?

"Now I don't know if this is relevant. Sherry was found with her head downhill. Georgina Pacheco was found with her head downhill. And Debbie Sloan was found with her head down facing downhill. With Andrea we will never know. Only part of her skull and jawbone were ever found."

Pam answered back, "I asked James if there is a fence at the place where John showed us. He thinks that there is. It is sort of hard to remember that spot. We haven't been there in over twenty-eight years. As far as power poles, they are all over the place up on that hill. I don't know if there is one at that particular spot.

"As far as the heads being downhill, that's interesting. Maybe it's the way he pulled them, you know—by their arms. Andrea was probably in the same position, too. They all seem to be found on a downslope or a ravine or something like that.

"I don't know who Sherry's boyfriend was at the time. She had a few boyfriends that she was really close to at different times. I've heard that Stillwell was one. She preferred the Indian guys. One guy was a little older and lived in Fortuna. He played in a band. Mom said that after Sherry's death, some boy Sherry had met in Santa Cruz called her. He was shocked that Sherry was dead."

A few days later, Harris informed Lisa, "According to reports, John said that Andrea had three purses and two wallets. He said she had a white purse made of macrame, a brown purse with a strap, and a blue or black purse with a strap. The purse that you never saw in the beginning, he said he found it on the bottom of the closet under a bunch of stuff. Now what woman would do that? Don't you usually put them on a table or hang them up by the strap? You wouldn't just throw them on a closet floor underneath some clothes, would you?

"Then John told detectives that Andrea had bought a new wallet around February 25, 1980. He said she liked it better than the old one because the new one had a mirror. How did he know about a mirror? Not too many guys look inside a woman's wallet.

"John said on the day he last saw Andrea, she was going to school wearing jeans, boots, and carrying a purse with a strap and books. One time he said she walked to the bus stop, and another time he said he drove her there. So which is it?"

To all of this Lisa answered, "I was told by police back then that they found the wallet stripped empty on the back of the toilet, not a purse. A purse was later found in Humboldt Bay and it was Andrea's favorite and most-used purse. It also contained her key ring with a leather initial "A" on it. Anghs probably had a few purses, but the other purses would have been for special outfits or something. Not everyday use.

"The police told me he had mentioned, in her missing-person report, that she was wearing the rust-colored jacket. This is why Detective Floyd Stokes was insistent I try to recall the jacket, even using hypnosis. However, during hypnosis the jacket, as I recall, was never brought up. I also remember that Mom had bought that jacket for Anghs for the Christmas of 1979. It was one of those nice ski jackets. I feel it crucial to see what other inconsistencies John brought up.

"John said the last time he saw her she was going to school. We both know she didn't have classes that day. In one report he also says she was going to the storage unit with a sheet and garbage bags because it had a leak or something. How did he know about the storage unit; or leak? In fact, when we checked later, the storage unit didn't have a leak at all. John was not supposed to have a key to that unit, he was not supposed to know it existed at all. Had he found one of Andrea's keys and forced her to tell him what it was for? I don't know.

"According to Max, Andrea was supposed to call him the morning of the seventeenth for him to pick her up and take her to cash her check for school. Max always helped Andrea cash her check primarily because she didn't have a checking account and she didn't have any transportation other than the bus.

"And according to John, one in a statement to the Fortuna PD, he was too upset to go to work after having a fight with Anghs the night before. The fact is, if they had a fight, Andrea would have been there waiting for Max to pick her up that morning. In fact, in a second statement John said he did go to work and mentioned nothing about a fight with Andrea. He said that when he got home Andrea wasn't there and she hadn't left him a note. I suspect he didn't go to work that day, and he spent the day trying to clean up the apartment. The detectives ought to have his employment attendance record. It would make sense to be afraid to tell the police about work, because they could check up on him.

"The real question is: Where were John and Andrea the night before? Did anybody see them the night before? Did Billy Ryan really see them at the Town Club? If Andrea was drinking, she might have said something that really pissed John off. He even told the detectives that she called him a mama's boy at one point. He said it bothered him a little bit. I'll bet it bothered him a lot. When did they go to bed that night? When did they wake up? So when was the last time John really saw Anghs alive?

"And one more thing: Sergeant Rogers said that Andrea never did cash her final school check."

Rumors still swirled around many aspects of the cases. Both Harris and Lisa had heard that the hacksaw had been found in the cabin that John and Andrea shared. There was also one police report that said it was found in the trunk of the car John had taken to Colorado. Which one was true? Or were there two hacksaws? And why was only one sent to the FBI lab if there were two?

* * *

In mid-April, Harris obtained a transcript of Mike Losey and Steve Rogers's comments on the stand in Debbie Sloan's preliminary hearing. Then-prosecutor Mark Kalina had been trying to get their testimony about Andrea into the Sloan trial without success but their testimony was still public record, and Lisa had never seen it. Harris sent her a copy which totaled almost 150 pages.

Lisa e-mailed him back in huge letters: "I JUST CAN'T BELIEVE IT!

"I'm in a state of shock. I know all cops and prosecutors aren't bad, but why didn't any of them in Humboldt show me this before? I can't tell which ones are the good ones and which ones aren't anymore.

"I've always believed the authorities were there to protect everyone, regardless of economics, nationality, or personal preferences. Even though that's the way the system was designed, that's not reality. I will never know what influence John Annibel might have had over anyone for them to totally disregard the value of another human being. I mean, they had no idea who would be the next victim. They had enough information to believe there would be another one, and when another unsuspecting victim was murdered, they again turned their backs."

Harris replied, "As far as good cops and prosecutors go, don't lose faith. There are always some bad ones, just like in every other profession. It's just human nature."

Bits and pieces of information filtered in to Harris from everywhere. He learned that Sherry had liked an older guy named Terry Robinson, and learned that Sherry had told Glenda that she was not going to visit her mom in Miranda after the dance because her mom would be asleep by that time. Harris learned directly from Pam that John had never dated Sherry, as he had indicated to detectives.

Pam told him, "John never dated Sherry. He never went on a double date with Tom and Terry. One time, Sherry did go to the movies with me and James and John. But that was no date. It was just my little sister wanting to tag along for the ride."

As far as guys Sherry did like, Pam said, "Terry Robinson is the guy she had a major crush on. Sherry and Mike Stillwell were real good friends, and Fred Lane sometimes came up and hung out with us, but Fred was about 5' 3" and Sherry was about 5' 8", so that would have been a funny match.

"Fred drove a Chevelle and he bought it from James's older brother, Ted. I don't know who Michael Moore is from back then. Sherry knew so many people and had so many friends that none of us even knew about. I don't ever remember anyone named Frank. In fact, James and I never hung out around the area. We were always up in Fortuna.

"Sherry called my mom and sister to say that she had been up at Alderpoint and that after the dance she would be home. If she told someone she was going to see me instead of going straight home, I didn't know about it, but that would make her ascent up Eel Rock Road make sense. Once they got to the top, though, and John did not turn left toward the Annibel home at the forks, Sherry would have known. She knew which way to come and see me. It could have been at that point that she probably started getting mad at John. He may have thought because she had danced a lot with him and he was giving her a ride home, she owed him something.

"If they left at around 2 AM, it takes about forty minutes to get from point A to point B. It would have taken that long to get from the spot where they found her. It would make it about 2:40 to 2:45 AM. That would take twenty-five minutes to kill her and hide her body and ten more minutes to get home. I saw John pull up at exactly 3:15 AM.

"If Sherry knew Ron Stone at all, it would have been through John. Ron's Falcon was brown in color. He had bought it from James and John's dad, Ted. Ted had used it as a work car. He drove it everyday to Scotia to work at the mill.

"How Sherry knew Paula Wise is very interesting. Paula was two years older than me. I didn't know she was hanging out with anyone at the time. She was kind of strange. I had never known her to have a boyfriend.

"Sherry did feel comfortable hanging around John. She would have been comfortable around anyone that he knew. Since Sherry had a lot of friends, she probably danced with a lot of them. As she danced with other people, John probably became enraged. He was like that. He could sit and let things fester and become very agitated. He could go off the deep end real easy. Both James and I can picture that happening.

"That was really something for John to say he didn't know Ron Stone that well. John and Ron were thick as thieves! They were always hanging out with each other back in those days.

"One more thing—Sherry would have fought for her life. I heard that she did have skin and blood under her fingernails."

It was strange that some elderly people Harris had talked to in Fortuna had once lived up on Fruitland Ridge and knew John and all the Annibels. They also knew Sherry Lynn Smith. These people told Harris that rumors were going around up there that Sherry's eyebrows had been burnt. *How could they know this?* he wondered. It wasn't in the newspapers. And yet they were almost right on. Her eyelashes had been singed, and that was pretty close to eyebrows being burned. So who had spread the rumors? Someone who had to have known the facts.

Harris realized that it had been a long time since Pam had thought about people and places in Humboldt County, especially dating back to 1976. He told her, "I might have covered some of this before, but I'll go through it again just in case. The first officer on the scene was Sheriff's Deputy D.R. Roberts. Also there was Reserve Officer John Hutchins. The scene was released from Roberts to Lieutenant Simmons when Simmons arrived. The little dirt road was 1.1 miles south of the Kinnebrew residence. Then you went down the little dirt road for about 250 yards.

"Much, much later, in December 1998, Sheriff's Sergeant Juan Freeman was called to Mendocino County. He had been given Sherry's case in 1997, after Detective Lonnie Lawson retired. In December 1998, Freeman and Investigator Mike Losey talked to John Annibel, who was in jail because of the Debbie Sloan murder. Freeman was there to talk about Sherry and Losey about Andrea LaDeRoute. Around this time they also talked to Beth Annibel.

"Beth was mad because the newspapers had said that John had dated Sherry. She said it wasn't true. Beth told the detec-

tives that the first ten years of their marriage were good, but
then John lost his job at Louisiana Pacific in Fort Bragg and
went to work for Harwood Lumber in Branscomb. She said he
would drink a bottle of rum each night during this time, and
was using drugs, too. He started throwing things around the
house. She told the detectives he did not hit her, but that he
was verbally abusive toward her.

"Beth told them that Andrea's name was mentioned seven
or eight times during their marriage. Then Beth said, 'Mike
Losey told me that he is sure Andrea was murdered and will
not be found alive.'

"Investigator Losey, according to a report, had seen a slide
of the vaginal smear taken from Sherry Lynn Smith's body. It
showed strong traces of acid phosphate, which was the test for
semen in 1976. On December 22, 1998, Losey reported that he
would send the slide to the Department of Justice for analysis."

Harris could tell that both Investigator Losey and Sergeant
Rogers did a lot of investigative work in late 1998 and early
1999, right after John was arrested for the murder of Debbie
Sloan in Mendocino County. They developed some new information, and then it just stopped. Did someone in higher authority tell them to stop, and if so, why? They both worked for
separate agencies, so the fact that they ceased about the same
time was puzzling in the extreme. By then Rogers worked for
the Fortuna PD, and Losey was an investigator for the district
attorney's office. Also puzzling was Paul Smith's comment
about Detective Juan Freeman, who worked for the Humboldt County Sheriff's Department. Paul said that Freeman was
all excited one day because he said that Sherry's case was going
to be solved. According to Paul, Freeman came back the very
next day dejected and said that key evidence was missing.

There was still a lot of hinky stuff going on in Humboldt
County, as far as Harris was concerned, and an e-mail from
Lisa to him only strengthened that resolve. She told him that
she had gone to the library once again to look up old micro-
filmed newspaper articles about a 1978 murder in Miranda.

Sixteen-year-old Debbie Holland was the murder victim in that year. This case intrigued her, because it had so many similarities to the Sherry Lynn Smith murder. Same locale, same type of girl, same MO. Lisa read everything she could on the subject in old newspaper articles.

Debbie Lynette Holland had gone missing after attending South Fork High School in Miranda on February 22, 1978. For four days the sheriff's office scoured the area to no avail. Holland's parents and thirty civilian volunteers also searched the surrounding area. Then on March 4, 1978, a sheriff's deputy found Holland's body in an area they had already searched. It was not far away from the school, but it had cleverly been hidden under a pile of debris, tree limbs, and brush. In fact, under what appeared at first to be a deadfall.

As a newspaper recounted, Holland had been "sexually molested and strangled to death. Her body had been hidden under debris and other vegetation." Once again there was fear in the Miranda area, as there had been after Sherry Lynn Smith's murder only two years before. According to the *Eureka Times-Standard*, "It was only a five-minute hike here from the school, but it seemed far removed from civilization and as peaceful as a cathedral. This is where they found the body of Debbie Lynette Holland on a trail down a steep bank and into the redwoods by the Eel River."

Detectives questioned nearly 200 people in the days after Holland's body was discovered. Most of them were questioned at the command post set up in the high school library. Teacher Shirley Foster described Holland as "a nice girl, and trusting." Those were the same words used about Sherry Lynn Smith in 1976.

Holland had been seen by friend Donna Burcia at lunch time in the cafeteria on February 22, where some girls had teased Holland about a boy she was supposed to like. Burcia saw Holland again in her fifth-period class where she discussed about joining the Rainbow Girls.

Just a few minutes before 3 PM, Principal Leroy Burger saw Holland in the hallway and asked her what she was doing out of class. It was nearly time for school to let out, however, so he let her go.

Sometime that afternoon Holland phoned her mother and said she was going to see about getting another rabbit to be a companion for the one she already had. Holland never got on the school bus or came home. The following day her backpack and jacket were found in the school library.

When her body was found, the newspapers noted that she was the fifth young woman to be raped, strangled, and left dead in an isolated area. Lisa was astounded, however, when the papers spoke of the Janet Bowman case and Karen Fisher case but not the Sherry Lynn Smith case. She said later, "The Sherry Lynn Smith case was the most obvious link of all! It had happened in the same vicinity of Miranda with a girl that looked like Debbie Holland, and had the same MO—raped, strangled, and left in the woods. But not one word about Sherry or John Annibel. According to the police, John was still the primary suspect in the Sherry Lynn Smith case, but there's no mention that he was ever questioned about Holland. Why not? It was amazing that none of the newspapers mentioned him in connection with Debbie Holland. It was the obvious link. Did he have any proof that he couldn't have done it? Did he have an alibi?"

Two hundred students and town's people crowded the school gym for a memorial service for Debbie Holland. The school choir, the same one of which she had been a member, sang songs such as "The Way We Were" and "You Light Up My Life." One of the students who spoke at the service was a boy named Tom Allman. Lisa was amazed at this. Allman later became Lieutenant Tom Allman of the Mendocino County Sheriff's Office, and she had spoken with him in 2004 about her sister and John Annibel.

Articles about the slain girl disappeared from the newspapers until March 13, 1978, and then there was a headline in the *Eureka Times-Standard:* SO. FORK BOY HELD IN SLAYING OF GIRL. The article stated that a fifteen-year-old boy from South Fork High was arrested as a suspect in the slaying of

Debbie Holland. There was a joint press conference by Sheriff Gene Cox and DA John Buffington.

The fifteen-year-old boy, who lived near Miranda, had a clean record at the time. He told investigators initially that he had talked to Debbie Holland the afternoon of the twenty-second about rabbits and left her at the school library. The detectives later noticed this same boy hanging around the command post in the school library, trying to overhear conversations. "That created suspicion," DA Buffington told a reporter. "They went back and took a look at him again."

Since the suspect was a minor, his hearing was set for juvenile court rather than regular court. His initial hearing was before Judge Charles Thomas. One source at school told a reporter that it was unlikely he would commit a rape and murder. "He didn't seem like that kind of boy," the person said.

The prosecutor against the boy was Bernard DePaoli. That name really sent up a red flag with Lisa. "DePaoli—the same guy who was later convicted of bribing a witness in a murder trial in Shasta County! The same guy who wouldn't proceed against John for the murder of Andrea! Now I really was suspicious of this whole Holland thing. Like maybe that boy was being set up?"

On March 15, 1978, the unnamed boy was formally charged with first-degree murder. Greg Rael was his public defender and a date was set for the boy to admit to or deny charges on March 23. DePaoli told the reporter that the boy would not face a jury trial, but there would be a trial decided by Judge Thomas.

Now Lisa was even more skeptical. She said, "No jury. No open court. No records that was available to the public. It was all very suspicious."

At his hearing, the boy denied that he had committed rape or murder. On the last day of March 1978, there was a closed session in juvenile court before Judge Thomas, where he heard more than five hours of testimony about whether to proceed or not. This was like a preliminary hearing in an adult trial.

One of the prosecution witnesses was school-bus driver Jack Dernedde. Dernedde testified that the boy got on the 4:30 PM bus that day instead of his usual 3:15 PM bus. Lead DA Investigator Robert Hickok "linked critical evidence" to the boy, the newspaper said, but it did not relate what this evidence was.

"There was another name out of the past," Lisa said. "Hickok was the one who initially said that John Annibel had passed his polygraph test. Then Hickok said he wasn't sure if John had. The DOJ technicians said John was lying on that polygraph exam. Why wasn't John even looked at for the Debbie Holland murder?"

Public Defender Rael called Sheriff's Investigator Phil Cox to the stand to help his client. Harris wondered, *why call Cox?* He was a sheriff's investigator, not an investigator for the public defender's office. What Cox said was not revealed in the newspaper. Here was another name out of the past. After five hours of this, Judge Thomas said there was enough evidence to proceed to trial. The trial was set for some undetermined time in the future. Look as she might, however, Lisa could not find one more bit of information about what had happened to the boy. Had he been convicted, pled out, and found to be innocent? She never heard another word about it.

What really raised her suspicions were several strange incidents that happened on her trips to the library. She had phoned Harris at one point, saying that she was going back to look at more microfilm about the 1978 murder of Debbie Holland at the library. Lisa started noticing a strange young man who was supposedly a volunteer at the library who sat down at a microfilm machine near her and seemed very interested in what she was doing. He was clean-cut and not just some homeless person, the type who sometimes hung around the library. He looked like he was a professional white-collar worker.

Lisa said, "So, I sat down next to the "volunteer" and turned on the machine. I had some "flat film." He looked over at what I had and said, 'That machine is for rolled film only." I thought, what business of yours is it what I have, and why are you looking at it? I turned directly toward him and said, 'Obviously, I'm not looking at anything right now.'

"I went to the reference table in the same room and looked in the 1980 reference book about Humboldt County DA cases.

I sat directly behind the volunteer. I saw that he was looking at microfilm of 1978 through 1980. I thought this was very odd, because those were the rolls I wanted to see. I also noticed he had a printed out e-mail that concerned Joyce Johnson!

"A few minutes later, he and I were the only ones in the room. I went to install the rolled film on the machine farthest away from him. I couldn't get the film to load for some reason. I struggled for at least three to five minutes, and you could hear the machine making the sound it does when it's not working right.

"About that time, the lady with the cart came in and she looked at me and smiled because she could see my frustration. I asked, 'Can you help me?' She said, 'Oh, I'm not the one to ask about those machines. I really don't know how they work.' Then she looked over at the guy and said, 'Winston is the one to ask.'

"He didn't respond at all until the lady finally asked him if he could help me. Then he came over to my machine and said, 'Oh, I've never seen this before. Maybe try a different machine.' I said, 'I just saw this machine being worked by somebody else. It's probably just something simple that I'm doing wrong.'

"He looked at the machine and said, 'Try closing the black arm. You know, where it says *push to open*.'

"Well, that made it work. But while I sat there, I got the feeling he was always looking over my shoulder. So I scooted as close to my screen as possible to block the view. I looked at the articles and noticed that Debbie Holland was last seen at 3:30 PM on February 22, 1978. I wonder if anyone ever asked John Annibel what he was doing at that time.

"For the first time in a long time, I felt like I did at the age of nineteen and twenty. The period of realization of Andrea's murder intertwined with the reflection of our lives together. While I drove home, a part of me really felt like bawling, while the other part resisted."

Harris was intrigued by the statement that "Winston" had an e-mail concerning a Joyce Johnson. That was the same name used by John Annibel in one of his alibis to detectives in 1980 as to why the bed he and Andrea shared was soaked with blood. In one instance, he said it was because Mr. Johnson supposedly had knee surgery. In another story to police, John said it was because Joyce Johnson had delivered a baby on the bed. And in yet another story it was because Andrea was menstruating there. John couldn't even keep track of his lies. Was he so arrogant from getting off on all these cases that he didn't even care?

Harris ran a portion of the transcript from a Humboldt County investigator's statements in 1999 that included Andrea.

Q. Prosecutor: "Have you had an opportunity to look at those photographs [of the crime scene in Andrea and John's apartment in Fortuna] back in April of 1980 to see whether they even came out?"

A. Investigator: "I don't recall looking at photographs in 1980. No."

Q. "Have you looked at photographs recently?"

A. "We have looked at photographs."

Q. "To your personal knowledge, have you seen photographs of what was in the apartment or the condition of the apartment during the execution of the search warrant?"

A. "I have not."

Harris told Lisa, "This is incredible! I have never heard of an investigator in a case not reviewing crime-scene photographs. And what happened to those photographs? Does the DA's office have them? Does Fortuna PD? Or the California Department of Justice? Do they even still exist, or did they ever exist?"

Questions kept multiplying in Harris's mind, and he threw a batch of them out for Pam Annibel to react to. "On June 3, 1976, DOJ agents interviewed John at the Humboldt County Sheriff's Office in Garberville. John told them the same story about he and Sherry at the dance. Then he said something new—he said he had talked to Doris Stone at the edge of the hall at 2 AM. This must be the woman who became Doris

Perna—Ron Stone's sister. When Doris talked to agents, she said she never had that conversation with John. Was this ever followed up by detectives? And why wasn't she questioned about Ron Stone, since a lot of people put him at the dance, and he was a friend of John's?"

Pam had her own set of questions and comments for Harris, which he answered in turn.

Pam: "Why was John being served beer at a bar when he was only eighteen?"

Harris: "I agree with you that John should not have been served beer at the bar. So he was probably trying to use this as an alibi, saying he was at the bar when he was actually somewhere else. He cannot say he didn't see Sherry at the end of the dance, because at least three people say that he did."

Pam: "Why did John get home at 3:15 AM and then leave again at about 5:30 or 6 AM? I believe it was to dump her suitcases. I remember how odd it was that he would leave after being home for a couple of hours. It just didn't make sense, and he didn't do that kind of thing before."

Harris: "I agree with you about this."

Pam: "Why did Ron Stone and Kathy think they needed to come to my house in Miranda while my mom was home? They never had done that before. Was he trying to see if we figured it out? Of course my mom was hysterical about who those strangers were, and yelled at them to leave. Which they did. But John, who was there too, didn't leave right away. Was he trying to see if we knew or what? We were so out of it then emotionally, we didn't think about anything except our loss."

Harris: "I didn't know that Ron and Kathy came to your place after Sherry was murdered. That is real suspicious, since they had never been there before. I'll bet you that they were checking to see what they could find out. At least Ron was. Remember, Sherry's body was not supposed to be discovered so soon. In fact, if not for the motorcycle rider on May 3, Sherry's body may not have been discovered for a long time. Sherry would have just disappeared and it would be blamed on the fact that she 'ran away.' Sherry might have become like Andrea—her remains not discovered for years, if ever. And then there was that comment by Ron back in 1976 that if anyone asked him what he was doing in the week that Sherry was murdered, he would definitely remember."

Lisa had an important message for Harris in late April. She said, "What a day yesterday! I met with Dave Douglas at the police department. He motioned me inside his office and gave me a hug. Then he closed both of his doors. He said, 'I spoke to Frank.'

Lisa: "Jager?"

Dave: "Yeah. Frank and I have talked and he thinks, well, he wants to give you everything."

Lisa: "Everything? In his files?"

Dave: "Everything. He has presented his report to the DA and he feels that they have done and documented everything that can be done. And Frank wants you to have the info."

Lisa: "Are you serious?"

Dave: "Yeah. It's a big deal. The reason I invited you back is because I wanted to keep my word to you. But it's really Frank that you need to thank if you get a chance. Now he's waiting to hear back from the DA. You should probably try calling Frank around May sixth. And if you want, I can call him to support you, if you'd like. I'm here to help."

Lisa: "Thank you. Wow, this is a big deal. But ultimately, it's still the DA's decision?"

Dave: "Yeah. But Frank really wants to help you close . . .

he just wants to make sure he has all his ducks in a row, so to speak. He's going to present his position to the DA."

Lisa: "Wow, I know this must be a big deal for him. I mean because he already knows the situation. The way I'm not allowed to even look at the files. So he must be going out on a limb."

Dave: "Yeah."

I thought to myself, *I wonder if Frank Jager is getting ready to retire. Like Glen Sipma did. And before Sipma did, he gave all that information about Sherry to Paul Smith.* But I didn't ask.

Dave asked, "So how are you, really?"

Lisa: "I'm doing okay. My day has been a little hectic. But just another day."

Dave: "Well, I'm just asking because your . . . well, all this information."

Lisa: "Yeah. It's unbelievable info."

At this point the conversation became obscure, because I could tell he wanted to say something to me, but he didn't want to say it directly.

Dave: "I'm concerned about your balance. We all have our responsibilities and pressures that we have to take care of. Must take care of. For example, as police officers we all have seen and experienced things that have ghosts. Even though they're always there, and we know they're there, we don't ignore them, we just know they are there. If we didn't, we wouldn't be able to do the type of work that we do. So as officers, we can also advocate for victims because as victims or survivors of serious crimes ourselves, we know how it affects them."

I still wasn't sure where he was going with this.

Dave: "So we feel, we hope that this info will help you with . . ."

Lisa: "Closure?"

Dave: "Yeah. That's what I was trying to say. Closure. Although it's not complete closure. I'm not saying that shouldn't happen. But separate from that, I'm just concerned that you maintain that balance. You say that with all this information and everything . . ."

Now I felt that he was questioning my stability. My ability to handle this. I said, "I've always been an anxious person. I thought this was just my personality. But a year or so after Andrea was found, my anxiety level increased, as did my beer indulgence. I started losing weight, which concerned me, even though some women would love to be 130 pounds. I was eating high-calorie food and still losing weight. So after a series of treatments, my doctor determined I was suffering from extreme anxiety. So she prescribed Zoloft, and a month later my husband said I was a completely different woman.

"I'm still high-strung, but before I would try to deal with my anxiety by obsessing and trying to resolve issues that were causing the anxiety, whether I had any control of a resolution or not. I can't say that what happened to Anghs caused this extreme anxiety, but I would be wrong to say that these situations didn't contribute. Since I began my Zoloft, I feel for the first time that both my feet are on solid ground. I'm still active with everything, but I've learned to shut things off when I need to."

He said, "That's not a confession. That sounds like you are balanced."

Teary-eyed, I told him, "My thoughts have been that if something happened to me, my sister would end up on a shelf with a number attached."

Later, Lisa asked Harris, "What does all of this mean? I mean, a month ago, Dave said he was unsuccessful in getting any of her remains released from the coroner's office. Now he says the coroner's office is still trying to persuade the DA. What makes them think they will change the DA's decision?

"Are people getting nervous? Is Jager really retiring, or is he formally washing his hands of everything?

"Anyone can see that this situation isn't about my obsessions, rather it's the fact that the Humboldt County DA's office refuses to give me the time of day, or even consider the fact that someone has killed at least two human beings after Sherry and is still at large.

"I'm not getting it. I almost had the feeling Dave was trying to warn me. I mean, he's been a friend all along. He's about the only one who has helped me consistently over the years. So who is he trying to warn me about?"

Lisa waited for May 6 to arrive. It came and went just like all the other days with no new word from the DA's office about her sister Andrea. Harris thought again about his analogy of the Humboldt County DA's office to a black hole. All information went in there and vanished as if it had never existed.

CHAPTER 13

Andrea's Ashes

On Friday the thirteenth, June 2005, Lisa and Andrea's "lucky day," Lisa contacted Harris to tell him how she viewed their teamwork. She said, "First, I'd like to address about the complexity of the case both you and I have endured, including the initial 'This can't be true,' feeling that the authorities would just ignore a homicide. I know, because for the last twenty-four years, I've thought of that over and over again.

"Before I met you, I always suffered from a high amount of anxiety, but because I was still able to function, I became an independent, productive person. I thought maybe it was just my personality. You have to remember, I was only nineteen when my sister disappeared. We had been raised under very intense and difficult conditions. So high anxiety was normal to me.

"Unfortunately, when Andrea disappeared, I was alone. My mother, who lived in the area, could not even discuss it. My aunt was preoccupied with her own struggles, and my two younger sisters had been removed, adopted out, years earlier. We had no other living relatives that were in contact with us.

"Up until the time Andrea disappeared, she was my life.

Everyone used to call us twins, I guess because you never saw one of us without the other. Anghs once told me, 'I think the reason you and I are so close is because we had to be a mother and father to each other.'

"That statement is the closest I can come to telling you just how much of my development and my life she was to me. She was always there for me from the time I was born. As a child she taught me most everything, from how to tie my shoes to how to ride a bike. I never knew life without her.

"A lot of my family members—my grandparents and other adults—always thought there was something wrong with me. It was the way they talked and treated me. I always felt different. Except for Anghs. She truly believed in me, and she gave me all the confidence one person could need. It came from just being around her. I never had to pretend to be anything I wasn't with her. She accepted and loved me unconditionally, just the way I was.

"The last time I saw her, smiling at me and waving good bye was at a very, very long stop light. I had no idea just how much I depended on her. Since then my life has been an endless mission to find her, and to make sure the person who took her away from me, never did this to someone else and their family.

"Of course, I've still tried to maintain a normal life. Some would say I've become a workaholic. I guess I tried disguising my being different by becoming as productive as I could, but only to the extent that after all my personal obligations had been taken care of could I spent every waking moment searching the river sandbars, the forests, driving by her old apartment, writing, letters to anyone I thought had influence, writing, writing, and writing.

"When I learned of yet another victim in 1998, I really felt that I had failed Debbie Sloan. If just somehow I had tried a little harder, then maybe she would still be alive and her poor sister and family would not be experiencing the same pain I knew they would have to live with for the rest of their lives.

"I stayed in Eureka, where we grew up, even though many times I was so discouraged I wanted to move away. I just couldn't bear to leave, though. I still drive by my grand-mother's house, which Anghs and I called home.

"I've spent numerous hours in the library as well as the court house, trying to find something, anything to help me with my mission. Most everyone, except for my husband, thought I was obsessed. Some of my closest friends and Sandy's family even asked that I stop pursuing my mission for fear of my health; or worse, that someone might harm me. So for many years, I became introverted and just continued to search and write in silence. I planted a rosebush on every anniversary of her disappearance, believing somehow, someday, my sister would be found.

"The day I read the news article that the authorities found unidentified remains, I knew it was Andrea. I had read over a dozen articles of unidentified remains that were recovered throughout the years, and a couple were similar to Andrea. But I knew these remains were Andrea's.

"When Andrea was found, part of my lifelong mission had finally been realized. However, the authorities refused to re-lease any information regarding her case or even release her remains, so that we could finally put her to rest. This was some-thing I had been waiting to do for twenty two years—bring her home.

"The lack of information only fired my persistence further. When my friends and Sandy's family would say, let it go, she's been found, I couldn't. Not as long as there was even one smidgen of a possibility that the individual who killed her could be released. I also felt a lot of anger toward the local DA's office. I couldn't understand how they couldn't feel some re-sponsibility for Sherry, for Anghs, for Debbie, and who knows how many others in the last twenty-two years.

"Again I suffered quietly, spending a lot of my free time on the computer, researching laws, victims' rights, news arti-cles, anything I could get my hands on. Then out of the blue, an angel called me. That's how I see you, Harris. As an angel. When you called me about Andrea's case, I was so suspicious of everyone, I almost didn't call back. But after a lot of care-ful thought, I agreed to meet with you and Georgina's sisters.

"Since then all of you have changed my life. It was like putting together a missing piece of the puzzle. I feel like everything I had worked on and saved throughout the years really had purpose, and [was] not just a waste of my time. I am no longer alone. I feel your caring and your support every day, even when there is no communication. Just knowing that people who don't even know me or my sister, are taking time out of their personal lives and even making sacrifices is one of the most heartfelt experiences I have ever known.

"I recently heard someone say, 'Justice may have been delayed, but not denied.' Who knows if Andrea or Sherry will ever have justice. But for all your hard work and support, Harris, and Chris, Tim [Kiely], Mark [Kalina], and Christy [Conrardy], and I'm sure many others, who don't even know me, thank you for believing in my sister's case and for giving me hope!"

If Friday the thirteenth was one omen, there was another on May 20. A small bear was seen hiding in some berry bushes at Allen McCloskey's residence on Hawthorne Street in Eureka. Something like this had never happened before. Lisa wrote Harris, "Did you see today's paper about the wild bear? That house where the bear was found is the house where Terry McCloskey grew up. I used to visit her there every day in high school. Her brother Allen inherited the house when Terry's mom died. Terry Lynn and her family were full Yurok Indians. I wonder what their culture thinks about a bear coming into their yard in the middle of the city, in the middle of the day? I'm sure they have some cultural belief about such a thing."

Who knows what the bear incident meant, but the portents for the DA's office in general, and Tim Stoen in particular were all bad in the Debi August case that very June. Many in Humboldt County, and Lisa in particular, saw the August case as a blatant "payback" for August's opposition to DA Gallegos in the recall election. She also blamed Gallegos and Stoen for putting so much effort into this "vendetta," as she called it, while ignoring all her faxes, phone calls, and letters asking about what the disposition of Andrea's case was. She viewed Stoen as Gallegos's point-man on this, and the Debi August case gave Lisa some new insights into the politics of the county and the DA's office in particular.

The Debi August affair began when she became the target of a grand-jury investigation. August, who was a real-estate broker as well as a councilwoman for Fortuna, was accused of "malfeasance, conflict of interest," over her decision to present a subdivision application to the Fortuna Planning Commission on behalf of a friend who was a developer. August also faced two counts of improperly filling out financial-disclosure forms and one count of allegedly revealing a grand-jury secret.

August wasn't taking all of this lying down. She hired a lawyer and stated, "I have rock-solid proof of perjured grand jury testimony." Her implication was that Gallegos and Stoen were improperly using the grand-jury process to "get her" for her opposition to Gallegos during the recall and her opposition to their lawsuit against PALCO.

The August case soon became a battle of wills when August's attorney, Bill Bragg, attempted to have Tim Stoen removed from the case, "Because Stoen has a vendetta against my client, and because August supported the recall against Stoen's boss District Attorney Gallegos." He also told reporters that, "It wasn't the grand jury, it was Mr. Stoen who took this and ran with it. Debi didn't do anything that would justify removing her from office."

Stoen, on the other hand, said that any attempt to remove him from the case was just a ploy to delay the trial. He added, "If there is a bias, there is a bias against me." He cited a contentious trial where Bragg had been his opponent in the previous year. In some respects, Tim Stoen was doing what a good number-two man should do—stick up for and be loyal to his boss.

All of this dragged on through the spring of 2005, and by May, Debi August had also hired Greg Rael as her attorney. Rael had been the unnamed boy's attorney during the Debbie Holland murder case in 1978. Lisa was intrigued by how so many names from the past kept cropping up on new cases.

Debi August had already spent $75,000 in legal fees by mid-May 2005. Rael told reporters, "It's an outrage that a local person, running for local office for the first time, should be subjected to these types of proceedings and have to spend a fortune to defend herself."

To Lisa it seemed as if the district attorney's office was in the throes of a meltdown, and the political heat seemed to have affected the top men. In a surprise move, DA Gallegos named Wes Keat as his number-two man in place of Tim Stoen. Gallegos tried putting the best spin on the situation by saying, "Tim's got his hands full. It was a decision I made and I felt it was appropriate. Tim's got a lot of work on his plate." Lisa saw things in a different light. She was sure that Gallegos was distancing himself from Tim Stoen.

Things would not get any better as far as Gallegos and Stoen were concerned. Superior Court Judge John Feeny dismissed three of the four counts against Debi August and only a conflict of interest count remained against her.

By June 25, 2005, the Debi August case had fully blown up in the DA office's face. A former grand-jury forewoman named Judith Schmidt was put on the stand by August's defense lawyers. Schmidt had been so upset by certain things during her tenure as forewoman of the 2003–2004 grand jury that she said, "The manner in which it was conducted as well as the advice provided to the grand jury bothered me. The advice came from Tim Stoen."

Schmidt said that inconsistencies in direction and instruction changes led to her keeping copies of Debi August–related documents even after her tenure was over. Schmidt was so concerned about what she deemed to be irregularities that she contacted the California State Attorney General's Office. When asked on the stand why she didn't go directly to the DA, Schmidt answered, "Because I didn't trust him."

Schmidt became even more concerned when she was contacted by the new grand jury forewoman, Darlene Marlowe, and told, "You don't have any e-mails [in connection with the Debi August case]."

Schmidt replied, "Yes, I do!"

To which Marlowe responded (according to Schmidt), "You don't understand. You don't have any e-mails!"

Schmidt understood this to mean that she was supposed to destroy any e-mails she had concerning the August case. Instead, she turned them over to the attorney general's office.

For days on end, Schmidt was kept on the stand, often sparring with Tim Stoen. When the judge asked how long he intended to keep Schmidt on the stand, Stoen answered five more days. Instead the judge gave Stoen two days in which to wrap up all his questioning.

In the end, Judge Feeny dismissed all charges against Debi August, saying that her due-process rights had been impaired and that he had grave concerns over the integrity of the Humboldt County grand-jury system.

When Debi August heard the news, she broke down in tears. She told reporters, "This case has completely changed my life. I will never be the same person I was before this started." She blamed Paul Gallegos and especially Tim Stoen for using the power of the office of the district attorney "to get her" for opposing Gallegos during the recall election.

A few days later, Tim Stoen let it be known in a surprise announcement that he was leaving the Humboldt County District Attorney's Office, and returning to the Mendocino County DA's Office as a financial-crimes prosecutor. He told a reporter, "There was just too much baggage that was being thrown on him [Gallegos] and it wouldn't be fair to go into an election campaign with that." Then he made an allusion to falling on his sword for Gallegos.

When asked about this surprise move, Debi August told a reporter, "The last time I said what I really thought about him [Stoen], it cost me more than $100,000. He's not someone you really want to say nasty things about. I'm sure someday Mr. Stoen will get everything that's coming to him!"

Lisa Lawler couldn't have agreed more. She said, "I felt like Andrea and I have been held hostage by the DA's office. I believe it was up to Stoen and Gallegos whether the case against John Annibel was going to proceed, but they were more interested with PALCO and getting even with Debi August than helping me. After all I did for Paul Gallegos during his recall election, I felt betrayed."

Lisa also wondered about news articles she'd read about Tim Stoen that had to do with allegations against him many years in the past. There had been a lot of irregularities in the 1975 San Francisco city elections, where Stoen at the time was a counsel for Jim Jones and the People's Temple. John Ritchie, head of the Fair Election Review Committee in 1976 said to reporters, "We want to know why in the 1975 elections there were so many irregularities. Was it a fraudulent election? And if so, who engineered it?"

Things would become even murkier when Ritchie and the FERC discovered that San Francisco DA Joseph Freitas, Jr. had been elected by the active help of Jim Jones and the People's Temple. Members of the People's Temple even confessed later that they had engaged in activities to swing the election results by busing people from outside areas to fraudulently vote in San Francisco. Freitas and Mayor George Moscone, friends of the People's Temple, had been voted into office by the margin of those illegal votes.

A *San Francisco Examiner* article stated, "Freitas appointed Tim Stoen, an officer of Jim Jones church to run the election-fraud investigation. Dozens of people were charged with individual activities of voter fraud, but the primary culprits behind the fraud were never investigated or charged."

Freitas later had the audacity to tell reporters that he'd never even heard of the People's Temple, but that he'd pulled Tim Stoen's "résumé out of the mail" when he appointed him to head the voter fraud unit.

A *San Francisco Chronicle* article stated, "A federal investigation has developed information that Assistant District Attorney Stoen misused his position to obstruct pending investigations that might have adversely impacted on the People's Temple, of which he was then a member." Because of these allegations, California State Attorney General Evelle Younger began an investigation of Freitas, Stoen, and the San Francisco DA's Office.

Lisa commented to Harris, "So here is this pattern of destroying documents in the San Francisco DA's office in 1975, and Humboldt Grand Jury documents in 2004. I want to know what crucial evidence and documents have been destroyed in Andrea's case. If they were, I want to know on who's orders that was done."

The political landscape was about to change in Humboldt County, however, and it would affect Lisa just as much as the DA's office. On June 22, 2005, Deputy DA Worth Dikeman announced that he was going to run for the position of district attorney against Paul Gallegos, even though the election was nearly a year away. He told reporters, "I will be compelled to discuss some things that Paul has done or neglected to do. If I thought he was doing a good job, I wouldn't be running." And in a reference to the August case he added, "To go forward with the prosecution of a case in the face of a valid defense constitutes an abuse of the district attorney's power and forces someone to defend against a charge that should not have been brought in the first place."

The fallout of Worth Dikeman's decision to run against Gallegos immediately was felt by Lisa. She received a fax from DA Investigator Mike Losey titled "RE: Murder Investigation." It was a copy of a letter that Paul Gallegos had sent to the coroner's office. The fax also had a critical portion as far as Lisa was concerned with the statement, "This case is still under review and it has now been assigned to Max Cardoza for review. As you know, the immense size of the case as well as technical issues with the case, will require time for Mr. Cardoza to become familiar with the facts."

Lisa was stunned. She told Harris, "They took the case out of Worth Dikeman's hands as soon as he began to run against Paul Gallegos! I had told Paul of my concerns about that very kind of thing during Terry Farmer's tenure as DA. Andrea's case had been passed from one deputy DA to another. Terry Farmer had never cared about the case and never really pursued it, as far as I was concerned. Paul had promised me he would not do that. And here he does that very thing!"

The copy of the letter from Paul Gallegos to Coroner Frank Jager about Andrea's remains was even more of a stunner to Lisa. In part it stated, "Whether there would be a need to present remains in any future hearings or have them available for examination by defense experts is unknown. There is a chance that the remains could be crucial in prosecuting a case. Therefore, we are not in a position to agree to releasing these remains."

There was one more portion of the letter, however, and it stated that Lisa and her family could have "a service over the remains, or in the presence of the remains." There were several stipulations attached, the main one being that someone within the coroner's office would have to always have the remains accounted for.

Lisa was outraged, and told Harris, "I pictured a gurney with flowers on it, and Andrea's remains in a cardboard box! What kind of memorial service is that? It was like a slap in the face. Andrea's the murder victim, and even though she's paid for the crime with her life, twenty-five years later, her remains are ordered to remain in custody of the district attorney while the perpetrator is not held accountable. If I had to sum up my childhood and my life without Andrea, the above scenario really has been the entire makeup of mine and Andrea's whole life. It seems that no matter what we did do to try and prevent these situations, or what I've tried to do to make things right, I keep running into similar problems my whole life. These are things that the everyday normal person should never be faced with.

"When I try and vent and explain what I've gone through, people just don't understand, I think because it's too unbelievable. It's like having several black clouds hanging over your head your entire life, and no matter what you do, you have to be prepared to fail, but keep fighting to succeed anyway."

Lisa had finally had it, as far as the Humboldt County District Attorney's Office was concerned. She told Harris, "I've had the same runaround for twenty-five years no matter who the District Attorney was—Bernard DePaoli, Terry Farmer, and Paul Gallegos. I don't believe things will be any different if Worth Dikeman is elected. Here's what I really think. I believe when charges were dismissed against John in April 1980, they were dismissed with prejudice. This prohibits charges from ever being refiled. I also believe that Annibel's attorney William Fer-roggiaro made a deal with then-DA DePaoli to have the records expunged. What agreement they came up with, I don't know. Since charges could never be refiled, there was no need to keep the records. However, according to law they were supposed to inform the victims involved, in this case Andrea's family.

"This is why everyone involved in the case continue to say publicly charges were never filed, even under oath, though he really was charged. But since the records were expunged, they must treat it as though charges were never filed. This is why I keep running into what appears to be a coverup situa-tion. The system is protecting itself and the suspect in this case.

"I don't believe I will ever be allowed to review the records under any circumstances. The sad truth is, the authorities should have let me know all along that charges were perma-nently dismissed. This may be where the favors were traded. Instead they continue their falsehoods that they don't have enough evidence. If they disclose the truth, they face a lawsuit. John Annibel got a get-out-of-jail-free card in 1980. He has nothing to worry about as long as Sherry's murder doesn't come up. Or maybe he even got a deal on that one too."

Harris wasn't so sure about the charges being dismissed with prejudice back in 1980, but he did agree with Lisa on one point—some kind of deal might have been made back in 1980 with then Humboldt County DA Bernard DePaoli. And Harris's reasoning came about by information he obtained in July 2005 concerning DePaoli, and it was dynamite. DePaoli had been caught redhanded bribing a witness in a murder trial.

Harris already knew a little about the case from very slim newspaper articles. When Harris found out about the partic-ulars of the case, they weren't pretty and they had all the ear-marks of what could well have occurred with John Annibel. If Harris's theory was right, it opened up a whole can of worms why the Humboldt County DA's Office might have treated Andrea's (and possibly Sherry's) case the way they had since at least 1980.

The information dealt with Bernard DePaoli in a murder trial in 1988. By that year DePaoli was no longer a DA, but rather a criminal-law attorney in Humboldt County. He had a client who was up on murder charges in Shasta County, named Philip Charles Kellotat. All of this stemmed from the murder of Vincent Capitan on February 6, 1987, in Shasta County. Capitan was an ex-convict from Oregon who had recently been paroled after serving time for solicitation to commit murder in which at least two persons were killed. Four months after Capitan's murder, the Shasta County DA's office charged Capitan's wife with the crime on the theory she had arranged for her husband's murder over a pending divorce and custody battle, as well as trying to get survivor's benefits for a dead spouse. The person she allegedly used as the hit man was Philip Kellotat.

All of this was discharged by a judge, but then the DA's office came up with a new theory, and it was that Philip Kellotat, who was now Linda Capitan's boyfriend, had ordered the male Capitan killed. According to evidence, Kellotat had first approached a person named Jody Seelye to kill Capitan. On March 1, 1988, Philip Kellotat was arrested in Bakersfield, California on a murder warrant and transported to the Shasta County Jail. Two weeks after Kellotat was arraigned, while awaiting a preliminary hearing, charges against him for the murder were dropped for lack of evidence, but he remained in the Shasta County jail because of a parole violation. At that time, Bernard DePaoli became Kellotat's lawyer.

The situation soon became even messier. A man named Alan Dale Bradley, who had nine felony convictions and was serving a seven-year sentence in a California state prison at Soledad for shooting a man in the head in Humboldt County, contacted Shasta County authorities and said if they would release him from prison, he would tell them all about how Kellotat had tried hiring him in June 1986 to kill Vincent Capitan. Bradley had not gone through with the plan, however, and a deal was hammered out between Shasta County DA Steve Carlton and Bradley. Bradley, in exchange for his testimony, would serve the rest of his time in the Shasta County Jail, and in fact, the time he had left to serve was reduced.

Because of evidence put forth by Bradley, Philip Kellotat was recharged on October 6, 1988, with the murder of Capitan. The charges were murder, murder for hire, murder for financial gain, and conspiracy to commit murder. On October 20, 1988, in the Shasta County Sheriff's Office, Detective Division, a meeting was held at the request of Alan Bradley for the purpose of further negotiations regarding a deal that he was trying to put together with District Attorney Stephen Carlton. A lawyer named Jere Hurley was also present on the behalf of Dawn Walker, Alan Bradley's girlfriend.

And now things got really interesting. At the meeting, Bradley told Carlton that Kellotat's lawyer, Bernard DePaoli, ex-district attorney of Humboldt County, had recently contacted him about making his own illegal deal. Bradley said that DePaoli had just tried to bribe him to change his testimony against Kellotat.

At first Carlton was skeptical about this story—after all, Bradley had served time for some serious crimes. But Carlton went ahead and arranged for Bradley to phone DePaoli in Eureka and have the conversation recorded. On October 28, 1988, Bradley phoned DePaoli from the Shasta County Jail and said that for $5,000 he would provide DePaoli with a statement that would clear Kellotat. DePaoli told Bradley no, but he seemed to be saying no to the amount, not to any outrage about a bribe having been offered in the first place. Carlton was still interested and he had Bradley still make phone calls to DePaoli.

On October 29, Bradley once again phoned DePaoli, and this time said he was not interested in money as much as he was in obtaining legal assistance for himself and his girlfriend, Dawn Walker. DePaoli responded that this might be a possibility.

Bradley made four more phone calls to DePaoli between October 29 and October 31, all with no clear deal in place between himself and DePaoli, but the stakes were soon upped. On November 1, 1988, Bradley, with Detective Jarrett listening in, began making collect phone calls to DePaoli, and there was one jailhouse visit by DePaoli to Bradley. On November 8, a fateful event occurred—$400 from a mysterious source was sent via Western Union to Bradley's girlfriend, Dawn Walker, and Bradley recanted his original statement about Philip Kellotat being involved in the murder of Vincent Capitan. It had all the appearance of a bribe being offered and accepted. Bradley said that DePaoli had agreed to this deal, and the $400 was just a test of good faith on DePaoli's part that more money would be coming later, according to Bradley.

On November 28, 1988, a date set for a discovery hearing in the Kellotat trial, Philip Kellotat and his lawyer Bernard DePaoli appeared at the Shasta County courthouse in Redding. DePaoli didn't get very far, however, and he was escorted to the Shasta County Sheriff's Office and told that he had best withdraw from the case since he might be charged with attempting to change a witness's testimony.

A charge was leveled against Bernard DePaoli—"Bribery of a witness in violation of Section 137(a) of the California Penal Code. The allegations are that between October twenty-seventh and November ninth of 1988, while defendant DePaoli was representing a Philip Charles Kellotat in *People v. Kellotat*, there were conversations between the principal complaining witness in that case, Alan Dale Bradley, and defendant DePaoli who was at that time the attorney for Kellotat, wherein Mr. DePaoli is alleged to have offered a bribe to Mr. Bradley to somehow influence his testimony against Mr. Kellotat."

Harris discovered that Bernard DePaoli, former district attorney of Humboldt County in 1980, made a plea bargain on the bribery charge in the 1988 Shasta County case during John Annibel's arrest for the murder of Andrea LaDeRoute. Just what the entire deal entailed wasn't clear, but a conclusion was reached by all parties. Harris wasn't even sure if the particulars of the deal were sealed, but he couldn't find out exactly what happened to DePaoli.

From there the information faded away except for a notation that on October 22, 1992, DePaoli's status in the State Bar of California was changed from "active" to "not entitled." On Christmas Day, 1992, it was changed to "resigned."

So there it was—rumors that had swirled around Bernard DePaoli for years came to light in valid documents that he had tried bribing a witness in a murder trial. The charges were brought forth by no less a person than the district attorney of Shasta County.

When Harris told Pam about what he had learned about De-Paoli, she had some very interesting things to say. Pam wrote him, "I do believe there was some kind of coverup regarding some of the authorities and detectives. I wasn't sure of this before, but I found out that John's parents paid a lot of money to his lawyer [William Ferroggiaro]. That lawyer had connections between himself and the judge's and the DA's office—especially DePaoli's office. This is my speculation, of course, but there is something more fishy than we all know.

"In fact, John's parents spent their life savings on the lawyer, Ferroggiaro, for John. I didn't know they had spent so much money, and I don't know for a fact if his parents knew all that was involved, and what the lawyer was doing, but it seems like a lot of money for back in the 1980s. There is definitely corruption in Humboldt County law enforcement, and we were wondering if Ferroggiaro was part of that. Of course, James was never told any details about after the time of John's arrest [for Andrea's murder in 1980], and why he was let go."

Harris passed this information from Pam to Lisa, and told her his theory why the charges against John Annibel in Andrea's case were never refiled. "You have to understand that this is my theory," he said, "but I think it has certain facts to back it up. Finding out what DePaoli did in Shasta County gives it more credence. I believe that in 1980, John Annibel, with the backing of his parent's money, was able to bribe Bernard De-Paoli to make sure that evidence would not be presented in time for the hearing on April 23, 1980. Hell, some of the key evidence wasn't even sent to the FBI lab in Washington, D.C. until April twenty-second. Whoever did that knew the results couldn't be back in time for John's arraignment. According to DePaoli, the lack of substantial evidence was the reason the charges against John were dismissed. DePaoli put on a dog-and-pony show that charges would be refiled when more evidence came in, but he knew he would never present whatever new evidence was discovered. He had no intention of ever letting John go to trial. Things were made easier for DePaoli because Andrea's remains were not found for so long.

"But then DePaoli was beaten in the election for district attorney by Terry Farmer in 1982. Without any remains of Andrea, Farmer had no real incentive to go forward on the case, as well. And then a nightmare happened—Bernard DePaoli was caught accepting a bribe on a murder trial, and made a plea bargain on the Shasta County charge. Now everything he had touched during his tenure as Humboldt County DA would look tainted in his handling of Andrea's case. Humboldt County could become entangled in lawsuits and litigations to overturn countless cases if it was proven that DePaoli was doing the same kind of thing when he was district attorney. The district attorney's office would be a shambles.

"An even worse event, as far as some were concerned, occurred when John Annibel killed Debbie Sloan in Mendocino County, was arrested and convicted. Now it could be proven that he had killed a woman, much in the same manner that Sherry Lynn Smith had been killed. And it made it seem even more likely that John had murdered Andrea. If somehow it was proven by Debbie Sloan's mother or sister that Bernard DePaoli had let John off on a bribe, the lawsuit that would follow from them on a wrongful-death charge could be enormous.

"Did a cover up in the DA's office go into high gear from that point on?" Harris asked her. "I don't know. It's possible. I'm not even saying one did at this point. All I know is documents started being expunged. When you or I asked clerks about any files connected to Annibel's 1980 case, they said they couldn't find them. This wasn't some traffic ticket—these were files on a murder charge, and court hearings had taken place back in 1980. So where are the public documents on that since it was done in open court? There had to be some kind of paper trail. And now they say that nothing exists. I don't buy it. I've seen public court records that go back to the 1940s. And they're telling us that records of murder charges from 1980 have somehow been expunged!

"And veiled threats against you seemed to pop up every time you tried to make the DA's office push forward on Andrea's case.

The incident with Roger Hudnall showing up at the court, when we indicated we were going there, is real suspicious. And so is the fact that the "volunteer" just happened to show up at the library and was real interested in what we were doing while looking at microfilm. He showed up every time you phoned me and said you would be there at a certain hour. He even fell for our ploy when you called me and said you wouldn't go at a certain hour, and then actually went there. Naturally, the 'volunteer' didn't show up. Most suspicious of all—he had the name of Joyce Johnson written down on an e-mail. That's the same name as one of John's supposed alibis as to why blood was found on the mattress that he and Andrea had shared.

"All of this became even more suspicious when he just happened to have the microfilm you wanted when you went to the library. A few of these kinds of things would just be co-incidence. A pattern seems to be the framework of collusion and coverups. What do you think?"

What Lisa thought was that she and Harris were on the same page about this. She even told him, when he became concerned for her safety, "I have always felt the presence of death around me. When I think about Anghs and the district attorney's office, I think they have contributed to my anxieties. I am human. I too am afraid of death and the unknown. And though I believe in truth, honor, and good will toward everyone, I have been faced with the unspoken reality that the truth is that my sister's murder may fall upon me, too. Either by the mur-derer, or by the authorities who have protected him all these years.

"My strength has come from God, and knowing that wher-ever my sister is in spirit, I do not have to fear, because I know she'll be there to greet me. I was taught from my mother to always stand up for what you believe in, and never, ever let someone take that away from you."

After reading that note, Harris was as proud of Lisa as if she was his own little sister. He admired her courage, honesty, and tenacity. She had lived a life no one should have ever been sub-jected to, yet had carried on with dignity and grace.

A few days later, Lisa e-mailed him with a note that was very evocative of everything that had happened. Lisa wrote, "Wow! I just had something very strange happen that I can't explain. My fingers can hardly type fast enough. I was out on the patio and I saw a butterfly in the backyard. As I mentioned before, I've always associated butterflies with Andrea. This beautiful orange butterfly just sat on the grass about five feet away, and kept flapping its wings while I was sitting on the grass.

"It sat there for a long time, and I was seeing Anghs in my thoughts, as if she was a ghost in my head. All of a sudden I heard Anghs's voice in my thoughts say, 'Lisa, you can do it!' That's when I realized I had been staring at the butterfly. As soon as I heard Anghs's voice, the butterfly flew straight up and out of sight. The feeling I was left with was one of serenity, because that's exactly what I would expect Andrea to say at times like these."

The next day, Lisa told Harris, "I dreamt I was a child again, back in elementary school, all the way through high school. Andrea was nowhere to be found. I made a report to the police and some woman at the school. She seemed to be someone I could trust throughout the dream, as I struggled to find Andrea.

"I noticed a pattern all through the school years. Every time I looked I found alterations to Andrea's records. At one point I looked at the elementary group pictures and they were using a new photo technology to erase Andrea's image.

"I never did understand who 'they' were, but they were just about to wipe her away from all of the school yearbooks. I confronted them and said I still had the originals.

"I went to my confidante, the older woman, who also worked in the public sector, and I was able to show her one of the group pictures with Andrea in it, and then the altered picture with her gone.

"My confidant didn't say much all during the dream, but this time I said to her, 'They can't do that can they?' She answered, 'No, but they will keep trying as long as they think they can, and unless someone stops them they will.'

"The more I confronted them, and showed them the pictures,

the more they told me things such as they were just updating the pictures and that it was all a mistake. I went back to school, or some place that had a thick glass window. They were all behind the window. I had to go up at least five stories to that room. I approached the window, furious about everything that had happened. I felt my body lifting from the ground, and when I was in midair, I started talking in a voice other than my own. I shouted at them through the window, 'The only way you're going to get rid of me is kill me, and you can't because I'm already dead!'"

In the last days of July 2005, Harris went up to Mendocino County one more time to see if there were any more files he had missed concerning the Humboldt County cases of Sherry and Andrea. He knew he would never get that information in Humboldt County—there was a brick wall there. In Mendocino County, however, there had been many Humboldt County documents that found there way into the files when Juan Freeman, Sergeant Steve Rogers, and Investigator Mike Losey came to interview John after he had admitted to killing Debbie Sloan.

It was an extremely hot day in Ukiah, when Harris pulled into town, and the courthouse felt cool and refreshing after being out on the street in the blazing sun. Harris wasn't really sure what he was looking for. He'd looked at those documents four times before and practically knew them by heart. He began plowing his way through the thousands of pages once again, and at 2 PM he nearly jumped out of his chair. There amidst all the other pages was a short document he had never seen before. How had he missed it?

Or had he missed it? The more he thought about it, he was sure it was not in that location before on past visits. It seemed as if it had been placed in there since his last trip to Ukiah in May. Who could have done that? It had to have been someone from Humboldt County. Mendocino County wouldn't have had this document on their own. Not this one.

It was the "smoking gun" he had been looking for. It was

a memo by a person either in law enforcement or the DA's office who asked themselves the same questions he had been asking himself for the last year and a half. Why had John Annibel escaped justice in the murders of Sherry Lynn Smith and Andrea LaDeRoute?

The document was merely listed as 26220. A secondary heading stated, "Annibel File Reviewed FPD, 3-4-99." Then there was a list of items, broken down into subcategories.

The document stated that there was no indication of certain items that had ever been examined for the blood of the victim. The list included a blanket believed used to transport the victim, twigs and leaves that needed to be analyzed for blood transfer, and a determination of the species and location of the leaves and twigs.

A second category was about blood in the apartment on Ninth Street in Fortuna and what caused DOJ tech Rynearson to determine that there was a "substantial supposition of violence." It asked if the FBI scrapings Q9 and Q10 were from the mirror frame. And were there photographs showing blood spray and could Rynearson testify to blood on the wall being from the result of a blow. The same went for Rynearson testifying that blood on the mattress, sheets, and pillowcase could have come from a punch. In fact, the person wanted to know if blood from the wall had ever been recovered and processed.

By 2005, Joe Rynearson was an instructor at the National Crime Investigation and Training center, which taught seminars to investigators and crime scene technicians from around the nation. Some of his seminars included Evidence and Crime Scene Reconstruction and a course in Bloodshed Interpretation. As he explained about this latter course, "It provides the student with the knowledge, skills, and ability essential to the investigation of bloodstain evidence." He delved into the area of blood dynamics within the body, such as flow rates, compression and ventilation effects, Rynearson also explained about "wound weapon correlation—wounds to pattern interpretation. He taught investigators how to examine and interpret stains in actual cases, and methods of pattern documentation at a crime scene.

Rynearson by 2005 had lectured at the California District

Attorney's Association on Homicides and Forensic Science, as well as the international Association of Forensic Scientists. In fact, he had been one of the driving forces behind the development of Criminal Investigative Response Teams comprised of special agents and criminalists. Because of Rynearson's qualifications, he obviously would be very beneficial in reconstructing what might have happened in that apartment on Ninth Street in Fortuna, back in1980.

Item three mentioned that blood from the mirror frame had not been resubmitted to the DOJ in February 1999 and wanted to know why not.

Item four dealt with Steve Rogers report and questioned why there was no indication that the throw rug and trunk mat found in John's Camaro was never submitted to the DOJ lab for testing. It also wondered if the FBI could do blood splatter analysis on Andrea's boot, her jacket, and the man's pair of shoes that were found.

Item five was about a woman named Sarah Smith, who as a child lived next door to the Annibel property. When she was young she had seen blood on a stump on the Annibel property, and also a bloody handprint in the barn. She had heard rumors as a child that a body was buried near the stump. The memo asked if a ground-disturbance test had ever been conducted near the stump.

Item six dealt with the question of why there had been no canvassing of John and Andrea's neighborhood in 1980. It also wondered why the nearest neighbor to John and Andrea's apartment had never been questioned as to whether he had ever heard John and Andrea fight.

Item seven asked if Evidence Tech Bud Thompson could still be questioned. It also contained a mysterious notation— "Reinterview Phil Cox" and questioned certain aspects of a previous interview.

Item eight wondered about the hand drawn map found in John's Camaro and it's significance. It was questioned why no details about it were given in the report.

Item nine was about the significance of the first seventeen

days of March 1980 being marked off the calendar found at John and Andrea's apartment.

That was it. No signature, no badge number, no ID number. The only thing that made it valid and significant was that it had a case number of 26220 on it, and it was written on official stationery. Whoever it was who wrote this memo had access to all the information and posed the same questions about which Harris and Lisa had been wondering. Harris wondered who had done it—and why? Why had it shown up in Ukiah now?

The more he pondered it, the more he began to think it had been done by someone within the system who had had enough. Enough of the double talk and runarounds that Lisa had been receiving for twenty-five years. Enough of the stonewalling in justice for Andrea. Perhaps they had done it out of a moral sense of duty. Perhaps they had done it for expiation of their sins. Perhaps they had done in regards to words written by Julia Butterfly Hill—"To see an injustice, and do nothing, is to become part of the injustice."

Because of the inconsistencies, irregularities, and just plain mysteries surrounding all the cases in Humboldt County, especially the ones concerning Sherry Lynn Smith and Andrea LaDeRoute, Harris compiled a file on these matters and went to see a superior court judge he knew and trusted. They had become friends after a grueling multiple murder case that had consumed two years of his life, and four years of hers. Harris knew that she was bright, learned in the law, and above all else, fair-minded. When he went to see her with his documents concerning how some of the Humboldt County authorities had treated cases connected to John Annibel, he expected her to give him about thirty minutes of her precious time. Instead she gave him an hour and a half.

As she read page after page of what he had brought, her face became more stern and the corners of her mouth turned down. It was as if she was gazing at something repulsive. Harris knew that she had almost twenty years in the judiciary system—first as a Deputy DA and then as a judge. What she saw before her now made her look angrier than he had ever seen her before.

Finally she looked up from him and almost threw the papers back across the table.

"Well, what do you think?" he asked.

"I think this whole thing reeks!" she replied.

"If you were me, what would you do now?" Harris asked her.

"I'd take all of this to the attorney general's office," she answered. She gave him a contact number for someone whom she had once worked with who was now an investigator with the California Attorney General's Office.

In early August 2005, Lisa sent Harris a letter she had written to Andrea. It was a letter to her in the twenty-fifth year of her loss. Lisa wrote:

There are so many things I want to tell you, I don't know where to begin. It's kind of hard to sum up twenty-five years of catching up in a simple letter. You know how I used to do when we were younger—I would write letters and greeting cards to friends and never send them. Well, this will be like that. I'll just save it for you.

I still regret not going with you and Max to see your new apartment. I struggled with myself for years, thinking that maybe if I had, you might still be here with me. Oh, I had plenty of things to feel bad about. I had to fight not to wallow in self-pity. Anytime I thought a crying jag was coming on, I would just think about when you told me, "I think when people cry and get all upset when someone dies, they're just thinking about themselves." Even in your "On Death and Dying" class at CRC, the collage you made was of happy things.

I think I'm still the same person deep down as when you were still here. I've just matured a lot. I think you would be impressed how much I've grown. It wasn't easy, that's for sure. I still have to struggle with my feelings of anger. Remember all the temper fits I had when I couldn't find a sock or something. You would laugh at me, while I was completely berserk, throwing things around. I remember the angrier I got, the harder you would laugh at me.

I'm so proud to have had you as a sister, Anghs. I really believe that although life has been tough on me, I have been blessed. Your approval, love, and acceptance was everything to me. I had a really hard time when I would achieve things like my first apartment, my first real car that was nice, my wedding—all these kinds of things. I always felt a void because I wanted so badly to run and show you, but there was no one to go to.

I can relate to your feelings of trying to find Donna and Corinna, our little sisters. Remember how Max and you would go to all the different schools for years and look through the chain-link fences trying to see if you could recognize our little sisters. Back then I thought it was a little strange. Now, I have to say I totally relate. The feeling of desperation and longing to find the ones you love.

You were right, we did have a pretty different childhood. I didn't really realize that until I was much older. Any time people would be sharing their childhood stories—when I would participate, the atmosphere in the room would change drastically. I've learned that people are afraid of what they don't understand. That's why I think people were so mean to us when we were kids. I get the sense that people might feel that way when they're around me after they know what happened to you.

I got a chance to meet two sisters, Zee and Laud. I had the fortunate opportunity to meet them in person. At first glance they reminded me so much of you and me together. Their personalities were completely opposite, but you could tell they really loved each other. Their sister, Georgina, was also murdered and at the time I met them; it had been sixteen years and the case was still unsolved. They were so sweet, they actually allowed me time to share my pain and were less concerned about their own. I was very touched. They were very supportive in my mission to find the truth, and I still get e-mails from them even a year later. I wish we could have met them together.

Boy, it feels good to write to you. I feel like you've been on a vacation for a very long time, and I'm trying to catch you up to speed. I could go on and on, talk and talk, and that part of me has never changed. I just want to take this chance to tell you about my husband Sandy. Anghs, you and Mom would really like Sandy. I wish you could have met him. His laugh reminds me so much of yours. He has truly been a blessing and an answered prayer from God. I had been praying to God for someone just like Sandy, and God answered my prayer and then some. He believes in trust, family, honesty, and friendship.

Sandy and I bought a home, which we both absolutely love, only a block away from the projects that you and I grew up in, and only two blocks away from the elementary school and junior-high school we went to. During the day, when the school is in session, I can hear the kids playing on the playground. And I think back on when we used to stand in line waiting our turn to play tetherball. Boy, you were good.

Anghs, I wish you could tell me what actually happened, although part of me is afraid to know the details. Why would John want to take your last breath from you? What could you have done or said that would have made him become such an animal?

Anghs I have to go for now. I don't know how to say good-bye. I've really enjoyed our time together today. I miss you more today than the day you left. Thank you so much for all the warm memories. I really rely on them when times are tough. Until the next time. I'll be here in the rose garden I planted for you, watching the butterflies.

I Love You!

It was one of those brisk windy San Francisco days when the wind whips off the bay and the sky is an azure blue. Harris walked up to the building that housed the attorney general's offices in that city, and stopped before crossing the portal. He hesitated and pondered what he was doing. He knew that once he crossed that threshold his life and many others would be changed forever.

He'd always spoken up for the prosecution and law-enforcement side of court matters. The defense end of a table just was not his calling. And now, the documents he had in his briefcase were accusatory of some members of the professions with whom he had always aligned himself.

Added to this was a conversation he'd recently had with a friend who had been a criminalist. This friend looked at all the evidence and wondered what role the Pacific Lumber Company had in all of this. She said, "John Annibel and his father were employed by Pacific Lumber, and John worked where Andrea's skull was later found by forestry workers on PL property. Lisa and Sandy got nowhere with Pacific Lumber, just as they got nowhere with the DA's office. Is there a connection?"

The truth of the matter was, Harris didn't know himself. It was time for others with authority to try and unravel all the layers surrounding John Annibel's years of eluding justice in Humboldt County.

For some reason, an image of John Annibel and Glenda Massey at the Garberville dance in 1976 popped into his mind. He could mentally see the throng of people dancing and hear the sound of the band. One of the people dancing was Sherry Lynn Smith. She wore a scarf in her hair and a white peasant blouse, and she had a big smile on her face. She was fifteen years old, and had her whole life ahead of her.

Harris recalled John and Glenda's words that night. Glenda had said to John, "Don't forget Sherry."

And John had answered, "I won't forget. I won't forget Sherry."

A moment later Harris muttered those same words to himself. "I won't forget. I won't forget Sherry."

And then he added, "Or Andrea, or Georgina, or Debbie."

He lifted his briefcase off the sidewalk and sighed. Then he crossed the threshold. There was no turning back.

ACKNOWLEDGMENTS

I would like to thank many people who helped on this book, including Captain Kurt Smallcomb, Investigator Tim Kiely, Investigator Kevin Bailey, Investigator Christy Conrardy, DDA Rick Martin, and DDA Mark Kalina. Thanks also to DA Norman Vroman and the entire staff at the Mendocino County DA's Office. Special thanks go to Lisa and Sandy Lawler, Pam and James Annibel, Laudalina, Zee, and Julie. I'd also like to acknowledge L. Carroll, M. Farrace, R. Belford, C. Anetsky, and P. Bunt. And thanks once again to my terrific literary agent, Damaris Rowland, and editor, Michaela Hamilton.